Person-C

Person–Centred Therapy

The Focusing-Oriented Approach

CAMPBELL PURTON

First published 2004 by
PALGRAVE MACMILLAN
Houndmills, Basingstoke, Hampshire RG21 6XS and
175 Fifth Avenue, New York, N.Y. 10010
Companies and representatives throughout the world

PALGRAVE MACMILLAN is the global academic imprint of the Palgrave
Macmillan division of St. Martin's Press, LLC and of Palgrave Macmillan Ltd.
Macmillan® is a registered trademark in the United States, United Kingdom
and other countries. Palgrave is a registered trademark in the European
Union and other countries.

ISBN 978-0-333-96916-8 paperback

A catalogue record for this book is available from the British Library.

A catalog record for this book is available from the Library of Congress.

10   9   8   7   6   5   4   3   2   1
13 12 11 10 09 08 07 06 05 04

Transferred to Digital Printing in 2011.

For Val, Dinah and Tom

Contents

Acknowledgements   viii

Terminological Note   x

Introduction   1

1. Rogers and the Development of Person-Centred Therapy   11

2. Fault-Lines in Person-Centred Theory   31

3. The Origins of Focusing   54

4. Focusing as a Taught Procedure   82

5. Focusing-Oriented Psychotherapy   96

6. Objections: Issues of Principle and Empirical Issues   143

7. Training and Supervision   163

8. Towards a Theory of Psychotherapy   175

Conclusion   207

Appendix A: The Wider Context   210

Appendix B: Resources   236

References   237

Index   250

Acknowledgements

I would like to thank Yoshihiko Morotomi for drawing my attention to the work of Fujio Tomoda. It was from that spark that my interest in focusing developed. Barbara McGavin was my first Focusing teacher, followed later by Rob Foxcroft. I owe much to both of them. My understanding of focusing has also been helped by attendance at Eugene Gendlin's 'Thinking at the Edge' workshop in New York, and by workshops run by Maarten Aalberse and Kevin McEvenue.

I am grateful to Rose Battye, Paul Cassell, Ann Weiser Cornell, Sarah Hawtin, Dave Mearns, Judy Moore and two anonymous publishers' readers, who kindly read and commented on parts of, or drafts of, the book. They have helped to make the book better than it would otherwise have been. I would also like to thank my Palgrave editors Alison Caunt and Andrew McAleer for their patient support during the writing of the book.

The 'Focusing and the Power of Philosophy' courses, on the Isle of Cumbrae, which I have taught with Rob Foxcroft, Barbara McGavin and Kye Nelson, helped a lot in clarifying my own under-standing of Gendlin's thinking. I benefited from the opportunity to discuss parts of the book – over wine and cake – at the UEA Counselling Service 'Writing and Research Group'; also from teaching focusing on the UEA counselling diploma course. I have learned a lot from our trainees, and I have very much valued the support of my colleagues, Caroline Brown, Ian Draper, Judy Moore, Eamonn O'Mahony and Louise Young, on the course.

My understanding of focusing has been helped greatly by my counselling clients; I hope that they have benefited as much from my involvement in focusing as I have from working with them.

I am grateful to Brian Thorne, with whom I have worked for so many years, for his initial encouragement to write the book and for his continuing interest in it; to Muriel Frankl, who helped me see that focusing, in spite of its being a way of helping people find their *own* path, can get in the way of precisely that; to Mary Hendricks, indefatigable Director of the Focusing Institute, for all her help along the way; and to Gene Gendlin himself. Gendlin has not read this book, though we have had helpful email discussions about some of the material. I am sure that in some places I will have unintentionally misrepresented his ideas, and I apologise to him in advance for that. I will have to leave it to the reader to assess how well I have done in this regard, after they have consulted Gendlin's own writings. I very much hope that readers will do this.

My daughter Dinah (now working on a PhD on existential themes) and my son Tom (now completing a Masters degree in psychoanalysis) have helped to make me feel that it is all worthwhile. Finally, my thanks to Val, who shares with me the pains and pleasures of trying to write in spite of the pressures of our over-busy lives.

Terminological Note

I have for the most part chosen to use the pronouns 'they', 'them', 'their' and 'themself' as singular forms in place of the gender-specific 'he', 'him', and 'his' and 'himself'. This is because I find that the consistent use of 'he or she', 'him or her' and so on often leads to impossibly contorted sentences (how, for example, could one live with such a rendering of 'He himself might feel that he would like his work to be more congenial to him'?). 'S/he' is unpronounceable, and the device of alternating the use of feminine and masculine pronouns runs into difficulties in contexts where gender-specific pronouns *are* required, and the distinction between a gender-specific 'him' and a gender-neutral 'him' is lost. There can be awkwardnesses in the singular use of the grammatically plural forms; for example, I have preferred forms such as 'while they themself think' to the grammatically correct 'while they themselves think' (though my word-processor keeps 'correcting' this); however, I find I can live with these awkwardnesses more comfortably than with any of the alternative ways around the problem. Singular uses of grammatical plurals are not unknown, although some readers may echo Queen Victoria's apocryphal 'We are not amused'.

Introduction

Person-centred therapy occupies a unique position within the wide range of psychological therapies available today. Just what its uniqueness consists in is one thing which I hope to show in the course of this book, through an exploration of the work of Carl Rogers' close colleague Eugene Gendlin.

I hope that the book will be of interest to counsellors, trainees, and anyone who is involved in person-centred therapy, or who is interested in looking at the ideas of Carl Rogers in a new way. Rogers himself always saw theories – including his own – as tentative constructions which were liable to modification in the light of further experience. Gendlin's work can be seen as one way in which Rogers' ideas can be carried forward. However, although Gendlin's approach grew out of his work with Rogers, it is deeply relevant to *any* form of counselling or psychotherapy. It provides a way of thinking about therapy which should be of interest to those who see themselves as working in 'eclectic' or 'integrationist' ways because it provides a plausible view of how such a way of working can avoid being superficial or incoherent. I hope also that the book will be of interest to people who are primarily interested in Gendlin's well-known 'Focusing' procedure, but who have not yet fully appreciated the richness of thought which lies behind the procedure. Finally, I hope the book will be of interest to anyone who would like to glimpse a genuinely novel way of approaching a range of issues which lie at the borders of psychotherapy – issues involving ethics, creativity, spirituality, and the relationship of psychotherapy to science and contemporary culture.

My aim is to take Carl Rogers' 'person-centred therapy' and to view it from the perspective developed by Gendlin. Gendlin's work is less known than that of Rogers, but I hope to show that it provides a solid, and much-needed, grounding for the practice of person-centred therapy. Although Gendlin's perspective does not entail radical changes in person-centred practice, it does present that practice in a new light. It also suggests a new way of seeing the relationships between the various 'schools' of therapy, and explains the remarkably persistent research finding that the practices of *all* the schools are equally effective.

Person-centred therapy centres the therapeutic work on the individual client in a way which is quite distinctive but not entirely easy to articulate. Carl Rogers initially characterised the form of therapy which he was developing as 'non-directive'. This term catches the idea that in this form of therapy the therapist's task is not to direct the client towards ends which the therapist sees as good or fulfilling, but to facilitate the client's efforts to determine their own goals, based on their *own* experiencing. Nor is it the therapist's task to direct the client along a path which the therapist sees as likely to lead to the client's goals, but to facilitate the client's movement along their own chosen path. Further, the task of the therapist is not to provide the client with ways of thinking about their situation, but to facilitate the development of the client's own ways of thinking about that situation.

These were revolutionary ideas when Rogers formulated them, and while there are many quarters in which they have still not been absorbed, there can be little doubt that Rogers' influence has been pervasive. 'Person-centred therapy' has, for many years, been one of the major approaches to counselling and psychotherapy in Britain. In the United States it is no longer prominent under that name, but the fourth edition of the American *Handbook of Psychotherapy and Behaviour Change* (Bergin and Garfield, 1996) now accords 'experiential psychotherapy' – that is, those forms of therapy which take 'the client's ongoing awareness of his or her own experience as the primary datum for therapy' (p. 509) – the status of a 'major approach', along with cognitive, behavioural and psychodynamic approaches.

I think that the principles of therapy which Rogers formulated are of enduring importance, but they have a simplicity which can be mistaken for a lack of depth. Person-centred therapy is often seen as lacking in theoretical sophistication, and while some practitioners delight in this, others are concerned about it and may seek to integrate person-centred ideas with theoretical principles drawn from other schools of therapy. However, there is already *within* the person-centred approach a developed body of theory. It is the theory of experiencing developed by Gendlin which I believe can provide a solid foundation for person-centred practice. This book is concerned more with practice than with theory, but I hope to show something of the relevance of the theory to the practice.

In the early days of the development of his approach, Rogers found that one simple and effective way of facilitating the client's process of change was simply to reflect back to the client what they had said. For Rogers this was a way of checking whether he had understood the client's meaning, although another aspect of this procedure – emphasised more by Gendlin – was that in hearing their words back the *client* can check whether their words really say what they meant to say. Then, having expressed what they were previously unable to express, the client can move on a step. This simple procedure of listening and reflecting, which Barrett-Lennard (1998) calls 'non-directive reflective psychotherapy', has remained important in the person-centred approach ever since Rogers introduced it.

It is clear that in listening and reflecting, the therapist is in an important way influencing what happens in the session. *Whatever* the therapist does will have an influence on the client, and person-centred therapists, like all therapists, do what they do in the expectation of having an influence which will be helpful to the client. Whether such conscious influence on the process of therapy should be called 'direction' is something we will need to address later. I think it is fair to say that there is in person-centred therapy at least some encouragement of a certain sort of process, that is, the sort of process which involves the client finding their own way forward. The person-centred therapist believes that it is in this particular sort of process that the client 'finds themself', so that it would be absurd for the therapist not to do things that help to bring about this sort of process.

So it seems that the term 'non-directive' is not entirely accurate as a description of Rogers' practice, and he himself later came to prefer the phrase 'client-centred'. The import of this new term was that the therapist should not try to formulate the client's experience or goals in terms of any external theory. What is important for the therapist is to be with the client in their *own* frame of reference, and to help the client to articulate their concerns in their own way. 'Client-centred' contrasts essentially with 'theory-centred', though it is important to see that this does not entail any disparagement of theory: if the client should formulate their experience in terms of concepts drawn, say, from Freud, and these concepts should have experiential meaning for the client, then the client-centred therapist should do their best to enter into the client's Freudian world. 'Client-centred' does not mean rejection of theories (after all, theories of all sorts are embodied in all our experiencing, even in what we call 'common sense'), but it does mean centring on the *client's* theories rather than on the therapist's theory.

One further terminological change in the development of Rogers' work was the shift from 'client-centred' to 'person-centred'. This change was primarily to allow for the fact that Rogers' approach to human problems came to be employed beyond the limits of psychotherapy. For example, Rogers came to think that in large groups the basic listening procedures of client-centred therapy could be helpful in facilitating mutual understanding. In this kind of context it would be inappropriate to speak of 'clients', so the term 'person-centred' is used to convey that the listener stays with the other person's way of being and experiencing. The person-centred/client-centred distinction marks a difference in the range of application of Rogers' ideas, not in their essential content.

One curious development has been that in spite of the approach being referred to as 'client-centred', Rogers and his successors have given far more attention to the attitudes of the therapist than to the experiencing of the client. This anomaly has begun to be noticed (Mearns and Thorne, 2000, p. 193), and Gendlin's work could be seen, in part, as a thoroughgoing effort to redress the balance.

Rogers came to see the therapist attitudes of empathy, acceptance and genuineness – what came to be known as the 'core conditions' of therapy – as the crucial ingredients in what made his non-directive reflective procedure effective. He went on to elaborate a theory of *why* this procedure was effective. This was, in brief, that psychological disturbance arises from the introjection of the values of significant others. He saw human beings as having a deep need for the respect and appreciation of others, a need which often conflicts with the other felt needs a person has. Such conflict does not itself constitute psychological disturbance, according to Rogers; there is such disturbance only when the person denies or distorts their own felt needs so as to develop a self-concept which fits the 'conditions of worth' of those around them. The process of therapy then consists in the undoing of the conditions of worth: in the situation where the therapist genuinely and empathically accepts the client for who they are, the conditions of worth dissolve.

Beginning from the observed effectiveness of the non-directive reflective approach, Gendlin's thought moved in a rather different direction. Before he became involved with Rogers' group in Chicago,

Gendlin had been working on a philosophical theory of experiencing. Essential to this theory is the idea that lived experiencing is distinct from the *concepts* through which we make sense of our experiencing. The ways in which we experience the world are determined in part by the conceptual patterns of the culture in which we are brought up, but at the same time, Gendlin insists, a human being is not a blank slate upon which just any old patterns can be drawn. The concepts and principles which we acquire from our culture are often modified by our own experiencing. We are not entirely trapped in the ways of seeing the world which are handed down to us; there is something in us which engages with the concepts and which determines whether these concepts are useful to us or not. This – our lived experiencing of the world – is something on which we can focus our attention, and to which all our ideas and thoughts are answerable.

I will discuss Gendlin's basic ideas later; for the present we need just to get a glimpse of them in order to see how it was that on encountering Rogers' work at the University of Chicago Counselling Center, Gendlin was struck by the fact that there was a group of people who were actually working in just that borderland between lived experiencing and conceptual understanding, which so deeply interested him. For, in client-centred therapy there are so often moments when the client is trying to find ways of *expressing what they are experiencing*. The stock concepts often will not do. For example:

> What I feel when I am with him is not exactly embarrassment, but there is a sort of awkwardness – there is something about how I am with him that is sort of 'pulled in', so I can't quite be myself...it is a quite specific feeling that goes with this situation...yet it is sort of familiar...a bit like I used to be with my uncle when he offered to help me when I was making those model planes...yes, *that* feeling. Aaah. [Takes a deeper breath].

Here there is an attempt to articulate, to find a form for, the feeling. And when the form is found there is a sense of release – 'Yes, that's what it is' – followed perhaps by a slightly deeper breath, or a sigh, or the shedding of a few tears. This is what Rogers (1956, 1961, p. 130) calls a 'moment of movement', and Gendlin (1996, p. 20) a 'shift' or 'change-step'. In such moments, something physically shifts a little, and in some sense the person 'moves on'.

Gendlin and Rogers see such movements as characteristic of the therapy process although, of course, they also occur in non-therapeutic contexts. It is important to realise that what is being described is something quite familiar. Novelists sometimes portray it. For example, in *The Glass Palace* (Ghosh, 2001, p. 328) Alison reflects as she is driving with Dinu:

> Now, when I wake up in the morning those things come back to me in just that way – I have to do this or that, for Mummy or for Daddy. Then I remember, No, I don't have to do any of those things; there's no reason to. And in an odd way, what you feel at those moments is not exactly sadness but a kind of disappointment. And that's awful too, for you to say to yourself – is this the best I can do? No: this isn't good enough. I should cry – everyone says it's good to cry. But the feeling inside doesn't have an easy name: it's not exactly pain or sorrow – not right then. It feels more like the sensation you have when you sit down very heavily in a chair: the breath rushes out of your body and you find yourself gagging. It's hard to make sense of it – any of it. You want the pain to be simple, straightforward – you don't want it to ambush you in these roundabout ways, each morning, when you're getting up to do something else – brush your teeth or eat your breakfast . . .
>
> The car veered suddenly towards the side of the road. Dinu snatched at the wheel to steady it. 'Alison! Slow down – careful.'
>
> She ran the car on to the grassy verge that flanked the road and stopped under a tree. Raising her hands, she touched her cheeks in a gesture of disbelief. 'Look,' she said, 'I'm crying'.

On the basis of the empirical studies with which he was involved as a member of Rogers' group, Gendlin came to believe that the kind of process that went on in client-centred therapy was in principle no different from that which went on in other forms of therapy *when they were therapeutically effective*. In all forms of therapy the crucial factor seemed to be whether the client was able to relate effectively to their own experiencing. Clients who spent their sessions in discussing external events tended not to make much progress. Nor did those who approached their problems in a purely intellectual way, and nor did those who simply allowed their feelings to take them over. The way of talking which did seem to be therapeutically effective was that which is encouraged by Rogers' listening-and-reflecting procedure. It is a way of talking in which the client gives attention to what is going on inside them and seeks to give expression to that experiencing. We will encounter many examples of this way of talking in the course of this book.

The differences between Rogers and Gendlin lie less in clinical practice than in the theory which underpins the practice. For Rogers the crucial point is that through embodying the core conditions the therapist provides a receptive, non-judging ambience which functions as an antidote to the conditions of worth which the client has absorbed. Rogers pictures therapy in terms of an agricultural metaphor: people are like plants which can flourish only if they are provided with suitable conditions for growth. Just as plants require sunlight and water, people require genuine acceptance and understanding. We will consider the aptness of this metaphor later, but it is by now well-recognised in person-centred thinking that there is another aspect of Rogers' thought which does not sit entirely comfortable with the agricultural metaphor. This second theme is Rogers' emphasis on the therapeutic relationship. In practice, person-centred therapists do not *simply* provide a receptive ambience of genuine empathy and acceptance. They *interact* with the client, reflecting what the client says, sometimes asking questions, and sometimes expressing their own feelings.

As we will see later, the practice of person-centred therapy changed significantly in the mid-1960s following the experience which Rogers and his colleagues had of working with schizophrenic patients in the large-scale Wisconsin Project. Instead of the emphasis on non-directive reflection there came to be an emphasis on how the therapist *interacts with* the client. The core conditions came to be seen more as ways of relating than simply as attitudes. For Gendlin, who had directed the Wisconsin Project, this emphasis on the interaction between client and therapist tied in closely with his understanding of human life as always an *interaction* between the felt flow of experiencing and *something else*. The 'something else' could be what someone else said or did, or it might be something which one had read, or the impact of a dream on waking experience, or of reading one's diary, or of watching a sunset, or of hearing a piece of music and so on. For Gendlin, human living is always a process of interaction between felt experiencing and all that which has an impact on our experiencing. It is through such interaction that our experiencing changes.

Gendlin sees psychological disturbance as due to difficulties which have arisen in the interaction process which constitutes human living. Such difficulties often arise through our spontaneous responses being blocked through our fear of what other people will think, but the crucial point is that *there is a block* in the ongoing interaction process. Provision of the core conditions often helps to free up the blocked process, but from his experience of schizophrenic patients, Gendlin became convinced that more than this may be needed. Even in cases of less-extreme disturbance it seems true that some clients are helped by empathic listening much more than others, and it is important to know why this is so.

Gendlin's view is that a lot depends on the *client*, a view which has been confirmed by much psychotherapy outcome research (for instance Orlinsky *et al.*, 1994). Some clients start from a place where they can respond to the therapist's interventions in a way which frees up their blocked process. These are rewarding clients for the therapist. But there are others who seem unable to make effective use of what is offered to them. For example, they may use the session to talk about the events of their week without referring to how these events struck them, or how they felt about the events, or what meaning these events had for them. Other clients speculate about the causes of their problems, perhaps analysing their difficulties in terms of some psychological theory. Still others simply remain immersed in their anxiety or depression and cannot *relate* to it. In the years following the Wisconsin project, Gendlin and his colleagues studied thousands of recordings of client sessions and were often able to identify *at the start* those clients who would be unlikely to make significant progress. This was a disturbing development because it meant that much therapeutic effort was quite likely to be unhelpful.

As a result of these studies Gendlin and his colleagues looked at the possibility of developing ways of reaching out to clients who would otherwise not be reached. The 'focusing' procedure was one possibility: clients could be *taught* to engage with their own experiencing in the way that successful clients did naturally. On the other hand, if the therapist assumes the role of a teacher this can have bad consequences for the client. The person-centred approach is premised on clients discovering their own resources, rather than relying on the knowledge of 'experts'. There is a tension here which I will explore in various contexts in this book. It is the tension between knowing that therapeutic change is likely to follow from the client's relating to their *own* experiencing, and the need in many cases to help the client to realise that this is so. In person-centred therapy we do not direct the client along a path which we think is best for them; we facilitate their following their own path. But what if the client is not on any path *of their own*? What if they are following rules laid down by other people, or tracks laid down by long irrelevant events, or generalised theoretical notions? Can we then in effect say to them 'Listen to *yourself*, listen to your own experiencing *now*. Don't even listen to me unless what I say resonates with you'? Whether this very particular kind of therapist directivity is alien to the person-centred approach will be one of the themes of this book.

In Chapter 1 I outline the theory of person-centred therapy as developed by Rogers, and the main developments in the years since Rogers ceased to write about the theory of therapy. In Chapter 2 I discuss some areas of person-centred theory which are problematic. Later in the book I hope to show how many of these difficulties can be resolved if we adopt Gendlin's view of therapy. In Chapter 3 we will look at how focusing developed in relation to the early development of client-centred therapy. Then in Chapter 4 I give a short account of 'Focusing' as a taught procedure. (I will always capitalise 'Focusing' when I am referring to this procedure.) Focusing understood in this way is the part of Gendlin's work which is best known, and it would be eccentric not to include this chapter. However, as will become clear in the course of the book, I think it is important to see that Focusing as a taught procedure is just one application of a whole way of thinking about therapy, and about many other aspects of human life. In Chapter 5 I discuss in some detail how Gendlin's ideas can inform therapeutic practice. This chapter is not in itself a manual for practice, but I hope it will provide enough material to entice some therapists to explore further how Gendlin's approach could enrich what they already do.

These chapters will inevitably give rise to questions and objections in some readers' minds, and in Chapter 6 I deal with what I take to be the main difficulties in Gendlin's approach, especially as seen through the eyes of more orthodox person-centred practitioners. The implications of Gendlin's approach for training and supervision are explored in Chapter 7, at least in connection with training which remains fairly close to the standard forms of person-centred therapist training. As we shall see, Gendlin's view of therapy involves a radical rethinking of the relationship between the person-centred approach and other schools of therapy. In brief, what is central to person-centred therapy belongs in *any* kind of effective therapy. The procedures of any school of therapy can be 'experientialised' or oriented towards the principles involved in focusing, so that Gendlin's work is relevant to *all* the schools of therapy. However, in this book I will, for the most part, restrict the discussion to the relationship between focusing-oriented therapy and the more standard person-centred approach.

In Chapter 8 I attempt to lay out the philosophical underpinnings of Gendlin's views. It has often been said that the person-centred approach is 'thin on theory', but I do not think anyone who has read

Gendlin will be likely to retain such an opinion. Gendlin's views are rooted in philosophical considerations which involve a thoroughgoing rethinking of many of the assumptions underlying our modern 'scientific' world view. Because of this, his thinking has implications far beyond the field of psychotherapy. This aspect of Gendlin's work will not be of interest to every reader, so I have relegated it to an appendix (Appendix A). However, I think myself that these further implications have an important bearing on therapy – for, if support for Gendlin's general approach can be found in how it illuminates these *other* areas, we will have extra reason to take his views more seriously when we turn our attention to psychotherapy itself.

While up to now Gendlin's contribution has usually been seen as the development of his Focusing procedure, I hope that this book will show how focusing-oriented psychotherapy embodies very deeply the spirit of the person-centred approach. I also hope that the book may whet the reader's appetite for further exploration of a deeply original view of the world which goes far beyond the realm of psychotherapy, while offering an explanation of just what psychotherapy is, and why it can be effective.

1

Rogers and the Development of Person-Centred Therapy

Rogers' work

In his book *Counselling and Psychotherapy: Newer Concepts in Practice*, published in 1942, Carl Rogers presents what he sees as a new method of therapy 'in which warmth of acceptance and absence of any form of coercion or personal pressure on the part of the counsellor permits the maximum expression of feelings, attitudes, and problems by the counsellee...In this unique experience of complete emotional freedom within a well-defined framework the client is free to recognise and understand his impulses and patterns, positive and negative, as in no other relationship' (Rogers, 1942, p. 113). The book contains the first complete recorded transcript of a series of therapy sessions, with a commentary by Rogers on how the therapist's responses in the session embodied the non-directive principles which Rogers was advocating.

During the following few years, while Rogers was based at Ohio State University, he and other therapists applied the principles of non-directive responding in a variety of contexts, including work with the adjustment problems of servicemen returning from wartime activities. It was in his next book (co-authored with John Wallen) *Counselling with Returned Servicemen* (1946) that Rogers first used the term 'client-centred', along with 'non-directive', as characterising his approach. It is the *client's* frame of reference which is emphasised, while '[i]t is the counsellor's function to provide an atmosphere in which the client, through the exploration of his situation, comes to see himself and his reactions more clearly and to accept his attitudes more fully' (Rogers and Wallen, 1946, p. 5). What the counsellor actually *did* in the sessions was mainly to accompany the client with reflective restatement and clarification of what the client said, without judgement, comment or interpretation.

This work became widely known, and in 1945 Rogers accepted an invitation to a senior appointment at the prestigious University of Chicago, where he proceeded to set up a Counselling Centre which incorporated both clinical and research activities. In the following years Rogers and his colleagues continued to refine their theory and practice of 'non-directive reflective' psychotherapy, and in 1951 Rogers published *Client-Centred Therapy*. As Barrett-Lennard (1998, p. 60) points out, there are, in this work, incipient changes of emphasis in Rogers' account. The emphasis on the therapist targeting the client's frame of reference is still there, but this mode of responding is now seen less as a technique than as the embodiment of certain attitudes. Also in this book Rogers begins to develop a theory of the self which was needed to explain why the client-centred approach was therapeutically effective. The essentials of this theory were that as a child develops, a 'self-structure' or 'self-concept' forms in which what is valued arises partly from immediate experiencing and partly from values introjected from others, which are experienced *as if* they were the child's own experience (Rogers, 1951, p. 500). As the child continues to develop, new experiences are assimilated into the self-structure *or*, if they are incompatible with it, are denied or distorted. Psychological disturbance is constituted by such denial or distortion. By contrast, psychological adjustment exists 'when the concept of self is at least roughly congruent with all the experiences of the organism' (p. 513). Any experience which is inconsistent with the self-structure is likely to be perceived as a threat, but the therapeutic situation provides a safe setting in which *all* the client's experiences can be examined, and the structure of the self then becomes re-organised so as to assimilate these experiences.

Two further important concepts in client-centred therapy were developed in the mid-1950s. Rogers took up Standal's (1954) notion of unconditional positive regard as a crucial element in effective therapy, and at the same time came to emphasise the importance of *therapist* 'congruence'. The 'congruence' involved was that between the self as it actually is and the self as perceived. 'Congruence' soon came to be used rather more broadly as a synonym for 'genuineness', which was seen as having two aspects: those of (a) consistency between experiencing and awareness, and (b) consistency between awareness and expression. Roughly speaking, people are fully congruent if they deceive neither themselves nor others.

In 1957 Rogers published his paper 'The necessary and sufficient conditions of therapeutic personality change'. In this he claims that just six conditions need to be obtained if there is to be therapeutic change. Three of these conditions have subsequently come to be known in client-centred writing as the 'core conditions' of therapy, namely the therapist conditions of empathic understanding, unconditional positive regard and congruence. The other conditions are that client and therapist are in psychological contact, that the client 'is in a state of incongruence, being vulnerable or anxious' (Rogers, 1957, p. 96), and that the client must register the therapist's empathy and unconditional positive regard. I will refer to the full set of six conditions as the 'therapeutic conditions', and to the three conditions which the *therapist* needs to embody as the 'therapist conditions'. (I prefer this latter phrase to the more familiar 'core conditions', since it does not misleadingly suggest that the therapist conditions are more central to therapy than the other three conditions.)

In subsequent years, much research effort was devoted to exploring the validity of Rogers' 'necessary and sufficient' claim, which was a claim about not just client-centred therapy but psychotherapy in general. Prior to 1957, Fiedler's research (Barrett-Lennard, 1998, p. 262) had already suggested that therapeutic effectiveness was correlated more with how experienced the therapists were than with their theoretical orientation. Further, work by Quinn (*ibid.*, p. 262) suggested what seemed to characterise the experienced therapists was essentially their receptive and sensitive *attitude* towards their clients. Heine (*ibid.*, p. 263) found that, regardless of the theoretical orientation of the therapist, what clients themselves found helpful were such things as 'assisting the patient by asking questions which have the effect of clarifying feelings or attitudes', 'expressing for the client straight-forwardly feelings which the client approaches hesitantly and hazily' and 'feelings of trust, of being understood, and of independence in reaching solutions to problems'. Further, at least some of the studies conducted around this time indicated that there was a correlation between therapeutic movement and how effectively the therapist embodied the therapist conditions (*ibid.*, pp. 82, 264–7).

In 1959 Rogers published his major theoretical paper, which explains in greater detail why the six therapeutic conditions are to be seen as causally effective. In brief, Roger's view is that human beings have, amongst their other needs, a deep need for the positive regard of others. This need can give rise to conflict in situations where the positive regard of others is conditional upon the individual having feelings or attitudes which they do not in fact have. The individual is then in effect faced with the choice of satisfying their own 'organismic' needs while losing the positive regard of significant others, or of retaining the positive regard while giving up their organismic needs. The latter option, however, is not really possible since the organismic needs *are there*. What *is* possible for the individual is to deny or distort their awareness of their needs. In this way a view of themselves, a self-concept, is set up which is congruent with the 'conditions of worth' set by others, but incongruent with their actual experiencing. Subsequently, when life situations arise which make it difficult to maintain the distortion or denial, the person will become anxious or behave defensively, and generally exhibit some degree of psychological disturbance. Further, because greater awareness of their own experiencing will render the person liable to anxiety, he or she will be disinclined to give much attention to their experiencing. Instead of looking within to determine what they really feel or value, they will look outwards to what other people are thinking or valuing; in Rogers' terminology they will have an 'external locus of evaluation'. This, while reducing anxiety, undermines the person's sense of themself as 'solid' and trustworthy, thus increasing the person's sense of vulnerability.

In Rogers' view, client-centred therapy is effective because it provides an antidote to the introjected conditions of worth: in their relationship with the therapist, the client has the experience of being seen as they are (the therapist is empathic), and of being unconditionally accepted for what they are. Further, the client experiences this empathic acceptance as being fully genuine on the therapist's part – it is not a pretence. In these circumstances the client no longer needs to deny or distort their experiencing, so that their self-concept can return to a state of congruence with their experiencing. As a result the client's psychological disturbance is relieved.

In the background of this account is Rogers' notion of the 'actualising tendency'. He held that the primary motivation of all human behaviour is the actualisation of the person's potentialities. However, once a concept of self is set up which is at variance with the person's organismic experiencing, self-actualisation becomes problematic. The person is torn between actualising that 'self' (self-concept) which is constituted by the conditions of worth (that is, becoming what one 'should be' in the eyes of others) and actualising their organismic potential.

Rogers sees the actualising tendency as common to all living beings. Given the right environmental conditions, an organism will grow –

actualise its potentials – without the need of any outside assistance. If the environmental conditions are less favourable then the organism will still grow, but perhaps in a bizarre way. Rogers (1980, p. 118) refers to the example of potatoes which, stored in his family's basement several feet below a small window, grew long, pale spindly sprouts as if they were seeking the light. This is not the 'natural' form of a potato plant; it is not the form the plant has in its natural environment. However even this distorted kind of potato is the result of the actualising tendency which moves the potato sprout to seek the light. Rogers sees this not just as an analogy for what happens in human lives, but as another example of the way in which organisms move towards actualising their potential. For human beings, as for potatoes, the environmental conditions may not be favourable or nurturing, and in that case the organism may develop an unusual form. For Rogers even the most bizarre and seemingly inappropriate forms of human behaviour are the results of the organism coping as best as it can with noxious environmental conditions. As with the potato an unnatural form of development renders the organism more vulnerable (the long potato spindles are easily broken), and there may be no way of reversing what has already happened. However, once the environmental conditions are changed (in the human case, once the conditions of worth are withdrawn) the organism will from there on be able to develop its potential more fully.

To summarise, Rogers first proposed a hypothesis, that therapeutic change will take place if and only if the six therapeutic conditions are present. I will call this the Therapeutic Conditions Hypothesis. Secondly he offered a theoretical explanation of why his hypothesis is likely to hold true, namely the Conditions of Worth Theory.

The Conditions of Worth Theory came relatively late in the evolution of client-centred therapy, some years after the client-centred practice had been established. It can look as though the theory simply emerged from the practice, but this seems unlikely, given modern views on the way scientific theories develop. In fact, Rogers' views were deeply influenced by his knowledge of Freudian psychotherapy. He does not use the word 'repression', but the 'distortion and denial of experience' of which he speaks are recognisably close to what Freudians mean by 'repression'. Indeed, Rogers (1951, pp. 498–503) himself makes this explicit. In connection with the internalisation of conditions of worth, Rogers uses the psychoanalytic terminology of 'introjection'. He avoids speaking of 'unconscious thoughts and feelings' but this is more an avoidance of the terminology, than of the concepts.

This is not to criticise Rogers; it is often worthwhile to say old things in new ways, and in addition there were many unwanted connotations of the Freudian terminology which Rogers wished to avoid. In particular, I suspect, Rogers wanted to get away from the Freudian idea that there is 'an unconscious' about which the therapist – armed with his theory – could know more than the client; for that idea runs counter to Rogers' fundamental belief that the therapist's aim should be to help the client articulate their experience *in the client's terms.*

Rather than seeing Roger's theory as simply growing out of his clinical experience I think we should see it arising from the interplay of that experience with Freudian ideas, with notions drawn from his knowledge of scientific agriculture, with ideas taken from many other thinkers. Nevertheless, it is true that Rogers' *own* theory emerged only some years after the practice of what Barrett-Lennard calls 'non-directive reflective therapy' had evolved. This is important for one of the themes of the present book, which is that while person-centred therapy is a demonstrably effective form of therapy, there are difficulties in its theoretical formulation which have some implications for clinical practice. It is important to be able to separate the *practice* of non-directive reflective therapy as it evolved in the 1940s and 1950s from the theoretical explanation of its effectiveness in terms of the Conditions of Worth Theory, which Rogers presented in a fully fledged form in 1959.

I will say more about the development of Rogers' theoretical ideas in Chapter 3, but two important points need to be made here about the later development of his thinking. One is that from the early 1960s, following his involvement in the Wisconsin schizophrenia project, Rogers came more and more to emphasise the importance of therapists being real and spontaneous in their relationships with their clients. One might say that the balance between the Therapist Conditions shifted from an emphasis on empathy and acceptance to an emphasis on genuineness. In practice this meant that client-centred practitioners were less restricted in the forms of response they might make. While previously questions, counsellor self-revelations, interpretations, suggestions and so forth were prohibited, such forms of response were now allowed so long as they were made in a way which still embodied the therapist conditions. The emphasis shifted from particular kinds of response (non-directive reflective responses) to the embodiment of particular attitudes (the therapist conditions) in whatever kinds of response came to the therapist spontaneously in the moment.

The other important aspect of Rogers' later thinking is that from the mid-1960s he became very much involved in working with groups. It was the time at which 'encounter groups' were becoming very popular in North America, and Rogers' interest was caught by the fact that the conditions which facilitated group understanding and co-operation seemed to be very much the same as the conditions which were facilitative in individual therapy. In the succeeding years nearly all of Rogers' professional energy was devoted to this new interest, and he wrote nothing significantly new in connection with counselling theory. Rogers' own enthusiasm for groups, together perhaps with something in the spirit of the times, led to a strong emphasis on unstructured group-work in the world of person-centred counselling, regardless of whether it was appropriate to the context. Mearns (1997, p. 11) recalls some of the more extreme examples of this trend, such as the trainer who 'began his weekend introductory course in person-centred counselling skills with a time-unlimited, unstructured encounter group without giving any warning or explanation'. Such episodes are less common today, although many people become interested in 'the person-centred approach' through encounter with person-centred group-work, and are sometimes surprised to learn that it was not in this context that Rogers' ideas originated.

Paths of development in PCT

In the years following the establishment of client-centred therapy as a distinctive school, several lines of development can be traced. I will briefly discuss each of these, with a view to seeing later how focusing-oriented therapy fits into the wider picture. Some of these alternative views within the broad spectrum of the person-centred tradition will be familiar to readers who come to person-centred therapy in what might be called the standard way, that is, through the writings of Rogers, and the experience of training courses which emphasise the centrality of the therapist conditions. Other views may be less familiar, and I will devote more space to some of these. In Britain, especially, there has been little awareness of how many distinct 'tribes' there are in the person-centred 'nation' (Warner, 2000a), although this situation is now beginning to change (Sanders, 2004).

The standard view

By 'the standard view' I mean the view of person-centred therapy which is set out in widely read books which frequently appear as 'recommended reading' on person-centred training courses. Examples of such books are Dave Mearns' and Brian Thorne's *Person-Centred Counselling in Action* (1988; second edition 1999), Tony Merry's *Learning and Being in Person-Centred Counselling* (1999) and Mearns' *Developing Person-Centred Counselling* (1994).

The 'standard view' follows closely what I have called Rogers' Conditions of Worth Theory. It sees psychological disturbance as originating through the imposition of conditions of worth which alienate the person from his or her 'organismic valuing process', and sees the role of the therapist as providing 'conditions for growth' in the form of the therapist conditions of empathy, acceptance and congruence.

Psychologically healthy persons are seen as those whose relationships with others have enabled them to develop self-concepts which allow them to be in touch with their own experiencing, and to trust in their own experiencing rather than in the judgements of others. Mearns (2003) puts it in Rogers' terminology: 'an implicit aim of person-centred working is to help the client to internalise his locus of evaluation'. Since the role of the therapist is seen as one of embodying the therapist conditions as a means of undoing restrictive conditions of worth, and encouraging the client to internalise their locus of evaluation, the main emphasis in the standard view of counsellor training is on the development of the core attitudes of congruence, empathy and acceptance in prospective counsellors. Hence on counselling training courses, 'personal development', in the sense of developing these attitudes, is seen as the most important aspect of training (Mearns and Thorne, 1988, p. 57; Mearns, 2003).

The standard view echoes Rogers' early concern about the imposition of theoretical categories on the client's experiencing. Mearns (2003), for example, speaks of 'the importance of centring the work in the experience of the client rather than in terms of other people's experience of the client issue'. The standard view opposes the introduction of diagnostic categories into counselling sessions, but allows that some general knowledge of conditions such as depression or post-traumatic stress can help the counsellor in understanding the client. Psychopathology is discussed largely in terms of conflict between conditions of worth and organismic experiencing (Lambers, in Mearns, 2003), and different therapist conditions are held to be especially important in connection with different pathologies: for example, congruence is emphasised in connection with psychotic clients (p. 114), and acceptance in connection with clients who have personality disorders (p. 120). The standard view thus allows for a differential emphasis in the therapist conditions depending on the nature of the client's difficulties.

Following Rogers, the standard view is wary of introducing specific therapeutic techniques. On the whole it remains committed to the view that the presence of the six therapeutic conditions is sufficient for therapeutic change. However, it does not insist that procedures which are employed in other therapeutic traditions are always inappropriate. It is rather that the bringing in of specialised techniques is seen as running into the grave danger that the client may come to trust in the expertise of the therapist rather than in their own experiencing. On the whole, the standard view discourages therapeutic moves which aim to teach or direct the client, but in the end the context and the therapist's own spontaneous feelings about what is appropriate to do at the moment are held to be paramount. The introduction of specific procedures does not necessarily go against the notion that the therapeutic conditions are sufficient; the employment of specific procedures can be seen as a manifestation of the therapist's congruent response to what the situation requires. In this respect the standard approach tends to take a pragmatic view of what is helpful, as against the 'purists' who would ban any kind of directivity on the part of the therapist. Brian Thorne (1992, p. 94) writes:

> I had always considered myself to be somewhat of a 'purist' until a member of the 'purist camp' walked out of a video demonstration of my work when he witnessed what was clearly, for him, a directive response from me to my client, even if delivered with extreme respect and tentativeness. At that moment, in his eyes, I had ceased to practice client-centred therapy. I sense that Carl Rogers would have stayed to see what happened next.

Thus the standard view follows the later development of Roger's thinking in that it allows the therapist to be active in the relationship so long as nothing is *imposed* on the client (Mearns, 2003, Chapter 19). Standard person-centred counselling training usually begins with an emphasis on listening and empathic tracking, but the trainees are later encouraged to develop their own individual ways of embodying the therapist conditions. The importance of the counsellor's *presence* in the relationship is emphasised. This reflects the development in Rogers' views to which I referred in the last section, that is, his increasing emphasis on therapist genuineness. Such genuineness involves the therapist in trusting, and where appropriate expressing, their natural responses to the client (Mearns, 2003). This is often referred to as 'use of the self in therapy', and it clearly requires a high level of self-awareness, if it is to be facilitative. Hence the growing emphasis on being genuine in relation to the client further reinforces the stress placed on personal development in counsellor training.

If Focusing procedures are discussed in training, they will normally be introduced as unobtrusive invitations to the client to move towards or remain in contact with what Gendlin calls the 'edge of awareness'. It is the counsellor's presence with the client at the edge of awareness that is emphasised, rather than Focusing as a matter of 'techniques' (Mearns, 2003; Mearns and Thorne, 1988, pp. 47–51).

The standard view has maintained something of Rogers' later enthusiasm for group-work, while letting go of any dogmatic assertion that such work is the only possible context for training in person-centred therapy. It is recognised that while personal development groups can provide experiences which are unattainable in one-to-one sessions, the converse is also true (Mearns, 1997, p. 102).

In sum, the standard view stays close to Rogers' principle of 'client-centredness' without taking this term in a completely literal way. The literalist or 'purist' approach, which I discuss below, would involve asserting that the person-centred approach has no goals for the client beyond those which the client has for themself. Mearns (2003) explicitly opposes the literal interpretation, asserting that person-centred therapists are at least committed to the goal of helping a client 'to find and exercise more of his own personal power with regard to understanding and evaluating his actions'.

Integrationists

Richard Worsley (2004) draws attention to two distinct ways in which person-centred therapists have sought to integrate their approach with ideas and procedures taken from other approaches. One way involves the attempt to integrate Rogers' theoretical concepts with those of other schools, through the development of a variant theory. The other is rather a matter of the individual practitioner assessing to what extent they can integrate ideas and procedures taken from other schools of therapy into their own conception of what it is to be person-centred.

An example of the first approach would be that of Wijngaarden (1990), who sees human beings as having destructive potentials which cannot be accounted for simply as the frustration of fundamentally positive impulses, and draws on Jung's work in elaborating a variation on Rogers' theory.

Examples of people who adopt the second approach include Worsley himself, Reinhard Tausch (1990), who advocates supplementing person-centred therapy with such procedures as relaxation techniques and behavioural counselling, and Rose Battye (2003), whose subtle position is hard to classify as either clearly person-centred or clearly integrationist.

There is something congenial to this second kind of integrationist approach in Rogers' thought itself. Rogers held that neither the theoretical orientation of the therapist, nor the techniques used, matter very much. So long as the therapeutic conditions are present, therapeutic change will occur regardless of the theoretical orientation of the practitioner 'whether we are thinking of classical psychoanalysis, or any of its modern offshoots, or Adlerian psychotherapy, or any other' (Rogers, 1957, p. 101). Similarly Warner (2000a) quotes Rogers as saying '[i]f a therapist has the attitudes we have come to regard as essential, probably he or she can use a variety of techniques'. But if it is unimportant what theoretical notions or techniques are employed by a therapist, then presumably a wide variety of notions and techniques can be brought together without detracting from the efficacy of the therapy.

There are two reservations which may be felt here. One is centred around the question of whether it really is compatible to use 'techniques' such as relaxation procedures or the Gestalt two-chair procedure with the person-centred approach. Many person-centred therapists would say that for the therapist to introduce such techniques is to go against the principle that the client knows best what will be helpful; others, including it would seem Rogers himself, have no objection to the use of special techniques so long as their use does not interfere with the person-centred therapeutic attitudes.

The second reservation centres around the question of whether the theoretical concepts of other schools can be employed along with the concepts of Rogers, but without going so far as to set up a variant theory as in the first kind of integrationist position. It would seem that to employ different and perhaps incompatible conceptual schemes at the same time can only lead to confusion, unless there is some meta-position which shows how the different schemes can all be used.

As we shall see, Gendlin's account can be seen as just such a meta-position, which allows for the possibility that almost any theory of psychotherapy, and almost any procedure, can be practised in a person-centred way. For Gendlin the person-centred approach does not exist on the same level as the theories and procedures of the other schools. I hope to show that it is in that way *fundamentally* different from all the other approaches.

Process-experientialists

Another path of development is that found in the work of Laura Rice, Leslie Greenberg and Robert Elliotz. Here the emphasis is on the micro-processes of therapy, and the development of particular forms of therapist intervention which are thought to be appropriate in different circumstances. The therapeutic conditions remain, but they are now more in the background. This kind of development in client-centred therapy is often now referred to as 'experiential psychotherapy' or 'process-experiential psychotherapy'. Gendlin's own approach is sometimes regarded as belonging here, and Gendlin (1973b) himself at one time used the term 'experiential psychotherapy' to characterise what he was doing. The development of the process-experiential approach can be briefly sketched as follows.

Laura Rice, who completed her doctorate at Rogers' Counselling Centre in Chicago, drew attention to a common kind of therapeutic event in which clients described and explored an incident in which they found themselves reacting in an inappropriate or unexpected way (Rice, 1974). She found that when clients were describing such 'problematic reaction points', it was often therapeutically helpful if the therapist encouraged the client to become more vividly aware of the detail of the incident. If the therapist did this, the client would often become aware that they were construing the incident in a way that did not adequately reflect their *experience* of what happened. For example, a client is unhappy about how he reacts when entering a room full of people, and they turn to look at him: he freezes or rushes out. The therapist reflects back what the client has been saying in a vivid way, such as 'You open the door, walk into the room and all the heads swivel. The eyes focus on you, they get big and terrifying.' This 'evocative reflection' gets the client back into his experiencing of the situation, and he may then notice things which are not part of his construal, for example, that the people are actually looking at him with indifference or even interest. In the therapy session the experiencing as a whole is recalled and reprocessed. There is no need for the therapist to give any interpretation of the situation; the client's own experiencing provides the corrective elements which enable the reprocessing to take place. Of course, if a client is to go back into frightening or painful experiences in this way, it is essential that they feel safe and supported. The therapist conditions are thus very important in maintaining that safe atmosphere, but the more evocative reflections go beyond this in helping the client to get into his or her own experiencing, so that the experiencing can be reconstrued in a more appropriate way. Rice acknowledges that there is an element of therapist directivity in this; the therapist is directing the client towards their own experiencing, but in all other ways the non-directive nature of the client-centred approach is maintained.

A little later Leslie Greenberg (1979), who also began his therapeutic career within the client-centred approach, drew attention to a kind of change event which is often referred to in Gestalt therapy. When a client is experiencing an inner conflict the Gestalt therapist may use a two-chair technique in which the client speaks from each 'part' of themselves while sitting first in one chair and then in the other. This brings the two parts more into awareness, and the resulting dialogue between the two often reduces the differences between them, so that the inner conflict is ameliorated. Greenberg presents evidence that the two-chair procedure can be more therapeutically effective than the procedure of staying empathically with the conflict, but whether or not this is generally so we have an example here of another *kind* of therapeutic procedure, marked this time by what Greenberg calls a 'conflict split'. It should be emphasised that Rice and Greenberg see Rogers' therapeutic conditions as providing an essential setting for procedures such as evocative reflection and two-chair work, and that the procedures are suggested to clients as possible ways of working which the client may prefer not to use. In that case the process-experiential therapist returns to a client-centred baseline of empathic responding.

Another type of therapeutic situation is marked by the client having 'unfinished business' with some significant person in their life. Here a helpful form of therapeutic intervention might be the suggestion that the client should imagine the significant other in an empty chair and express to him or her what the client needs to express.

Of especial interest in the context of this book is the kind of therapeutic situation in which a client has a vague sense of a problem, but is unable to articulate it. Here the most appropriate form of intervention might be Gendlin's Focusing procedure, which Greenberg and Rice (Greenberg *et al.*, 1993) see as one example of an 'experiential search' procedure.

Greenberg and Rice (joined later by Robert Elliott and others) have thus developed a form of therapy in which the provision of the therapist conditions is supplemented by attention to the kind of 'process difficulty' which the client is having. By 'process difficulty' they mean such things as the client being in conflict, finding themself responding to situations in problematic ways, not being able to 'let go' of something in their experiencing and so on. These difficulties are not content-specific: what the conflict is about or what the situation is, is another matter, and only the client can speak with authority about that content. In classical client-centred therapy the client is the expert on what they are experiencing; however in process-experiential therapy the therapist is seen as having special expertise in *ways of working with* one's experiencing. The importance of the therapeutic conditions is not denied, and the process-experientialists emphasise that the conditions can be *directly* effective in therapy (where for instance the client's main need is to be understood or valued). However, they add that the conditions may also provide a setting for work with specific difficulties which are arising in the client's processing of their experiencing. There is a *diagnosis* of process difficulties in process-experiential therapy, and the therapist assumes a directive role in suggesting procedures which may help with the difficulties. The therapist makes no diagnosis in connection with the content of the client's experiencing (there is no 'interpretation'), and does not in any way direct or suggest ways in which the client might view their situation. The slogan of the process-experiential school is 'Direct the process but not the content'.

One further development in process-experiential theory has been the work of Greenberg and his associates on the nature of emotion (Greenberg and Safran, 1987; Greenberg *et al.*, 1993; Greenberg, 2002). In their view it is therapeutically important to target those places where the client's experiencing is constrained or distorted by construals that are inappropriate to the full range of the client's experiencing. These construals should not be seen, as they tend to be seen in some other forms of therapy, as essentially cognitive. They are, rather, *emotional* schemes, and the function of procedures such as Focusing or Two-chair work is to access, and hence allow the restructuring of, these emotional schemes. The theory of emotion and hence of psychotherapy which Greenberg and his associates have developed is rather different from that of Gendlin, but the details lie beyond the scope of the present book.

Process-experiential therapy is not widely known in Britain, although this situation is beginning to change with the recent publications of Worsley (2002) and Baker (2004). However, in Europe and in the United States it has become a quite widely researched form of therapy, with its own literature, clinical handbooks and training courses. In addition to Greenberg, Rice and Elliott, who have been the central figures in this approach, there are others who are more or less closely aligned with it, such as Alvin Mahrer (1996) and David Rennie (1998). All these workers see themselves as operating within the broadly client-centred tradition, emphasising the centrality of the client's conceptualising of their experiencing, as opposed to a conceptualisation based on the categories of a psychotherapeutic theory. They differ from many client-centred therapists in that they see the client as needing context-sensitive therapeutic help in working effectively with their own experiencing. The client is the ultimate authority on what they are experiencing, and on what that experiencing means to them, but a client may need very specific forms of help from the therapist in getting to know what that experiencing and meaning are.

Within the process-experiential tradition, Focusing is seen as a procedure which is appropriate in connection with certain specific client problems, which are marked by the fact that the client has a vague sense of something which they are currently unable to articulate. Gendlin's view of the place of focusing in psychotherapy is rather different, as we shall see, but there is much in the work of the process-experientialists which is relevant to focusing-oriented psychotherapy.

'Purists'

The development of 'integrationist' and 'experiential' approaches within the broad sweep of person-centred therapy has led to a reaction from those who think that such developments undermine the crucial insights of Rogers. These theorists hold that the therapist should have no goal but to follow the client's goals. Barbara Brodley has for several decades resisted what she sees as distortions of the person-centred approach. She writes (Brodley, 1991, her emphasis):

> Any specific goal for a client, systematically pursued by a therapist for a client, *functions and communicates as an expression of authority over the client.* It is an expression of knowing what is good for the client. Having specific goals for clients, including process goals, expresses a conception of the therapeutic relationship that *assumes the capability and the right of the*

therapist to constructively direct the client. I believe that these are deluded assumptions.

And:

the client-centred therapist, guided by his non-directive attitude, has no *directive intentions* in relation to the client. The therapist's intentions are distinctly and only to experience and to manifest the attitudinal conditions in such a way that unconditional positive regard and empathic understanding can be perceived by the client. (Brodley, 1990, p. 90)

Very similarly, Jerold Bozarth (1998, p. 12) writes

The therapist's intent is not to promote feelings or to help the client become more independent or 'to get' the client anywhere. The goal is not self-actualization, actualization, independence, or to help the client become a 'fully functioning' person. The only therapist goal is to be a certain way and by being that way a natural growth process is promoted in the client.

Bozarth grounds his view in his understanding of Rogers' theory:

Rogers' view of psychological dysfunction is that individuals are thwarted in their natural growth by conditions of worth being introjected by significant others. Psychological growth results from the individual being freed from these introjections. When the individual experiences unconditional positive regard from a significant other, the person begins to develop unconditional positive self-regard. As this occurs, the individual becomes increasingly able to deal with problems and life. If the therapist is congruent in the person-centered relationship, experiences unconditional positive regard and empathic understanding towards the client, and if these attitudes are, at least minimally, perceived by the client, then therapeutic change will occur. (p. 117)

Bozarth's understanding of Rogers' theory makes the client's 'actualising tendency' the cornerstone of therapeutic change. The therapist's task is simply to create the conditions under which the actualising tendency can operate effectively. Interestingly, Bozarth (pp. 41–2) concludes from this that the therapist conditions are not strictly necessary; other things may elicit self-regard, and the actualising tendency will make use of whatever is available for constructive change:

There are certainly individuals who report significant change and improved function from experiencing a religious conversion, a sunset, a smile, a traumatic experience, and so on ... The remarkable resiliency of humans in terms of the actualising tendency leads me to conclude that the conditions may not necessarily be necessary.

What Bozarth does insist on is that the therapeutic conditions are sufficient. He sees the 'fundamental curative factor' as the client's perception of the therapist's unconditional positive regard. Empathy is seen as 'the purest way to communicate unconditional positive regard' (p. 51), and congruence is entwined with empathy in that the therapist's awareness of their own experiencing is bound up with their openness to the client's experiencing (p. 80). The therapist conditions are aspects of a way of being in which the therapist is fully receptive of the client, and it is that full presence and receptivity which dissolves the conditions of worth. Bozarth notes that late in his life Rogers himself remarked:

> I recognize that when I am intensely focused on a client, just my presence seems to be healing ... (and) I am inclined to think that in my writing perhaps I have stressed too much the three basic conditions (congruence, unconditional positive regard, and empathic understanding). Perhaps it is something around the edges of these conditions that is really the most important element of therapy – when my self is clearly, obviously present. (Rogers cited in Baldwin, 1987, p. 45)

So far as the use of specific procedures such as 'reflection of feeling' are concerned, Bozarth sees these as possible vehicles for communicating the therapist's positive regard and empathy. Bozarth follows Rogers in holding that other procedures (even such things as interpretations and advice) are acceptable if they communicate the crucial attitudes. What matters is not what the therapist does, but whether what is done conveys the healing attitude.

Tomoda

Another development in person-centred therapy lies in the work of the Japanese therapist Fujio Tomoda, who was a major figure in the introduction of client-centred therapy to Japan. Tomoda had been having deep doubts about the value of advice-giving in student counselling sessions, when in 1948 he was given a copy of the book to which I referred at the start of this chapter, Rogers' *Counselling and*

Psychotherapy. He was deeply impressed by Rogers' approach, and proceeded to translate the book into Japanese. In 1955 he published a translation of *Client-Centered Therapy*, followed a year later by his own major work in Japanese. He continued to play a major role in translating Rogers, and the *Complete Works of C.R. Rogers* was published in Japanese, in twenty-three volumes, in 1969.

While much of person-centred therapy in Japan has subsequently followed the 'standard' path, Tomoda has a distinctive perspective which emphasises the role of the therapist in helping the client to be alone with their own experiencing (Hayashi *et al.*, 1998). Tomoda was very struck by an episode in the earliest published transcription of a complete series of psychotherapy sessions, which was included in Rogers' *Counselling and Psychotherapy* as 'The case of Herbert Bryan'. The therapist is not identified, but is widely understood to be Rogers himself. The central passages which struck Tomoda are (Rogers, 1942, pp. 393, 412):

In Session Six:

> Bryan: So the ideal for me would be to – well, perhaps it's too yogi-istic or something, but I want to sort of effect a cure by myself, apart from the environmental problem. Then after the cure, why, I'll go out and tackle the problem.
>
> Therapist: You feel that growth can sort of take place in a vacuum, and then once you have developed the growth, then you would be capable of dealing with the situation.
>
> Bryan: Well, growth hasn't occurred in the environment, so perhaps it could occur by some sort of solitary meditation or whatever you'd want to call it. That doesn't sound so good, does it?
>
> Therapist: Well, I don't know of growth taking place that way, but I can understand your feeling in regard to it.
>
> Bryan: You know certain religious mystics will meditate in solitude for a long time. Then that seems to gird their loins, as it were. Then they go out and make achievements. So there must be some sort of building up of power there while they're in their solitude.

In Session 7:

> Bryan: ... a person can resolve in a vacuum when they really sincerely mean it, but it's too hard to keep meaning it in a vacuum.

Tomoda comments: 'The true leap or growth of a person occurs when he is utterly alone. It is in human relationships or in the actual world that he makes sure of his own leap or growth. But it is not in the actual human relationship that true growth occurs.' This helped Tomoda to 'grasp the significance of the Zen ascetic standing under a waterfall on a mountain or sitting in religious meditation in solitude. In regard to counselling, the true meaning of the Rogerian techniques is that these techniques help the client to be in a state of being utterly alone' (Hayashi *et al.*, 1998).

As Hayashi *et al.* put it, 'Rogers' core conditions... have crucial importance and are absolutely necessary, but they are themselves not the sufficient conditions for therapeutic personality change. They are, in fact, prerequisites for the vacuum state... The essential meaning of client-centred therapy is in the paradoxical relationship in which a person becomes "utterly alone" through another person's empathic understanding' (p. 113). The way in which this happens is, briefly, that when we sit down with our troubles by ourselves we tend to remain caught in them. We are physically but not psychologically alone (p. 114). The presence of the therapist helps to create a safe space, a 'vacuum', within which we can be with ourselves without being distracted by what Tomoda calls the 'inner strangers', all those parts of ourselves which criticise, undermine and distract us from being who we really are. This kind of view, as Hayashi *et al.* point out, is very closely paralleled in some of Gendlin's concepts, such as those of 'clearing a space' and 'the client's client'. Tomoda's work gives us a different perspective on person-centred therapy, a perspective which connects in a fascinating cross-cultural way with that which Gendlin has quite independently developed.

Rennie

David Rennie's (1998) approach 'fits between the person-centred and experiential genres' (p. *vi*). Rennie follows Rice (see Chapter 5) in emphasising the value of 'evocative reflection' and the use by the counsellor of metaphor and imagery. He follows the process-experientialists generally in seeing a need for process identification and process direction (Chapter 7) in certain circumstances. However, he does not emphasise the use of specific techniques (such as two-chair work) in response to 'markers' of process difficulties (such as 'inner conflict'). Rather, he sees clients as sometimes needing help in dealing with themselves, which can take the form of either process identification or process direction. In process identification the counsellor draws the client's attention to what they are doing, such as 'remembering' or 'telling a story' or 'complaining'. One function of such process identifications is to facilitate the client's awareness of what they are doing, thus opening up the possibility that they may not wish to be doing it. In process direction the counsellor suggests that the client might do something different from what they are currently doing, for example, by suggesting that the client *give some attention* to a feeling, or asking the client if they can *identify what it is* about their situation which is so threatening.

Rennie's approach emphasises throughout the self-reflexive aspect of human experiencing. We not only have our experiences, but also reflect upon them, and this self-reflection is crucial to our sense of ourselves as active agents in the world. As Rennie acknowledges (p. 143), the ideal form of living may be one of non-reflective 'flow', but when the flow is blocked, or is in some way unsatisfactory, we need to stop and reflect, to turn our attention to our experiencing. 'Process identification' is involved in the reflexive awareness of what we are doing, such as 'I am experiencing fear' in contrast to the non-reflexive awareness of simply being afraid.

As Rennie (pp. 4, 12) remarks, while Rogers' *theory* has nothing to say about reflexivity, his practice suggests otherwise. Fred Zimring (1990, p. 442) in effect draws attention to this when he concludes from his analysis that 'Rogers's focus was on the person's present reaction to and interest in his or her problem or concern, as well as on the problem or concern itself.' Rogers did not respond just to the problem or to the feeling; he responded to the client's response to the problem or the feeling.

As we shall see, this separation of the immediate experiencing from the awareness of the experiencing (the creation of a space between me and my fears, for example) is something that is central also in Gendlin's approach. Like Rogers, Gendlin relates to the client in a way that will help the client to relate to their experiencing.

2

Fault-Lines in Person-Centred Theory

Any theory has its weak spots or 'fault-lines' – those places where it is not fully consistent, or where what it predicts does not entirely fit with actual experience. These fault-lines are places from which the theory can grow. In this chapter I will discuss several such fault-lines in the theory of person-centred therapy, and later in the book we will see how Gendlin's work suggests ways in which the theory can be re-structured in ways that eliminate *these* fault-lines. Of course, new fault-lines may then develop!

The agricultural metaphor

The picture of human beings as organisms which actualise themselves in environments which may be more or less favourable is central to Carl Rogers' thought. However, as Brian Thorne points out, it is not altogether consistent with Rogers' emphasis on the importance of the client's relationship with the therapist. It seems, as Thorne (1992, p. 88) puts it, that the therapist 'only has to provide a particular psychological environment and the therapeutic process will unfold spontaneously and inevitably'. Thorne remarks that Rogers' 'tendency to employ images culled from agriculture and his emphasis on the actualising tendency and the wisdom of the organism can lead to a highly positive view of the human being but one which is strangely non-relational'. Thorne simply acknowledges 'the inconsistencies and, at times, the logical contradictions in Rogers' point of view' (p. 89), but I think we see here a fault-line in client-centred theory which needs to be taken seriously.

Rogers uses the life of plants as an analogy for human life. He sees a plant as an organism which has certain innate developmental tendencies, which will be realised if 'environmental conditions' are favourable, 'environmental conditions' being such things as adequate air, warmth, sunlight and water. The analogy is that human beings have an innate actualising tendency which will be fulfilled if their environment contains the favourable interpersonal conditions of genuine empathy and acceptance.

However, even in the case of plants, to think in this way is a serious oversimplification. In order to live fully, a plant needs not only background conditions such as air and sunlight, but specific interactions with elements in its environment. It needs insects to come and pollinate it, and it needs its flowers to be open at the time when the insects are abroad. It needs birds to come and eat its fruit so that its seeds can be distributed. A plant has, or rather *is*, a set of complex *interactions* with elements of its environment.

The same is true for human beings. In order to live fully, a human being needs not only favourable environmental conditions such as understanding and respect, but a whole range of interactions with other people, animals and material objects. Consider for example the learning of language which is so crucial to being human. A child learns one particular language through detailed ongoing interactions with other people. It is not that the child is ready-programmed with its language (although *some* aspects may be innate), and only requires the favourable environmental conditions for speech to emerge. And what is true for language is true for everything that involves the child's initiation into its culture, and that culture's ways of seeing and doing things. The background conditions of empathy and respect are crucial, but much detailed interaction needs to go on in the foreground if the child is to develop normally.

The picture of a human being as an organism which will flourish so long as its natural growth process is not interfered with has a deep appeal, but I would like to probe it a little more. A picture may help our understanding, but if pressed too far it may mislead. A religious person may say, and mean, that 'the eye of God sees everything' but if someone then insists on asking about God's eyebrows, we know that they have misunderstood the use of the picture. It was not meant to be developed along *those* lines (Wittgenstein, 1966, p. 71).

Let us press Rogers' picture of the biological organism a little bit. First, it is clear that that the natural growth and behaviour patterns of organisms are not oriented entirely towards the survival and flourishing of the individual. Think of the bee that dies as a result of its stinging behaviour. Bees are 'programmed' to sting intruders and it is generally to the benefit of the species that this should be done, even if the individual bee dies. Human beings also may well be 'programmed' with instinctive tendencies that involve self-sacrifice. The human mother who will risk her life for her children can be seen as motivated in the same way as the bird mother who makes herself visible to a predator in order to lure the predator away from her nest. Tennyson (*In Memoriam*, Lyric LV), reflecting on the death of his friend Hallam in relation to Darwin's theory, wrote of Nature as 'So careful of the type she seems/So careless of the single life.'

In the background of biological thought is the principle not of the flourishing of the individual but of the species (or, in modern biology, of the genes involved). This is not altogether consonant with Rogers' ideas. But also, according to Darwinian principles, there is no 'goal' or 'general tendency' towards the evolution of the species. It is just that, under the pressure of competition for resources, organisms which are structured in certain ways survive better and leave more offspring than the others. In circumstances where there is no competition for resources, the form and behaviour of organisms (e.g. trilobites) can remain unchanged for millions of years. What was so distinctive, and disturbing, about Darwinian biology was that it eliminated any need for the notion of 'purpose' or 'inherent tendency' in the formation of the organic world.

In terms of the evolutionary process we can see how it is that the structure and instinctive behaviour of organisms are oriented towards the occurrence of certain states or the activation of certain processes. There are indeed these specific tendencies, but there is no overall tendency oriented towards the survival or flourishing of either the individual or the species. In other words there is no single 'potential' to be 'actualised'. This way of rethinking (or eliminating) the notion of the actualising tendency is similar to that suggested by Seeman (1988) and by Greenberg and Van Balen (1998, p. 46). The latter suggest that 'it is the biologically adaptive emotion system which provides the scientific basis for the actualising tendency and the associated organismic valuing process'. They accept the actualising tendency as a tendency towards increased complexity which results in greater adaptive flexibility, but reject the notion that it involves the actualisation of potential, or the 'becoming of all that one can be'.

However, we do not have to take what Rogers says about 'the organism' as literally as this. Instead we can take what he says as a metaphor for what he knows about certain aspects of human life.

If we follow that line of thought, the notion of human life can be *illuminated by* the notion of organic life, rather than reduced to it. Our hopes and fears, and our needs and tendencies can be seen as the many interacting processes which go on in a living organism. Our plans develop and come to *fruition*. We take time to *digest* a surprising experience. We hear a new idea, and a *seed* is planted in us which later develops. Overall, our lives involve the *growth* of experience, maturity, and then the autumn of our days in which we can allow the leaves to fall away. There is an overall pattern in our lives to which all the particular events and processes contribute. Our life is the life of a living whole and we can, if we give attention, become aware of what this living whole needs at any particular time.

The metaphor of a human being as an organism seems a very apt one. Indeed, we may now feel unsure again about whether it really *is* just a metaphor – for, surely we *are* living things, as well as being conscious animals and rational thinkers. We really do grow, breathe, feed, reproduce and decline in the same way as plants and animals do. We are alive in those ways, as well as 'having a life' in the way that only a human being has a life. If it is said that human beings are different because they are *social* beings, and that they exist only in interaction with a whole social context, it could be replied that, as I suggested above, plants too exist only in interaction with a whole environmental context. There is no doubt that we really are living things and that therefore our sense of ourselves as actualising wholes must in some way be embodied in our organic nature.

Gendlin (1997a) argues that what this shows is that the concepts of modern biology themselves need to be re-thought to allow for creatures like ourselves to be in the world. I will touch on this matter later in the book (in Appendix A), but here I just want to suggest that while it may not be useful to tie Rogers' notions to the scientific concepts of evolutionary biology, there is every reason to relate them to our *everyday* notion of a living thing. The issue which then remains is not one which relates especially to Rogers or to psychotherapy; it is the issue of how modern biology can connect with our ordinary sense of the distinctive nature of living things. Gendlin has much to say about this in his more philosophical work.

'Being oneself' and 'social restraint'

The notion that the nature of human life is essentially social and interactional is very widely accepted today. However, as a number of commentators (e.g. Thorne, 1992, p. 88; Holdstock, 1996; Schmid, 2000) have pointed out, this notion seems not to fit well with some aspects of Rogers' thinking. Rogers tends to see human beings as individual organisms which would develop happily, and flourish, if only other human organisms did not come along and impose conditions of worth on them. It can seem, at least, that in Rogers' scheme society comes into the life of the individual in an inhibiting and potentially damaging way. Conflicts are set up between the 'actualising tendency' which is rooted in the organism's biological needs and the requirements – the 'oughts' and 'shoulds' – of society.

In the 1960s and 1970s this aspect of Rogers' thought was warmly welcomed by those involved in the 'human potential' movement. It provided support for a counter-culture which, as Mearns and Thorne (2000, p. 178) put it, had a strong preference for

> 'feelings' over 'thoughts'; for non-self-conscious 'being' over considered action; for 'free expression' over 'censoring'; for 'radical' choices over 'conservative' choices and for 'volume-up' expression of feeling over 'volume-down' expression of feeling.

In short, Rogers was seen as advocating 'following one's feelings' rather than 'adapting to society'.

In response to this, Mearns and Thorne (pp. 177–86) suggest a reformulation of Rogers' theory which replaces the notion of the actualising tendency with the notion of a balanced interaction between actualising tendency and social restraint. They see human beings as social beings in whom the actualising tendency generates a reaction of concern for the impact of one's action on one's social relationships. Their examples include such cases as 'I fought my way out of a relationship previously, and I lost more than I ever imagined' or 'Everything seemed to point in the direction of leaving the job – I needed to be free of it. But my family would have lost too much – and that would mean *me* losing too much. So I rolled up my sleeves and made the best of it.' These are examples in which there is a pull towards doing something which one wants to do, which is counteracted by a concern for the impact on other people and on one's relationships with them.

However, I think that *without* any modification to his theory, Rogers can (and did) allow that people have social impulses as well as purely individual impulses. A man both wants to get out of his job *and* wants his family to be secure. Both these impulses can be seen as aspects of his actualising tendency, just as an animal may have an impulse to protect its young as well as an impulse to seek its own safety. The examples which Mearns and Thorne give are not obviously examples of conflict between actualising tendency and conditions of worth; they seem rather to be examples of conflict between wanting to promote one's own well-being and wanting to promote the well-being of others.

I think that the distinction between impulses which come from the actualising tendency and impulses which come from conditions of worth is not a distinction which can be specified (a) in terms of the content of the impulses *or* (b) in terms of where the impulses come from.

(a) I think that it is not simply that the person's actualising tendency favours the welfare of that person, while what comes from the conditions of worth favours the welfare of others. It *is* often that way, but it need not be: imagine a residential community which is devoted to self-development principles which include the principle of living out one's own needs and not being drawn into 'rescuing' others when they get into emotional difficulties. Everyone agrees that during their time together they will resolutely 'look after themselves'. Then there comes a day when one participant is deeply touched by someone else's pain. Her spontaneous feeling is to put aside her own very real concerns and reach out to this person, but the conditions of worth which she has internalised in the group are very strong, and they prevent her from doing what is natural for her to do. Here her actualising tendency is directed towards the welfare of the other person, while the conditions of worth are directed towards her own welfare. (And situations similar to this really can arise in person-centred training courses.)

The distinction between actualising tendency and conditions of worth needs to be made in a quite different way. To act from the actualising tendency should be seen as a matter of acting *authentically*, which is a matter of giving attention to one's whole sense of the situation one is in, noticing the conflicting impulses, being aware of the moral and prudential principles which seem to apply, and acting from one's *felt sense of all that*. To act from conditions of worth, by contrast, is to act from some *general rule*, such as 'You don't reach out to people in this group', without checking the appropriateness of following the rule against everything else which one thinks and feels. The actualising tendency is a tendency that gives expression to the whole person's experiencing of a particular situation, and only that person in that situation can know what the appropriate expression will be. Conditions of worth, by contrast, embody general rules which it is important to take into account, but which cannot possibly do justice to the intricacy of the lived situation.

The important distinction, then, is not between impulses which will benefit self and impulses which will benefit others, but between impulses which come from deep down in one's whole felt sense of a situation (which takes into account the needs of both self and others), and impulses which arise directly from general principles or rules *without any sensing of whether, or how, the rules apply in this situation*. The relevant distinction is not that between 'my needs' and 'the requirements of society', but that between 'what I deeply sense is best, taking everything into account' and 'what the rules say'. It is very easy to run these two distinctions together, and then we get caught in the equally unsatisfactory positions of either 'We need to follow our feelings and set aside the rules of society' or 'We need to follow the rules, and set aside our personal feelings.'

Part of the confusion here comes from the ambiguity of the word 'feelings' (Gendlin, 1959; Moore, 2002). I think that what Rogers meant when he advocated following one's feelings was what Gendlin means when he says we should be guided by our felt sense of situations. Following feelings is not a matter of indulging emotions or ignoring the needs of others or setting aside moral principles. It is a matter of getting a bodily sense of what the whole situation requires, a feeling which implicitly takes into account one's own emotions and needs, those of others, one's past experience, various principles of morality and so on. Acting from feeling means acting from what Gendlin calls the 'felt sense', rather than acting simply from some strong emotion, or out of habit, or in deference to 'the rules'.

(b) A second confusion which complicates the discussion of 'conditions of worth' is that it can look as if conditions of worth are bad because they come from outside us, whereas the actualising impulses are good because they come from inside. This again fuels the idea that if we are to be ourselves, if we are to be authentic, we should always go by our feelings, in the sense of what *we* want, and take no notice of what anyone else says.

It is true that some of our feelings and attitudes seem to come from inside us, and others seem to come more from what we have learned from others. But it is often hard to know which feelings come from where. A child may develop a strong feeling that people should always be truthful, and we might trace this to certain strongly held principles in their family. But the fact that the child has in this way learned to be truthful does not mean that they have 'introjected a value' which is not theirs. When they grow up they may be genuinely grateful to their parents for having taught them the value of truthfulness. It is a value to which they can authentically and wholeheartedly assent. The fact that it 'came from their parents' does not challenge its authenticity any more than the fact that our knowledge that water is H_2O is invalidated by the fact that it 'came from our teachers'.

Whether an attitude or value is 'ours' is not a matter of where it came from but that of whether we *now* can give it our full assent, whether it resonates for us so that we can live it. Of course, some of our feelings and attitudes which 'come from other people' are *not* authentic. We have taken them in and maybe even act from them, without *feeling* their validity. But what makes this undesirable is not that the feelings or attitudes have 'come from others' but that they have come from others without our checking whether they are right for us. Much of what is valuable to us 'comes from others' (otherwise education would be impossible); the point is that if our feelings and attitudes are to be authentic, we must not skip the step of checking what has 'come from others' against our own felt experiencing.

One final point is that there are cases where we cannot *yet* feel what other people say is good and valuable, though we can sense that we might come to feel it if only some other things in our makeup could shift. We can sometimes sense, after the matter has been brought to our notice, that it would be a good thing to feel a certain way (for instance to feel accepting of some minority group), but we do not yet feel that way. Working towards such a change in our feelings in the light of a general principle which others have suggested to us need not be inauthentic. It is only inauthentic if 'in our heart' (that is, if, taking everything into account, our felt sense is) we do not really want to change.

In this section I have made use of Gendlin's notion of the 'felt sense'. I will be explaining, examining and using this notion throughout the book, but hope to have given a sufficient glimpse here of how such a notion is essential if we are to make sense of Rogers' idea of 'following one's feelings', and to defend it against distortion and trivialisation.

The necessary/sufficient debate

The issues here are central to the disagreements between the purists and other person-centred practitioners. The most common version of the disagreement is over whether Rogers' therapeutic conditions are sufficient as well as necessary for therapeutic change to occur. (The necessity of the Conditions – as I shall call them for brevity – tends to be conceded by the integrationists although, as we saw in Chapter 1, Bozarth, who can reasonably be called a 'purist', has doubts about it, on the grounds that circumstances other than the Conditions can be facilitative.)

The issue here may seem a straightforward empirical one. That is, it may seem at first sight that what are needed are more studies of whether the Conditions by themselves really are sufficient. In reality, of course, there is no easy way to set up such an empirical test. The classical research studies in client-centred therapy suggest that where the Conditions are present, therapeutic change often does ensue, but not always. The question then is whether in the cases of 'failure' this is because the Conditions were not sufficiently embodied in the therapeutic situation, or because there was some further necessary condition which was absent in the 'failure' cases. Or again it might be that it is not the Conditions which are *ever* sufficient because there is some other factor which often, but not always, tends to accompany the Conditions. The difficulty here is that although it has been dem-onstrated fairly conclusively that there is some correlation between the Conditions and therapeutic progress, it has not been shown what the causal connections actually are (Watson, 1984). I will return to this question in Chapter 6.

In the absence of conclusive empirical studies, the question of the sufficiency of the Conditions can be approached only through con-sideration of whether it is theoretically plausible. The purist position would be that what is central to the client-centred view of the person is the actualising tendency of the human organism. The only thing which stands in the way of the actualising tendency, and of therapeutic progress, is conditions of worth, and all that is needed to neutralise conditions of worth is the presence of the Conditions. This is a valid argument, but it presupposes that the only thing which stands in the way of the actualising tendency is conditions of worth. I doubt that this is true, for reasons which I will give in the next section.

Psychological disturbance and conditions of worth

According to the Conditions of Worth Theory, the aim of therapy is to provide an antidote to the introjected conditions of worth. This view follows from the idea that it is the setting up of conditions of worth which is at the root of psychological disturbance. I think most therapists would agree that a great deal of psychological disturbance does originate in this way, but does it all?

For example, traumatically induced phobias and post-traumatic stress difficulties are not obviously related to the imposition of conditions of worth. There are several hypotheses about what is involved in the generation of post-traumatic stress, but the introjection of conditions of worth is not one of them.

Many clients come to counselling because they are faced with some predicament in which they have to choose between equally difficult courses of action. For instance, Barbara is a young mother who, before her marriage, had begun a promising musical career. She now has a young son, and a husband whose pattern of work allows little time for childcare. There is the possibility of some regular musical performance which would help her to pick up her career again, but this would mean leaving her son in the care of people she does not altogether trust. She is torn between the responsibility she feels for her son's welfare and the responsibility she feels she has to her own personal and professional development. Of course, conditions of worth may lurk in the background here (Barbara's parents might have strong views about 'looking after yourself' *or* about 'putting your children first'), but equally that may *not* be so. Certainly there can be deep anxiety and confusion in such predicaments without the addition of conditions of worth.

Then again, in bereavement and other cases of loss, such as miscarriage, or loss of a job, or loss of opportunities, there is psychological distress which can be worked on through counselling, but there is no necessity for conditions of worth to be involved.

Consider also cases where the roots of a client's difficulties lie not in the parents' imposition of conditions of worth but in their being physically or emotionally absent. Disturbance often seems to arise from a client's not having been related to adequately in their early life. If for any reason a mother is unable to 'mirror' her child effectively then the child may not find it easy to acquire a strong sense of what they feel and want. The psychological disturbance comes not from the mother imposing conditions of worth, but from her being unable to connect sufficiently with her child.

I think it will be agreed that examples such as these are not exceptional. They and probably dozens of other kinds of case which do not involve introjection of conditions of worth are part of the daily experience of most counsellors. Person-centred therapists as much as any other therapists work with clients who come with issues such as these.

The Conditions of Worth Theory suggests that person-centred therapy is effective because the client's perception of the therapist's congruent and empathic unconditional positive regard provides an antidote to the conditional regard which the client has experienced in the past. Once the conditions of worth are removed, the client's actualising tendency will automatically propel the client towards fuller functioning. But this cannot be the explanation of why person-centred therapy is effective in the cases I have just referred to, that is, those in which conditional regard played no role in the generation of the disturbance. I know of no empirical research which would suggest that person-centred therapy is ineffective in these kinds of case, and I will assume that such a suggestion is too implausible to be taken very seriously, although the matter is of course open to empirical investigation.

It is an interesting question why, in spite of these rather obvious counter-examples, the Conditions of Worth Theory has been so widely accepted in person-centred circles. Part of the reason may be that difficulties due to introjection of conditions of worth *are* very common, and that even where such introjection is not the primary factor, it can exacerbate the trouble (for instance, conditions of worth which interfere with the expression of grief). More speculatively, it may be that in Rogers' own life conditions of worth played a very prominent role, so that his attention would naturally have been drawn to *that* kind of difficulty. Then, as the person-centred approach became better known, people with that kind of difficulty would themselves be drawn to the approach and feel that Rogers had expressed what they 'had always known'. (This speculation no doubt appeals to me partly because it fits with *my* personal experience, in which early trauma seems to have played as prominent a role as conditions of worth.)

However that may be, it seems clear that there is a range of common-enough kinds of case in which, it is reasonable to assume, person-centred therapy can be effective, but in which the *reason* for its being effective cannot be that which the Conditions of Worth Theory asserts. What is needed is a theory of person-centred therapy which will explain its effectiveness in *these* cases, as well as in those cases which do involve the introjection of conditions of worth. As we shall see, Gendlin provides such a theory.

Directivity

In the early days Rogers characterised his approach to therapy as being 'non-directive':

> The counselling relationship is one in which warmth of acceptance and absence of any form of coercion or personal pressure on the part of the counsellor permits the maximum expression of feelings, attitudes and problems by the counsellee. (Rogers, 1942, pp. 113–14)

> Nondirective counselling is based on the assumption that the client has the right to select his own life goals, even though these may be at variance with the goals that the counsellor might choose for him. (Rogers, 1942, pp. 126–7)

Later, the term 'non-directive' was dropped in favour of 'client-centred', although it is not clear whether this terminological change reflected any significant change in Rogers' views (Wilkins, 2003, p. 87).

Directing a client needs to be distinguished from having an influence on them (Brodley, 1999, p. 79; Wilkins, 2003, p. 90). Clearly, whatever the therapist does has some influence on the client, and there would be little point in the therapist being there if they had no influence. But the client may not be influenced in the way the therapist intends. Jung once said that it is usually quite safe to give clients advice because they so rarely take it! A client is quite likely to respond to the therapist's advice by doing the opposite, because they wish to be independent, or because when they hear the advice it brings into focus that they do not wish to follow it. The important issue is not whether the client does what the therapist suggests, but whether the client reflects and consults their own experiencing before going along with, or against, the therapist's suggestion.

Mearns and Thorne (2000, pp. 190–5) argue in a similar way that the important issue is not whether the therapist is 'directive' but whether the client is directed. They give a nice example:

> *Jeri*: Okay, Dave – tell me what I should do – should I take this job or not?
> *Dave*: Take it. Ring them now before they change their minds. It's a great job.
> *Jeri*: [pauses]...No, it doesn't feel right...I don't know what's wrong with it yet...but it's not right.
> ...[Jeri] is entirely uninfluenced by the therapist's opinion but she can make good use of it as a means of 'focusing'...it allows Jeri to imagine her Self, in that moment, telephoning to accept the job...and immediately she

experiences the reaction which tells her that something is not right. She makes good use of the therapist's advice.

There is also a difference between directing a person and coercing or manipulating them (Lietaer, 1998, pp. 62–4). An air traffic controller directs the aircraft into a safe landing, but does not coerce or manipulate the pilot. The controller can see what the pilot cannot see, so the pilot follows the controller's directions. This is close to a model of therapy in which the therapist can see better than the client what is going on and what is needed. But this is precisely what Rogers denies. His view is that the therapist simply is not in a position to know what the best course is for the client. Bozarth (1998, p. 121) quotes Rogers as saying 'If I thought that I knew what was best for a client, I would tell him.'

What the therapist can do, and this is a central theme in Gendlin's work, is to help the client to experience more fully and more explicitly what their situation is, and what the possible ways forward may be. But given this, the therapist has a responsibility to behave in ways that will facilitate the client's *own* experiencing of their situation. The therapist should, for example, discourage the client from taking what the therapist says as necessarily right, or from dwelling inordinately on what other people want the client to do. Following their belief that the client is the only person who can really know what they should do, the therapist will want to direct the client away from what other people think, and gently press the question 'And what do *you* think? How is it for *you*?'

There is directivity here, but not of the sort that would come from the therapist having a superior understanding of the client's situation. The therapist cannot know the client's situation better than the client, but they do know something that the client may not know; that therapeutic change is likely to follow if the client can move from an external locus of evaluation to an internal one. That is, what the therapist knows is that for anyone's life to move forward the person must give attention to their *own* perceptions and values. It is *their* life that is in some way blocked, and *their* life is constituted precisely by *their own* experiencing. If the client wishes their life to move forward, the client has to begin by giving attention to where they are. This is not to deny that reflecting on what other people say can be important, or that it may be valuable to reflect on and take seriously the attitudes of society or the position taken up by one's secular or religious teachers. But in the end the individual has to decide whether they wish to identify with these views and attitudes of others. The point here is that elucidated by existential philosophers such as Sartre; that if there is anything essential to being a person it is that people have choices in what they are to become.

Perhaps because of the ambiguities in the term 'directivity', Rogers later came to call his approach 'client-centred': it *centres on the client*. But this does not imply that the therapist is totally non-directive. On the contrary, one of the aims of the therapeutic situation is that of facilitating the *client-centredness of the client*. This aim is not a personal aim of the therapist which they, as it were, *impose* on the client; it arises rather from the fact that the client has come for therapeutic help and that in the client-centred view of things what is central to therapeutic helpfulness is the centring of attention on the client's *own* experiencing. Should the client have different views on what is therapeutically effective, should they for instance believe that therapy involves the therapist discovering what is going on in the client's unconscious and informing the client of what has been found, then the responsible client-centred therapist would need to point out that they cannot work in terms of that assumption.

Client-centred therapy *is* directive in that it holds that therapeutic interventions should normally be responses to the *client's* experiencing. If the client moves towards centring the sessions around what the therapist believes, or around what significant others believe, the responsible client-centred therapist will gently direct the client back to the question of what the client themself thinks or feels. The responsible client-centred therapist will do this because they believe that it is only through attention to one's own experiencing that one can change, and after all the client has come to therapy precisely because in some sense they do wish to change.

The directivity towards the client's own experiencing is, however, the *only* way in which client-centred therapy is directive. The client-centred therapist does not try to direct the course of the client's experiencing, or its content, or its evaluation as satisfactory or unsatisfactory. This is not, as is often assumed, because the therapist does not wish to be powerful in the relationship; therapist power, harnessed to the client's aims, would be helpful to the client. (To repeat Rogers' words, 'If I thought that I knew what was best for a client, I would tell him.') Rather, the therapist does not try to direct the course, content or evaluation of the client's experiencing, partly because he or she usually just does not know enough even to make helpful suggestions, and partly because if the client is to know what to do, this knowledge – to be real knowledge – must be rooted in their own experiencing.

It is not that the ideas or advice of a therapist can never be helpful; *of course* they can, but for there to be therapeutic progress the client has to reflect and digest what the therapist and other people have said, to check it against their own experiencing. There is nothing opposed to client-centred principles in the therapist offering their own ideas about the client's situation, but the extent to which this is done has to be very limited because for each comment of the therapist the client needs time to reflect on how that feels for *them*.

In sum, the therapist *cannot* direct the course of the client's experiencing; it is not that they *should not* because of ethical considerations about the exercise of power. The attitude of the person-centred therapist is 'I really don't know how your difficulty can be resolved, but I may be able to help you to stay with your own experiencing so that out of that a way will emerge.' It is *not* the attitude 'Of course, as an experienced therapist I know precisely what the way forward is, but it will be better for you if you find it out for yourself.' But while the therapist cannot direct the client's experiencing, what they *can* do, and need to avoid doing, is to *block* the client's experiencing. With a client who is not well grounded in their own experiencing, an instruction to do something will take them out of their experiencing and centre them in the therapist's frame of reference.

The difficulties about the notion of directivity can thus be resolved if we place the emphasis on the client's experiencing, which, as we shall see, is what Gendlin's focusing-oriented therapy consistently does.

The nature of congruence

The notion of congruence plays a double role in Rogers' theory. Congruence in the therapist is one of the Conditions for therapeutic movement, but it is also what is lacking in the client. The psychological disturbance of the client is understood theoretically as a lack of congruence, a lack of 'fit', between the client's experience and their conceptualisation of their experience. From the point of view of Rogers' theory, progress in therapy consists in the increasing congruence of the client and reaches its ideal term when the client becomes fully congruent and therefore fully functioning.

Rogers' (1959, p. 206) explanation of congruence is:

> when self-experiences are accurately symbolized, and are included in the self-concept in accurately symbolized form, then the state is one of congruence of self and experience.

Rogers took the term 'congruence' from geometry (Kirschenbaum, 1979, p. 196), where two triangles are congruent if they are of exactly the same shape and size, and therefore correspond exactly to each other. For Rogers, self-concept and experience are congruent if they exactly match up and if the self-concept accurately represents the experience. Rogers continues:

> This is a concept which has grown out of therapeutic experience, in which the individual appears to be revising his concept of self to bring it into congruence with his experience, accurately symbolised. Thus he discovers that one aspect of his experience if accurately symbolized, would be hatred for his father; another would be strong homosexual desires.

Congruence, then, is essentially the accurate symbolisation of experience. And 'experience', for Rogers, is 'all that is going on within the envelope of the organism at any given moment which is potentially available to awareness. It includes events of which the individual is unaware, as well as all the phenomena which are in consciousness' (p. 197).

Thus a man who discovers that he hates his father has moved from a position in which his experience of his father was inaccurately symbolised as, for example, 'admiring', to a position where he symbolises it accurately as 'hating'. The experience of hatred was there all the time, but it had not until now been symbolised (conceptualised, recognised) as hatred.

It is important to see that the term 'experience' is being used here in a novel way. The more usual thing to say would be that the man did not at the earlier time *experience* hatred; his hatred was there, but unconscious and therefore *not* experienced. If asked at the earlier time whether he experienced hatred, the man could truthfully say 'No'. Later he may truthfully say he *now* experiences hatred, but up until now he had not been aware of it. Using the term 'experience' as it is normally used, if a person says they are not experiencing something then they are not experiencing it (assuming that they have an adequate command of the language, and are not lying).

Rogers' way of thinking here is little different from Freud's. For Freud the man does not consciously experience hatred; this experience has been repressed, and is *unconscious*. Rogers (1961, p. 237) himself occasionally uses the term repression:

Our theory is that in the psychological safety of the therapeutic relationship the client is able to permit in his awareness feelings and experiences
which would ordinarily be repressed, or denied to awareness.

Rogers does not explicitly speak in terms of 'the unconscious'
because he sees that once we allow that sort of talk, it opens the way
to the therapist knowing better than the client what the client's
experience is, and that would go against the basic principles of his
approach. However, as Ellingham (2001) has recently argued, Rogers
does follow *very* closely in the footsteps of Freud.

It seems to me that Rogers cannot have it both ways. Either there
are, as he says, events in the client's experience 'of which the individual is unaware', 'experiences denied to awareness', or there are not. If
there are, then his position is not significantly different from Freud's;
if there are not, then we need a new way of thinking about situations
in which a person, for example, comes to realise that they hate their
father. How can we think about this if not in terms of the Freudian
kind of picture of something having been there all the time,
unknown to the client, but quite possibly known to the therapist?

For Rogers, as for Freud, the experience of hatred may be there
even if the person *says* the experience is one of admiration. But what
is the criterion for saying the person experiences hatred? Perhaps his
behaviour shows subtle signs of aggression which can be seen by
others as typical of hatred. But it is notorious that feelings, especially
more intricate feelings, cannot be read off from a person's behaviour.
Suppose that instead of realising that he hated his father the man realised that he experienced his father as someone who subtly put him
down. We could easily see that his father subtly put him down, but
how could we see whether he *experienced* (in Rogers' sense) his father
as subtly putting him down. In the ordinary sense of 'experience' he
clearly *did not* experience this at the time; in Rogers' sense there is no
way of knowing.

Rogers was aware of this difficulty. At the end of his 1959 paper
he writes (p. 250):

We are urgently in need of new and more ingenious tools of measurement...
most urgently needed of all is a method whereby we might give oper-
ational definition to the construct *experience* in our theory, so that discrep-
ancies between self-concept and experience, awareness and experience,
etc. might be measured. This would permit the testing of some of the
most crucial hypotheses of the theoretical system.

Needless to say, no such 'ingenious tools of measurement' have ever been devised. It is hard to see how they could be, since the problem is one about concepts rather than about measurement. If we stick to the phenomenological view of 'experience' as that which is in one's awareness then 'unconscious experiences' is a contradiction in terms. On the other hand if we allow that there are unconscious experiences then there must be ways of establishing when these experiences occur. The client, by definition, cannot know when they occur, so if they are accessible at all they must be accessible by others, such as therapists or researchers. But then the therapist or researcher knows better than the client what the client experiences.

A similar problem arises in connection with the *therapist's* congruence. If incongruence is a matter of the therapist having certain experiences of which they are not conscious, how can the therapist know that they are having such experiences? And if they do not know, how can they know whether they should be trying to be more congruent? Rogers (1963, p. 11) himself acknowledged that 'a lack of congruence is usually unknown to the therapist himself at the time', but as Haugh (2001, p. 121) says 'he does not adequately address this problem, and it is not possible to get out of the dead end of Rogers' reasoning'.

Gendlin has important things to say about this issue. His view is that talk of what is 'unconscious' needs to be replaced by talk of what is 'implicit'. The process of therapy, for Gendlin, is not a matter of making conscious what was unconscious, but of making explicit what was implicit. We will be exploring this view in later chapters. For the moment I hope at least to have shown that there are serious problems with the notion of congruence as Rogers understood it.

The client-centred response

The hypothesis which Rogers formulated in the late 1950s – what I have called the Therapeutic Conditions Hypothesis – is not specific about the form which therapist responses should take. What is seen to be crucial is that the response should be genuinely empathic and accepting. Nevertheless, one important way of embodying these attitudes so that the client will experience them has remained that of 'active listening' or 'non-directive reflecting' of the client's experience. Just what is involved in this distinctively client-centred mode of therapist responding has not often been made explicit. In person-centred training courses it is often said that 'reflection' should not be done in a 'wooden' way. That is, it is unlikely to be helpful if the therapist simply repeats back what the client has said with appropriate changes of pronouns. For example,

> Client: I have been feeling really low this week.
> Therapist: You have been feeling really low this week.
> Client: It has actually been worse since I talked about all that stuff...
> Therapist: It has actually been worse since you talked about all that stuff...

If the session continues like this, the client may well feel that they might as well have bought a parrot! Rogers himself said (1986a, p. 376):

> I am *not* trying to "reflect feelings". I am trying to determine whether my understanding of the client's world is correct – whether I am seeing it as he or she is experiencing it at this moment.

On the other hand, *clients* could experience what Rogers was doing in a different way: for example, Slack (1985) writes:

> It was like Dr Rogers was a magical mirror. The process involved my sending rays towards that mirror. I looked into the mirror to get a glimpse of the reality that I am ... This experience allowed me an opportunity to get a view of myself that was untainted by the perceptions of outside viewers.

Rogers (1986a) says in response to Slack only that 'in understanding the client's experience, we can realise that such responses do serve as a mirror', which rather suggests that he saw the mirroring function as incidental; he was not *intending* to mirror the client. On the other hand, around the same time, Rogers (1986b, p. 202) writes in connection with a reflective response he made in a demonstration session: 'My response has the advantage of bringing fully into awareness her positive aims and goals. There is value in holding up a mirror to the client.'

It is as if Rogers rather *reluctantly* accepted the mirroring function of reflection. It was not what he was primarily trying to do, but he saw that it could be of value to the client.

Rogers usually reflected what his clients said in his own words, which is clearly important if the main concern is to check understanding. However, it is also true that at times the literal reflection of the client's words can be therapeutically effective. Consider the following example taken from Leijssen (1993, p. 137):

C45: A kind of…hum…a mixture of things I think. (T: Hmh.) Something to do with darkness and something to do with, hum…I can only…can I give you an image?

T46: Hmh. Please do.

C46: A sort of fog.

T46: A sort of fog.

C47: Mhm, a creeping fog. (T: Mhm) That's what I'm sort of picking up. (T: Mhm) A creeping fog.

T47: A creeping fog.

Here the client is moving a bit more deeply into their experiencing, and there is considerable evidence that such movement is associated with therapeutic change. Rogers would say that what matters is that the therapist has understood, and has conveyed that understanding to the client. Yet while it is undoubtedly true that feeling understood is likely to be helpful to the client, it is not obvious that such understanding is the only helpful factor in the kind of interchange just considered. In Leijssen's session the therapist, not being a native English speaker, *did not understand* the words 'creeping fog'. She decided to wait to ask for an explanation, meanwhile just reflecting the keywords. Here in spite of the lack of understanding, the therapist's response still served the function of helping the client to articulate her experiencing, and go further into it. This second therapeutic function of reflection seems to be undervalued by Rogers. It is central to Gendlin's therapeutic practice, and we will encounter many examples of it as we proceed.

There is, I suspect, a third therapeutic function of reflection which is not discussed explicitly by Rogers, though Gendlin (1996, Chapter 22) makes some reference to it. It is that in 'seeing their own experiencing in the therapist's mirror' the client gets a stronger sense of that experiencing and of their own existential reality. Psychodynamic writers as different as Winnicott, Kohut and Lacan have all emphasised the importance in early childhood of the mother's mirroring of the child. The child gazes into the mother's eyes (or the equivalent in other sensory modes) and becomes aware of their own reality through their awareness of the mother's awareness of them. (This is an experiential version of Bishop Berkeley's famous philosophical dictum 'To be is to be perceived.' It is also something which is strongly suggested by some of Henry Moore's sculptures in which the reflective 'lines of force' between mother and child are portrayed by threads connecting the eyes.) Where the mother is unable to provide good enough mirroring, because of the pressures in her life, or her own troubles, or her self-absorption, or her lack of interest in the child, the child finds it more difficult to acquire a strong sense of their own reality.

However, such a developmental deficit is remediable (Schore, 1994, 2003). It simply requires other people, later on, to respond to the client in the mirroring way which is characteristic of much person-centred therapy. The difficulties of clients with this kind of background come not from the imposition of external conditions of worth on a strongly felt and differentiated experiencing, but from the relative lack of such experiencing. If person-centred therapy is effective with such clients, it is not through restoring the client's sense of their own experiencing through the dissolution of conditions of worth, but through helping the client to find their own experiential centre for the first time. All this is implicit in Gendlin's theory of therapy, which emphasises the interactional nature of human life, and the fact that often in the early stages of therapy the client can only be themself in the relationship with the therapist (Gendlin, 1964b/1973, p. 469). I will return to that theme in Chapter 3.

The counsellor as well-functioning

In the person-centred approach there is sometimes a tendency to disparage expert knowledge and skills. This attitude derives from the person-centred belief that in the end it is only the client who can be an expert on their life. Instead of valuing a therapist's knowledge and skill, the person-centred approach tends to value the therapist's attitudes and 'way of being'. Therapeutic movement is seen as movement from incongruence to congruence under the benign influence of a congruent, empathic and accepting counsellor, a counsellor who if not fully functioning, is at least well-functioning. For trainee counsellors this takes away one problem (you do not have to be an expert) but replaces it with another (you do need to be well-functioning). I suspect that person-centred counsellors are not always aware of how, from the perspective of other schools, the person-centred position can seem to be setting itself up as morally superior. In other schools of therapy the view is that a trainee therapist works hard to acquire their knowledge and skills, becomes to some extent an 'expert', and then uses their expertise to help their clients. No claim is made that through their training the trainee becomes a better *person*. Yet that is how the person-centred view can come across: the training should make the trainee more understanding, more accepting and more genuine. These traits that the training should develop are morally tinged attitudes; they are not 'neutral'. To be a good counsellor it seems that one has to be a good person.

This is a tangled area. I think it is undeniable that a counsellor (of whatever school) is likely to be more effective the more they embody the attitudes of genuineness, empathy and acceptance. But I imagine that that is true for almost any profession in which one is working with people. Person-centred therapy does not have a monopoly on the values of understanding, respect and honesty. In professions other than person-centred psychotherapy the 'core conditions' are *facilitative* of what is being done: the empathic teacher teaches better than the unempathic teacher. But embodying these conditions does not *constitute* teaching; someone could embody these conditions to perfection but fail to have the knowledge and skills of a teacher. There is a question here of to what extent psychotherapy resembles teaching in this respect. Is it that there are therapeutic skills which are facilitated by the presence of the therapist conditions, or are the Conditions *all* that is required? Person-centred therapists are very wary of reducing therapy to the possession of skills, but I think it is important to appreciate the other point of view, which is that being a good therapist should not be identified, in effect, with being a good person. That is surely to set the standard for being a good therapist far too high, and to invest it with a moral tone that is not entirely comfortable or plausible.

Gendlin remarks in this connection, 'The essence of working with another person is to be present as a living being. And that is lucky, because if we had to be smart, or good, or mature, or wise, then we would probably be in trouble' (Gendlin, 1990, p. 205). Just what Gendlin means by 'being present as a living being' we will need to explore later.

The equal effectiveness of the major approaches

In his early research work Rogers was trying to establish what are the conditions of therapeutic change. His aim was not to establish a new school of therapy but to determine what was involved in effective therapy, whatever the school. Out of this work grew the view that there are certain therapist *attitudes* which are conducive to therapeutic change, together with the stronger suggestion that these attitudes are *all* that is needed. Thus what I am calling the Therapeutic Conditions Hypothesis came into being.

The assertion of the Therapeutic Conditions Hypothesis in effect established a new school of therapy. If this theory is correct then all other schools either leave out at least one of the Conditions, or add other things, which according to the Therapeutic Conditions Hypothesis are unnecessary. The effectiveness of other schools of therapy should therefore be less than that of the person-centred school because the work of the other therapists will either leave out something that is essential for therapy, or waste time and effort on things which are not essential. But in fact the evidence suggests that all the major forms of therapy are about equally effective, including the person-centred form (Smith and Glass, 1977; Stiles *et al.*, 1986; Lambert and Bergin, 1994; King *et al.*, 2000).

The question arises of whether this is because the research studies are inadequate (or in some way biased against person-centred therapy), or whether the Therapeutic Conditions Hypothesis is flawed – for, if it really is true that there is little difference between the effectiveness of the different therapies, *including person-centred therapy*, then it means that we have not in fact identified satisfactorily the necessary and sufficient conditions of effective therapy.

As I will detail in Chapter 6, what the research studies suggest is not that there are no differences between the effectiveness of therapists, but that effectiveness is not correlated significantly with the type of therapy. What does seem to make a significant difference is the quality of the therapeutic interaction and the client's own capacity to engage in the therapeutic work. This is not quite what the Therapeutic Conditions Hypothesis says. The Hypothesis says nothing about client capacity (only that the client is anxious or vulnerable), and restricts the notion of therapeutic interaction to the providing of the therapeutic conditions. A more satisfactory view would have more to say about the client side of the relationship, and also more about what exactly is involved in effective therapeutic interaction.

As we shall see, Gendlin's theory has much to say about both of these issues. In Chapters 3 and 4 we will look at his views in some detail, and then return to the question of how his 'focusing-oriented psychotherapy' relates to the more familiar formulations of person-centred therapy.

3

The Origins of Focusing

Eugene Gendlin joined Carl Rogers' group at the Counselling Center of the University of Chicago in 1953. He was at the time working on his PhD in philosophy, having completed a philosophy MA three years previously. Gendlin's interest in philosophy centred around the question of how we symbolise our experience, and what the relation is between our experiencing and the symbols in terms of which we articulate our experiencing. The philosopher Richard McKeon (to whom Gendlin referred as 'my great teacher') had emphasised what today has become a commonplace: that there are *alternative ways* of conceptualising our experience. The world is not simply there, already divided up into natural categories; rather, our ways of thinking and living have an important part to play in how the world is for us. Today this is often referred to as the 'social construction of reality'. But for Gendlin it is not the whole story. Although there are many ways of conceptualising our experience some of these ways lead somewhere, or 'carry us forward', while others do not. Gendlin holds that in thinking about the relationship between concepts and experience we have to avoid not only the trap of saying that there is just one way in which our experience can be conceptualised, but also the trap of saying that an experience can be conceptualised in any way we please.

When, in the early 1950s, Gendlin came across the work of Rogers' group it struck him that these people in psychotherapy were doing just the thing which interested him. Gendlin (1983, p. 78) says in an interview:

> I actually went into the Counselling Center while I didn't belong there, and discovered that the papers the staff members were writing were available in the waiting room...And so, I sneaked in there and pretended I was a client, so that I could borrow one of those. And then I got more

and more interested, since indeed they were doing this; they were letting a person have directly this experience and slowly to work at how to express that, how to symbolize that, how to say that.

Gendlin was trained in 'non-directive therapy' by Rogers' group and began to participate in the research work of the Counselling Center. One important study by Kirtner and Cartwright had strongly suggested that it is often possible to predict from the first few sessions whether a client was likely to be successful in therapy. Much seemed to depend on the personality of the client (Kirtner and Cartwright, 1958a), and on how the client related to their own experiencing (Kirtner and Cartwright, 1958b). Recalling this period Gendlin (in Rogers and Russell, 2002, p. *xviii*) remarks:

> In 1956, when Kirtner distributed his study, the center staff was outraged. We could not believe that we worked with some clients in a way that was failure-predicted from the first few interviews. Surely there must be an error in the study, we declared. Only Rogers was calm. He told us, "Facts are always friendly." When I came to his office to argue about it, he said "This study will help us with the next study." As I was leaving and we stood in the doorway, he put his hand on my shoulder for emphasis and said "Look, maybe *you* will be the one to discover how to go on from this." He meant me only as an example, but I may have heard him on a deeper level.

One early question which Gendlin worked on in the 1950s was the role of the counsellor–client relationship in the process of psychotherapy. Many theorists, including Freud and Rogers, held that the interpersonal relationship is crucial, yet some research studies had suggested that there was in fact no correlation between therapeutic outcome and the extent to which clients focus on the relationship in therapy. With Richard Jenney and John Shlien, Gendlin (1960) designed a study that would 'distinguish between observations of relationship focus as a topic of discussion and observations indicating use of the relationship for significant experiencing' (p. 211). The conclusion was that there was no general correlation between therapeutic outcome and the degree to which the client focused on their relationship with the counsellor; what was significant, rather, was whether in referring to the relationship the client was involved in his or her own immediate experiencing, for instance: 'I feel guilty when I want to be independent. And I feel that way with you also' or 'I've never been able to let go and just feel dependent and helpless, as I do now.' Similarly, this study suggested, there is an important difference in connection with the question of whether client reference to *feelings* is important. The conclusion was that clients who simply *talk about* their feelings (e.g. 'I was scared last night'; 'Often I am depressed') make little progress, whereas those who *express* their feelings (e.g. 'It comes to me now how scared I was last night'; 'Gee, I feel low') are more likely to make progress.

Gendlin, along with others in Rogers' group, believed that much psychological disturbance is associated with a 'structure-bound' manner of experiencing. Freud (1936, p. 105) spoke of 'repetition compulsion' where past perceptions are imposed on, and distort, present perception, but Gendlin emphasised not so much the *content* of the perceptual distortion but the *manner of experiencing* which is involved. 'There is experiencing of structures and patterns instead of the richly detailed immediacy of present events' (Gendlin and Shlien, 1961, p. 69). Gendlin held at this time a view which he has held ever since, that the efficacy of psychotherapy has much to do with whether the client can direct their attention to their own immediate experiencing. Such directed attention has physiological effects, as Gendlin and Berlin (1961, p. 73) demonstrated in another early paper, on 'Galvanic skin response correlates of different modes of experiencing'. Gendlin and his colleague wrote in this paper, 'Personality change during psychotherapy is held to involve many brief periods during which the individual refers his attention directly, and in a continuous way, to these immediately felt data of experiencing.' The results of the study showed that attention to one's immediate experiencing results in increased galvanic skin-resistance (and hence tension-reduction), even in cases where the *content* of what is experienced might in normal circumstances be associated with increased tension. As we shall see, this is a phenomenon which is characteristic of the 'focusing' procedure.

Working with Fred Zimring (Gendlin and Zimring, 1955) Gendlin developed a Process Scale which was designed to measure the extent to which clients refer directly to the process of their own experiencing. A version of this scale was used in the large Wisconsin study on schizophrenia, and it was later refined as the Experiencing Scale.

In this period, the mid-1950s, Rogers had been developing two lines of thought about what is involved in successful psychotherapy. One was concerned with what the *therapist* was doing; the other was concerned with what takes place in the client. The line of thought concerning the therapist is what is best known about Rogers' work, that is, that therapy is effective when the therapist embodies the

Conditions of genuineness, empathy and unconditional regard. As we have seen, Rogers presented his first full statement of this view in the paper 'The necessary and sufficient conditions of therapeutic personality change' (Rogers, 1957).

However, Rogers was equally interested in the question of what happens in the client. In 1956 he gave an address to the American Academy of Psychotherapists on 'The essence of psychotherapy: moments of movement' (Rogers, 1956). This address was unfortunately never published, but shortly before his death Rogers sent a copy to Jerold Bozarth with the comment 'I just discovered this 1956 paper and I like it' (Bozarth, 1996, p. 495). In the paper Rogers says:

Is it possible, in the richly interactional relationship of psychotherapy, to discern some essential or crucial element, to which all the rest of the experience is subsidiary? This is a question which has compelled my interest for a long time. It is a question to which, during the past two decades, I have given a variety of answers. In years gone by I believed that insight, properly defined, was such a crucial element. I have long since given up this view. I have spoken as though the relationship is the crucial element, and in one sense I think this is true. It is the crucial element for the therapist, since the quality of the relationship is the one element he can directly influence. But when I think of psychotherapy as personality change, and ask myself whether there is any one essential or crucial element in such change, then I find myself giving a different answer . . .

He goes on to say that he is

not going to try to specify the conditions which lead up to this experience, though I believe they are specifiable. In a recent paper [this is his 'necessary and conditions' paper, at that time in press] I have tentatively formulated these conditions, and several research projects are now getting under way to test this formulation.

The experience itself he characterises partly by an example taken from an earlier book, *Psychotherapy and Personality Change* (Rogers, 1954). It is from the transcript of a session with Mrs Oak:

In the thirty-first interview she is trying to discover what it is that she is experiencing. It is a strong emotion. She thinks it is not guilt. She weeps for a time. Then:

Client: It's just being terribly hurt! . . . And then, of course, I've come to see and feel that over this . . . see, I've covered it up.

A moment later she puts it slightly differently.

Client: You know, its almost a physical thing. It's . . . sort of as though I were looking within myself at all kinds of . . . nerve endings – and bits of . . . things that have been sort of mashed. (weeping)
Therapist: As though some of the most delicate aspects of you – physically almost – have been crushed or hurt.
Client: Yes. And you know, I do get the feeling, oh, you poor thing.
Therapist: You just can't help but feel very deeply sorry for the person that is you.

This moment in her experience is what I have come to think of as a 'moment of movement' in therapy, generally as a moment of personality change. I would hypothesise that therapy is made up of a series of such moments of movement, sometimes strung rather closely together, sometimes occurring at long intervals, always with periods of preparatory experiences in between . . . . It is not a *thinking* about something, it is an *experience* of something at this instant, in the relationship. . . . There are of course many qualities in the relationship which lead up to it and make it possible, but once it has occurred, it has an almost irreversible quality, even though it may take the client a long time fully to assimilate what has occurred.

The following year Rogers presented a paper to the American Psychological Convention on 'A process conception of psychotherapy', a shorter version of which was published in 1958 (Rogers, 1958). Rogers revised the paper again to form Chapter 7 of *On Becoming a Person* (1961). I will quote from this final version in some detail, since much of what Rogers says here is almost indistinguishable from Gendlin's views. Rogers (p. 128) writes that

during this past year I have spent many hours listening to recorded therapeutic interviews – trying to listen as naively as possible. I have endeavored to soak up all the clues I could capture to the process, as to what elements are significant for change. I have tried to abstract from that sensing the simplest abstractions which would describe them. Here I have been much stimulated and helped by the thinking of many of my colleagues, but I would like to mention my special indebtedness to Eugene Gendlin, William Kirtner and Fred Zimring, whose demonstrated ability to think in new ways about these matters has been particularly helpful, and from whom I have borrowed heavily.

In this paper Rogers distinguishes again between the experiential process of change in the client and the conditions which facilitate this change. He refers to his 'necessary and sufficient conditions' paper, but says 'For our present purpose I believe I can state this assumed condition in one word...that the client experiences himself as being fully *received*' (p. 130). Given this condition, clients will change in a characteristic way (p. 131):

> Individuals move, I began to see, not from a fixity or homeostasis through change to a new fixity, though such a process is indeed possible. But much the more significant continuum is from fixity to changingness, from rigid structure to flow, from stasis to process. I formed the tentative hypothesis that perhaps the qualities of the client's expression at any one point might indicate his position on this continuum, might indicate where he stood in this process of change.

As in his 1956 paper, he speaks of 'moments of movement – moments when it appears that change actually occurs' (p. 130). He then goes on to lay out the continuum of change, roughly dividing it into seven stages.

In the first stage the client typically talks about external events, and is unwilling to communicate anything of him- or herself. 'The ways in which he construes experience have been set by his past, and are rigidly unaffected by the actualities of the present. He is (to use the term of Gendlin and Zimring) structure-bound in his manner of experiencing' (p. 133). In the second stage there is more reference to self, but in a rather external way, such as 'Disorganisation keeps cropping up in my life.' In the third stage there is a freer flow of expression about the self, and much talk about feelings in the past, some recognition that the client's way of constructing their experience *is* a construction, rather than a settled fact. In the fourth stage there is a further loosening of constructs, a greater tendency to experience feelings in the present, though little acceptance of those feelings. At the fifth stage, feelings in the present moment are freely expressed and '[t]here is a beginning tendency to realize that experiencing a feeling involves a direct referent' (p. 140). 'Gendlin has called my attention to this significant quality of experiencing as a referent' (p. 150).

The 'direct referent' is what Gendlin later came to call the 'felt sense'. Rogers (p. 140) gives the following illustrations:

> Example: "That kinda came out and I just don't understand it (*Long pause*) I'm trying to get hold of what that terror is."

> Example: Client is talking about an external event. Suddenly she gives a pained, stricken look.

Therapist: "What – what's hitting you now?"

Client: "I don't know (*She cries*). I must have been getting a little too close to something I didn't want to talk about, or something."

Example: "I feel stopped right now. Why is my mind blank right now? I feel as if I am hanging on to something, and I've been letting go of other things; and something in me is saying, 'What more do I have to give up?'"

Rogers comments (p. 140) on these three examples:

In each case the client knows he has experienced something, knows he is not clear as to what he has experienced. But there is the dawning realization that the referent of these vague cognitions lies within him, in an organismic event against which he can check his symbolization and his cognitive formulations. This is often shown by expressions that indicate the closeness or distance he feels from this referent.

Example: "I really don't have my finger on it. I'm just kinda describing it."

At this stage

There is a strong and evident tendency toward exactness in differentiation of feelings and meanings. Example: "...some tension that grows in me, or in some hopelessness, or some kind of incompleteness – and my life actually is very incomplete right now...I just don't know. Seems to be, the closest thing it gets to, is *hopelessness.*" Obviously, he is trying to capture the exact term which for him symbolizes his experience. (p. 142)

In Rogers' sixth stage of process

The moment of full experiencing becomes a clear and definite referent. The examples given should indicate that the client is often not too clearly aware of what has "hit him" in these moments. Yet this does not seem too important because the event is an entity, a referent, which can be turned to again and again, if necessary, to discover more about it. The pleadingness, the feeling of "loving myself" which are present in these examples, may not prove to be exactly as described. They are, however, solid points of reference to which the client can return until he has satisfied himself as to what they are. It is, perhaps, that they constitute a clear-cut physiological event, a substratum of the conscious life, which the client can return to for investigatory purposes. (pp. 149–50)

In the seventh and final stage, which Rogers says often occurs beyond the end of formal therapy,

Experiencing has lost almost completely its structure-bound aspects and becomes process experiencing – that is, the situation is experienced and interpreted in its newness, not as the past....Personal constructs are tentatively reformulated, to be validated against further experience, but even then, to be held loosely...There is the experiencing of effective choice of new ways of living. (pp. 152–4)

The view of therapy which was emerging in the 1950s from the work of Rogers, Gendlin and others in the group at the University of Chicago Counselling Center, can be summarised in the following way: Therapeutic change takes place when the therapist can, in Rogers' phrase, 'receive the client'. Such reception of the client leads to a kind of experiencing in the client which is increasingly less 'structure-bound'. The therapist's part in the process consists in creating the 'receiving' atmosphere, which Rogers explicated further in terms of genuineness, empathy and unconditional regard. What goes on in the client is a new mode of experiencing which increasingly involves attention to that experiencing followed by loosening of the structures in terms of which the experiencing is symbolised.

This view of the therapeutic process seemed to be open to experimental testing. Rogers' group already had some experience in working with psychometric techniques, and it seemed an appropriate time to set up a large-scale test of their theory. What was required was a battery of tests which would assess (1) to what extent, on the therapist's side, the conditions of empathy, congruence and unconditional regard had been present, (2) to what extent, on the client's side, the client's experiencing had become less structure-bound and (3) to what extent the therapy had been effective. Rating scales for therapist empathy, unconditional regard and congruence were developed by members of Rogers' group; Rogers' seven stages of process were operationalised into a Process Scale, and Gendlin developed a related Experiencing Scale which measured the extent to which the individual was remote from, or engaged with, their experiencing; finally, the effectiveness of therapy was measured by a variety of indices, such as the MMPI personality questionnaire, hospitalisation release rates and the judgement of clinicians (Rogers, 1967).

Since up to that time client-centred therapy had been used almost exclusively with 'neurotic' rather than 'psychotic' clients, it was decided to centre the project around a schizophrenic population in a psychiatric hospital. Rogers and his group believed that their theory of therapy was a general one which would apply to any kind of psychological disturbance, so that in choosing a schizophrenic client group they hoped that they would be able to demonstrate the general applicability of their theory along with the more specific hypotheses about therapist conditions and client process change.

The 'Wisconsin project', as it came to be known, was one of the largest projects ever developed to test a theory in psychotherapy. Involving over a hundred researchers, counsellors and assistants, it took five years (1958–63) and something like $500,000 to complete. Rogers maintained an overall responsibility for the project, but handed over its direction to Gendlin. In a letter written in 1966 he says 'I felt so gleeful because Gene [Gendlin] had agreed to come and initiate the project and I knew he had the skills and aptitudes which would make that possible where I did not. I felt then and feel now enormous gratitude that he was willing to undertake that task and for all he has done since to carry the project through' (Kirschenbaum, 1979, p. 286).

The project was beset with difficulties: there was its sheer scale, the difficulties of working within the setting of a psychiatric hospital and the extraordinary theft by one of the participants of a significant part of the data (which then had to be re-worked) (Kirschenbaum, 1979, Chapter 9). It was nevertheless brought to completion, and the results are of great interest, though they have been little discussed in person-centred circles. Rogers (1967, Chapter 5) wrote a summary of the findings for the published account of the project. The first of these findings was that 'a theory of therapeutic change can be put to empirical test' and that this 'may in some respects be our most important finding. . . . Some of our hypotheses were at least partially confirmed. Others were disproved. New evidence was unearthed which did not fit the theory from which we had started. Thus a rethinking of the theoretical basis of our therapy became necessary' (pp. 74–5).

More specifically, it was found that the schizophrenics generally rated very low on the Experiencing Scale, and 'showed little change in the level of experiencing over the period of therapy' (p. 79). Regarding outcome,

> In many respects the therapy group taken as a whole showed no greater evidence of positive outcome than did the matched and paired control group. It had, however, a slightly better rate of release from hospital. And this differential was maintained a year after the termination of therapy. The therapy group also showed a number of positive personality changes which were not evidenced by the control group.

Regarding these apparently rather minor effects of therapy Rogers comments that members of the control group were receiving occupational and recreational therapy from which they may well have benefited, while in the therapy group there were a number of patients who were particularly resistant to any helping relationship, so that 'the question might be raised whether they were actually in therapy at all' (p. 82). In short, it was not altogether surprising that the effects of therapy were not great; rather, it is significant that there was at least some observed difference between the therapy group and the control group.

Turning to the relationship between therapist attitudes and client process, Rogers (pp. 82, 83) acknowledges that one of the findings was disappointing:

> there seemed to be no significant relationship between the degree of therapist empathy, congruence and acceptance, and the degree of process movement shown by the patient...Thus, in general our expectations and hypotheses in regard to a progression of stages of development in therapeutic movement throughout the process of therapy were not upheld in our work with these schizophrenic individuals.

On the other hand (p. 83, Rogers' emphasis):

> The story was quite different when we examined the relationship between the therapist attitudes and conditions and the process *level* exhibited by our schizophrenic individuals. Here we found that *the deeper the level of the therapist's understanding and genuineness in his relationship with his patient, the more his patient was likely to exhibit a deeper level of self-experiencing and self-exploration at every point of therapy – initially, throughout therapy, and at termination.*

These results were puzzling. The expectation had been that high levels of the therapist conditions would lead to an increased process level in the client, which would in turn be associated with a better therapeutic outcome. Rather, it turned out that client process level was not increased by the therapeutic interaction, but that clients who *began* at a higher level made better therapeutic progress. Curiously, though, the therapists of the clients with higher process levels showed higher levels of the therapist conditions.

Rogers concluded that what needed to be re-thought were the causal connections between the three variables: therapist conditions, process level and positive outcome (p. 89). The facts appear to be that both high process level and high therapist conditions are correlated with constructive personality change, and with each other. But it is not that the high therapist conditions *cause* the high process level; that level remains as it is from the start of therapy. So why is it that high therapist conditions are correlated with high process level from the start? Rogers writes:

> The main thrust of these findings . . . appears clear. *The characteristics of the client or patient influenced the quality of the relationship which formed between himself and his therapist.*

In this connection Rogers notes other factors which were correlated with higher therapist conditions, including higher client socio-economic status, higher verbal IQ and greater expressivity in the early interviews. He then concludes (pp. 89–90, 91):

> High levels of empathic understanding, genuineness, and warm acceptance in the therapist's behavior are more likely to be evident when he is dealing with a reasonably expressive individual with a socio-educational level closer to his own. The therapist's attitudes are clearly important, but the patient's characteristics appear to play a definite part in eliciting these qualities. . . . All of this points to the conclusion that an early assessment of the relationship qualities and the process level of any given relationship is a good prognosticator of the probability that constructive personality change will occur.

Thus what this mammoth study suggested was not that therapist conditions lead to a higher process level in the client which is associated with constructive personality change. Rather, some clients begin therapy at a higher process level than others, and it is this higher process level, maintained throughout, which helps to elicit the higher therapist conditions *and* the constructive personality change. Rogers was pleased that the study had been completed successfully and that its design had enabled new discoveries to be made. The content of these discoveries was, however, a disappointment to him (p. 82). Clearly the theory needed modification, but Rogers had meanwhile become deeply interested in another field of study, that of the application of his basic ideas to groups. On completion of the Wisconsin project in 1963 (although four years before its publication) Rogers moved to La Jolla in California, and from then on most of his writings were concerned with groups. Because members of groups could not appropriately be referred to as 'clients' he changed the name of his approach from 'client-centred' to 'person-centred' and it is in this form that 'person-centred therapy' has become widely known.

We might try to imagine how Rogers felt in 1963. He had developed a striking and plausible theory of psychotherapy which had received some empirical confirmation. His new book *On becoming a person* (1961) had been an almost instant success. He had expected the Wisconsin project to be a large-scale confirmation of his theorising over the previous ten years. But the project had run into many practical and interpersonal problems, and the final results were disappointing insofar as they failed to confirm his theory. Kirschenbaum (1979, p. 275) refers to this period in his life as 'a time which Rogers himself often wished he could forget. He once called it "the most painful and anguished episode in my whole professional life".' Yet whatever the findings of the project suggested, Rogers clearly did not take them as refuting his view that the attitudes of empathy, acceptance and genuineness are deeply helpful in human relationships. This was for him an experiential fact which was increasingly confirmed for him in his new work with groups. To continue from where the Wisconsin project had ended would have involved more theoretical work, and more again of the time-consuming empirical research which had yielded such a meagre harvest of clear results. By contrast, the development of the person-centred approach outside of the therapy room must have seemed full of promise. In a 1963 letter to Godfrey Barrett-Lennard (1998, p. 154) Rogers wrote of some of the early groups, '... with the establishment of a few simple conditions, which are close to but not identical with the conditions we have described for establishing a therapeutic relationship, these ... groups all went through an experience that must have been so parallel as to be almost identical'. Thus Rogers at the age of 61 was launched on a whole new phase of his career, through which his work became much more widely known.

Meanwhile, Gendlin's experiences in Wisconsin led to a deeper articulation of the theory of therapy, and to changes in his therapeutic practice. I will discuss the changes in practice first. Gendlin (1983) recalls that although the schizophrenics in the Wisconsin project had not shown very marked changes as the result of therapy, the *therapists* were significantly changed by the experience. Working with hospitalised schizophrenics was very different from working with clients in an office in the University of Chicago Counselling Center. There were often long periods of silence, but it was not the sort of silence in which a client is exploring or sensing into their experiencing; it was, rather, an empty, resisting silence. The schizophrenics did not come to therapy with a sense of having problems with which they wished to work; they were not oriented towards personal exploration. They were isolated, disconnected people who would often reject the therapist. Gendlin (1964a, pp. 169–70) wrote of his experience:

> I was not, at least then, accustomed to seeing someone who did not want to see me. It had always been the other person's need that was my excuse for being there, for living, for working. *He* needed me and I had nothing to do with it . . . . But here was a person who said "Leave me alone. Go away. I don't want to talk. I talk to *some* people, but I don't want to talk to *you*. Aren't there other patients you can see?" . . . I slowly learned that there is another reason why I might go to see someone. It might not be because he needs me, which makes it very easy. Instead it might be because I want to, because I decide to . . .
>
> This happened repeatedly to almost every one of the therapists. And it is invariably a painful experience . . . The patient is ill, afraid and with-drawing. You know that but it is still painful – particularly painful not to be *able* to reach out to him for such a long period, when you want to.

In the face of these challenges the Wisconsin project therapists found that they had to drop many of their preconceptions and favourite methods.

> This, more than anything else, has moved us away from a concern with technique, a concern with being 'client-centred' or being any other particular way . . . We have shifted from talking about the optimal response behavior to much more basic and global factors: the attitudes of the therapist, the approach that as one person he takes towards the other person, how to make interaction happen where it isn't. (Gendlin, 1964a, pp. 171–2)

Rogers had already made the theoretical move from the technique of reflection towards the embodiment of therapeutic attitudes, but it was only through working with schizophrenics that it became clear that some clients may absolutely require 'a much wider range of what one might do, what one might be pushed into doing by one's own feelings and own needs, in order to reach a person not being reached' (*ibid.*, p. 172). In the post-Wisconsin years Rogers expressed the same conclusion through his increasing emphasis on the importance of therapist congruence.

To 'reach a person not being reached' requires the therapist to be more active in their relationship with their client, and this can seem to clash with the original principles of non-directive therapy. The therapist may need to make interpretations, express their own feelings, ask questions, answer questions, express opinions, refer back to what the client said previously and so on. These forms of therapist response were deliberately inhibited in non-directive therapy because they were seen as having the undesirable effect of distracting the client from his or her own therapeutic track. Yet with the schizophrenics such inhibition had the consequence that no therapeutic relationship was established. The schizophrenic *was not on any therapeutic track* and did not make any use of what the therapist was offering. In these circumstances the Wisconsin project therapists found themselves doing just the things which non-directive therapy would have ruled out. Now in Gendlin's view the therapists were not going against the spirit of Rogers' approach – the point of the non-directive 'rules' was to avoid deflecting the client from their own process. But in schizophrenia a person's process is blocked; personal process flows primarily in relation to other people, and the schizophrenic's estrangement from their own process is all of a piece with their estrangement from other people. Hence what is needed is the re-establishment of relationship: the relationship of the schizophrenic to other people and to his or her own experiencing. This requires the therapist to do things which could in other circumstances detract from the client following their own therapeutic track. The 'relaxation of the non-directive rules' must of course be limited and appropriate to what is happening in the relationship. The therapist needs to make some move (ask a question, express a feeling and so on) and then check how that is with the client. The therapist is not directing the therapeutic process, but *enabling it to occur*.

One way of understanding Gendlin's focusing-oriented psychotherapy is to see it as extending the principles of the work with schizophrenics to psychotherapy clients in general (Gendlin, 1963/1968). The problems of working with schizophrenics could be seen as the general problems of psychotherapy writ large. That is, when clients come to psychotherapy what happens in the session is not always therapeutic. In particular, clients may talk continually about external events in their life, or analyse in Sherlock Holmes style the connections between childhood events and present troubles, or live out the same feelings they have lived for years in other relationships. After a while the therapist becomes uncomfortable, in the way that the Wisconsin project therapists became uncomfortable with the schizophrenics. If the client always just talks about the events in their week, even the most orthodox client-centred therapist is unlikely to let this go on indefinitely. There is a sense that 'nothing is happening', and the therapist might express their discomfort, or ask a question such as 'And how did that strike you?' Similarly with the client who continually analyses or intellectualises the therapist is likely after a while to want to introduce a feeling or experiential element into the conversation. 'It does seem likely that you feel this way because of the way it was in your family, but I'm wondering how all that feels for you right now?' And with the recurrently emoting client the therapist may come to the point of saying something like 'This anger you are feeling again . . . maybe we could try to stand back from it a little and just see what is in it . . . what this is all about?'

In these situations, as with the schizophrenics, the therapist is trying to reach out to the client in a way that will help the client to engage in a therapeutic process. These moves which the therapist makes do not interfere with the therapeutic process; they help to initiate it. One of Gendlin's early insights was that psychotherapy does not always take place in what are *called* psychotherapy sessions; what goes on may be largely non-therapeutic externalising, intellectualising or emoting. Of course, talking about the events of one's week, or reflecting upon childhood experiences or releasing pent-up emotion *may* be therapeutic, but it is not always so, and what is crucial for an understanding of therapy is what it is that makes the difference.

Let us return now to the theoretical implications of the Wisconsin project findings. As we saw, before his departure for California, Rogers was at least considering the possibility that high experiencing level in the client tends to bring about therapeutic progress while also eliciting high therapist conditions. The evidence for the second point was not very conclusive (Gendlin *et al.*, 1967, p. 61), but what did seem clear was that in therapy much depends on 'where the client is' at the start, as well as on what the therapist does. The Wisconsin results strongly suggested that therapist conditions do not cause high experiencing levels, if by that is meant that the stronger the conditions the higher the experiencing level.

My own interpretation is that it is rather that if the therapist conditions fall below a certain level they will tend to block the client's experiencing. It is not so much that high therapist conditions are the cause of high experiencing and hence of therapeutic progress, but that *low* therapist conditions block the process which would otherwise take place. An analogy might be: a car cannot run if it does not have wheels, but also the tyres on the wheels must be pumped up.

Pumped-up tyres are a causal factor in the car's running effectively, but it is not that the more you pump up the tyres the better the car runs. It is misleading to say that pumped-up tyres cause cars to run effectively; it is rather that *flat* tyres cause cars to run *ineffectively*. Similarly it is misleading to say that therapist empathy, acceptance and genuineness result in therapeutic progress; it is rather that therapist misunderstanding, criticism and phoneyness *block* the therapeutic process. Such a view is consistent not only with the thinking of Gendlin but also with that of Rogers. For Rogers, personal development is driven by the 'actualising tendency'; other people can have an impact on growth but it is not that the therapeutic conditions cause the growth. Rather, it is that their opposites stand in the way of growth. To see things this way is to put the *client* back at the centre of client-centred therapy. Too much emphasis on the therapist conditions can distort our view of what takes place in therapy. As we shall see, it is important for the therapist to *be there*, but it is equally important for the therapist not to get in the way of the client's process. The therapist conditions, from this perspective, are a matter of *not blocking* the client, rather than a matter of giving the client anything.

We can turn now to Gendlin's own account of psychotherapy. The essence of it can be found in a paper published in 1964 entitled 'A theory of personality change', which drew upon his more philo-sophical work in *Experiencing and the Creation of Meaning* (1962/1997). It was in this paper that he first introduced the term 'focusing'. Central to Gendlin's thought is the idea that human experiencing has a rich intricacy which can be rendered conceptually and linguistically only to a limited extent. There is always far more to our experiencing than we can put into words or concepts. Yet it is not that our experiencing is ineffable; if we stay with our experiencing, words and symbols may arise which then do render the experience in a communicable form. We can check the words against the experience, and then sometimes at least we are able to say 'Yes, that expresses it exactly.' Gendlin often uses the example of a poet who is struggling to complete a poem, the last line of which eludes him. He reads the already written lines over and over again and has a *sense* of what the last line needs to be. This sense – what Gendlin calls a 'felt sense' – is definite enough for him to be able to reject various possible lines which come. The felt sense is vague in that there are as yet no words for it, but quite precise in that only certain words will 'fit' it. When those words come the poet takes a deep breath and says 'Ah, *that's* right', and then he can move on. This is clearly similar to what often happens in psychotherapy. A client may say 'I have a strange feeling about all this which I can't put into words. It's not that I feel guilty about it...it is something else...it's more a sort of fear...a fear of what people will say...no, I don't really care what they say...what is this?...it's as if I'm afraid of really being me...(sigh)...yes, that's it...if I did it I would *really* be me, and then I couldn't pretend any more...' In looking at psychotherapy transcripts one finds endless examples of this characteristic form of reflecting. The client is focusing their attention on their own experiencing and trying to formulate it in words or images. When the 'right' word or image comes there is a feeling of release, which has nothing to do with whether the client *likes* what has come. It may be that in the course of reflection on a problem that the client says 'Now I see what it is...(release)... and it's much worse than I thought. Now I *really* don't know what to do.'

In Gendlin's view the articulation of our implicit experiencing is what is central to psychotherapy. This is what for Gendlin corresponds to what in Freud is conceptualised as 'making the unconscious conscious' or in Rogers as 'bringing the self-concept into congruence with organismic experience'. To understand Gendlin's view of psychotherapy we need first to see how it differs from the views of Freud and of Rogers.

Consider this example from Gendlin (1964b/1973, p. 485. Page references to this paper are to the 1973 version):

> An individual leaves a certain situation feeling quite happy. Four days later he becomes aware that really he has been quite angry about what happened. He feels that he 'has been' angry all along but 'wasn't aware of it'.

Freud would say that this person has been *unconsciously* angry during those four days; Rogers would say that his organismic experiencing has been that of anger, but that he has not conceptualised it as such: his (self-)concept has been incongruent with his organismic experiencing. Gendlin's view is that the individual's situation was one in which anger would have been the natural response, but that this response has been blocked. In the four days since the events occurred, the person has *not* been angry; rather he has been in a state which 'implies' anger, a state in which anger is incipient, but not yet occurring. Now, four days later, the anger is there. He says he has been 'angry all along', but what this amounts to is that he has been in a blocked state of incipient anger, which is now being expressed.

The expression of the anger is not a matter of him having had the anger all the time, but is only now able to verbalise or conceptualise what he felt. His now exclaiming 'I'm really furious about that!' is not a *description* of a feeling which he has not up to now been able to describe accurately; it is the 'discharging' or 'completing' of the condition he has physically felt for the past four days. I will discuss this aspect of Gendlin's theory further in Chapter 8.

Gendlin's view is that effective psychotherapy involves the release of blocked process. By 'process' he means the natural flow of our experiential interaction with the world. Rather analogously to Rogers' notion of the 'actualising tendency' Gendlin sees people (and other organisms) as in constant movement-towards-future-states. A person cannot be understood fully in terms of what they are now, but in terms of what they are becoming. Or rather, what we are now can only be specified in terms of where we are going. To be hungry now is to be on the way to eating. We may not get there, but the 'implication' of eating is there now, and constitutes the hunger. (Even in the physical world, Gendlin suggests, the present states of things cannot be expressed independently of where they are heading. That a body has such-and-such a momentum tells us something about the future as much as about the present.)

The present state of an organism 'implies' future states, but these future states may not be realised; for example, there may be no food for the hungry animal. This leads to a state of physiological tension and the animal begins to search for food. In its hunting behaviour we see the implying of feeding, but that implying is not yet satisfied. Similarly the insulted person is in a state which implies angry behaviour, but there may be no safe way of being angry. This leads to physiological tension and the person becomes irritable with his wife, phones a friend, goes for a drink and so on. In this unsettled behaviour we see the implying of anger, but that implying is blocked, not yet satisfied. In human beings the ways in which our living and experiencing can be blocked are multifarious, but in each case there is the failure to express or satisfy something that is implied. We are stuck; our experiencing does not, in Gendlin's phrase, 'carry us forward'. Nevertheless, in that 'stuck' state there is the implying of what would release it. The present state implies what needs to come in order that there will not any longer be that implying. Hence through giving attention to our stuck states we may find what it is that needs to come. This, for Gendlin, is the fundamental principle of psychotherapy, but it needs more elucidation.

Our lives may become blocked in many ways which do not require the help of psychotherapy. Because of circumstances we may no longer be able to continue with our work, or with a friendship, or with an activity. Then we are sad and upset and cast around for other ways in which the 'implying' can be carried forward. When we are blocked our lives do not stop; they carry on in new, and perhaps strange, ways which involve a seeking for something which will satisfy the blocked 'implying'. If we can stay in touch with our experiencing we can sense what does or does not lead in the direction of satisfying or expressing the implying. At such times we often feel painfully alive. It can help to have another person there to be with us in our searching, but it is not absolutely essential.

At other times we lose touch with our own experiencing. Instead of noticing how we are right now feeling about the situation in all its intricacy, we respond to it in what Gendlin (1964b/1973, pp. 461–3) calls a 'structure-bound' way. For example, someone reacts to their boss's behaviour in the same way that they react to *anyone* whom they perceive as an authority. They react to him just as 'an authority' and not as a person in this particular situation. They experience their boss only in this very limited schematic way. It is as if their experiencing has become frozen into a particular form, rather than being a living awareness of the present situation. In the structure-bound way of experiencing there is a lack of immediacy which may extend to a sense of one's life as a whole. Then we feel 'I do everything right, but I'm not in it' or 'Life is going on all right, but I'm in some back room. I merely hear about it, I'm not living it' (*ibid.*, p. 461).

When we are in this kind of state and reflect on our problems we tend to move along intellectual and conceptual tracks. We may say 'I am in this situation because I am that sort of person, and I got to be this way because of this and this, so I suppose what I really need to do is such-and-such, but when I do things like that they always go wrong, but what else can I try...' This way of thinking moves from one idea to another in a logical fashion, but does not dip down into the felt sense of the situation. Nothing new emerges because the problem has already been structured in a particular way, and we are circling around within that structure. For something new to emerge we have to let ourselves dip back into the rich intricacy of our immediate experiencing, and see if some new structure can emerge, which may then again be checked against our experiencing, so that it may itself be replaced by something new.

Structure-bound states are states in which our experiencing is stuck in particular forms, in particular ways of seeing and being. When we are in such states we do not respond effectively to the intricacy of our situation. From the structure nothing new can *come*, but if we can, as it were, get behind the structure, into what it is rooted in, then there is the possibility of a restructuring which will truly express what has become blocked. For example, so long as the man with a problem about his boss keeps saying to himself 'I have an authority problem, and this comes from the way it was with my father, and I need to distinguish between my father and my boss, of course, don't I? . . .' little change can occur. Everything he says is true, but such understanding of one's problem does not make it go away! What might make a difference would be if he took some time to stay with the whole felt sense of his problem with his boss. He sits down and gently asks himself 'Now what is all this? . . . what am I feeling about this whole thing with the boss . . . ?' He may notice a tension in his chest, and a sinking feeling in his stomach. His *body* is responding to the situation in a quite definite way. There is a whole 'something' there which he physically senses. He immediately thinks, 'Well of course I'm feeling like this – it's fear – I'm afraid of the boss aren't I? People get all tense like this when they are afraid, don't they? And I got to be like this because . . .' But now instead of following the well-trodden track which he usually follows he pauses and comes back to the physically felt sense of the situation. There it is – *that* feeling. If he stays with the felt sense new aspects of the situation may emerge. For example, there, in *all that*, along with the fear, is a kind of pain . . . a memory comes, or an image . . . something to do with his longing to connect with his father . . . the pain is disturbing, but the sense of being in touch with something new is releasing. Tears come to his eyes, he does not quite know what all this is. But the felt sense of the situation is a bit different. *He* is a bit different, and the next time he sees the boss he will behave a little differently.

'Focusing' is Gendlin's term for the whole process which takes place when we give our attention in a sustained way to our felt sense of something. For some people this kind of attending comes naturally, while for others it may be quite a novel idea that one can turn one's attention to 'how it feels in here about all that business to do with such and such'.

In his 1964 paper Gendlin divides the focusing process into four broad phases (*ibid.*, p. 451). There is first the felt sense of some whole issue or problem. 'I always feel this when people do that to me' or

'There is something about this which could lead to dreadful things happening to me.' We can refer directly to the 'this', bring our attention to it. It may be conceptually vague, yet experientially it is quite distinct. In Gendlin's terminology the felt sense is a 'direct referent' for us. It is interesting that if what is involved is anxiety-provoking, then giving attention to the felt sense *decreases* the anxiety. Gendlin's interpretation of this is that through giving attention and expression to the felt sense we are already carrying a process forward. The interaction between the experiencing and the attention results in a change in the experiencing. This process is often seen in therapy, where the client formulates their experiencing in one way, and then finds that this formulation must be replaced by another which now feels more 'accurate'.

Gendlin's concept of the felt sense developed partly through his philosophical work on the nature of experiencing (Gendlin, 1962/1997). In this work he was concerned with the important fact that in a conversation people can make *the same point* in different ways. If one way of getting my point across fails, then I can reformulate it in different words. Similarly, if two people approach an issue from very different standpoints they may be able to agree that they are making the same point in two different ways. This situation can often arise when therapists belonging to different schools discuss a client issue. They do not share the same framework of concepts, but may be able to agree that they are 'saying the same thing' in their different ways. Gendlin's way of expressing this is that in spite of there being a difference of words and concepts, the two people share a felt sense of the point that is being made. It is a sense of *that point* which they wish to make; each of them can sense *it*. The words which they use are attempts to formulate *it*; but they may need to stay for some time with the uneasy feel of *it* until words come which effectively express *it*.

It should be clear from this that by 'felt sense' Gendlin does not mean *any* kind of feeling which we may notice when we turn our attention to our experiencing. We may notice body sensations of soreness or tightness, or we may be conscious of emotions such as fear or anger. But neither body sensations (of that sort) nor emotions constitute a felt sense of a situation. A feeling of soreness may be caused by the way we are sitting, but that is different from having a *sense of* oneself as sitting in an odd way. A felt sense is a felt sense *of* something.

Unlike body sensations, emotions *are* of (or about) something. Fear is fear of something, anger is anger about something. Where the felt sense differs from emotion is that emotions are specific to *kinds* of situations. Fear is the way we feel inside when danger threatens, anger is what we feel inside when something important to us has been violated. Emotions like these can *get in the way of* a felt sense of our situation. When we are frightened or angry we are less able to sense the intricacy of the whole situation (Gendlin, 1973a, 1991a). Some emotions, such as remorse or hope, come closer to involving a felt sense. Such emotions have no universal form of physical expression (as anger has fighting or stomping), but they are still characteristic of specific *kinds* of situation. The felt sense, by contrast, is the sense of *this* situation. If we give our attention simply to the remorse, we can miss what is specific to this situation, what it is in the situation which generates the remorse. The remorse is not the felt sense of the situation; rather the felt sense of the whole situation *includes* the emotion of remorse.

It may help to clarify the distinction between emotion and felt sense if we reflect on another distinction: that between emotion-in-action and emotion as something we feel inside (Gendlin, 1997a). Take anger as an example. By 'emotion-in-action' I mean shouting, stomping around or hitting out, in a situation in which something we value is in some way being violated. Here the emotion is there *in the action*. Animals can have emotions in this way. But as human beings we can also turn our attention to what we are feeling inside, to how our body is registering the situation. We can sense the anger *as a feeling*.

Now behaviour such as stomping around is a very specific, 'narrow' form of behaviour. In stomping we are likely to lose track of the intricacies of the situation we are in. We are, as we say, 'overcome' by the emotion. But most of the time we are not stomping around; most of the time we are acting in terms of a much broader sense of our situation. We are sensitive to the context and to the implications of what we are doing. In moving our chair to make room for another person we are sensing the whole situation, the need for this person not to feel excluded, the positions of the other chairs, the impact which the movement of our chair will have on the people next to us, the disturbance which this will make....There is an implicit sensing-in-action of what the situation requires, which it would be impossible fully to put into words. Again, it seems clear that animals have this sensing-in-action of whole situations. The dog adjusts its behaviour not only to the direction and speed with which the rabbit is running, but also to the shouts of its human companion. There is an implicit weighing up of the situation which results in a particular form of behaviour. Now just as we as human beings can bring our attention to how our body is registering specific aspects of the situation (e.g. as 'violating', or 'threatening', corresponding to the emotions of anger and fear), so also we can bring our attention to how our body is registering the current situation *as a whole*. To bring our attention to an aspect of the situation as of a specific kind is what is involved in experiencing an emotion as a feeling. To bring our attention to how our body is registering the situation *as a whole* is what is involved in having a felt sense. (I will say more in Chapter 8 about the theory which lies behind the notion of the felt sense.)

The felt sense is usually less noticeable than an emotion. It can take a little time for it to come into focus. We look at a painting and are aware of the colours and shapes. We try to get a sense of this picture as a whole. That sense is not yet there, but we try out some words or phrases, such as 'formal', 'civilised, but with an undertow of something' or 'energy contained'. As we do this the felt sense of the picture begins to form. We may not be able yet (or ever) to find words which are quite right, but as we focus our attention on our response to the painting a felt sense of it begins to form for us – there is *that* feeling. We can, as it were, gesture at it, and continue to seek for a way of expressing it. The felt sense is now there, and as we continue to 'stay with it' or 'probe' it we may find that it 'opens' for us, and we say 'Oh, yes...this is about containment *creating* energy... (deeper breath)...yes...I see it now...' And then further thoughts, feelings and images may come.

This takes us to the second and third phases of focusing. The second phase Gendlin (1964b/1973) calls 'unfolding'. Through giving attention to the felt sense one finds that it begins to 'open up'. For example:

> Yes, *of course* he is afraid, he realises. He has not permitted himself even to think about dealing with *this* and *this* aspect of the situation, and this has been because he has not believed that these aspects really existed. Well, yes, he did realise they existed, but he also felt compelled to blame himself for them as if he merely imagined them. And if they do exist (and they do), he does not know how he could possibly live with them. He has not allowed himself to try to deal with them (he how realises) or even to consider them anything other than his imagination, because, my God, if they are really there, then he is helpless. Then there is *nothing* he can do! But they are there. Well, it is a relief to know at least that. (p. 454)

In that felt experiencing which was initially labelled as 'fear' there is a whole multiplicity of aspects, and in making some of these aspects explicit there is a change in the quality of the experiencing. Sometimes the unfolding of the aspects may lead to a different view of the problem, such that action can now be taken to do something about it, but this is not always so. As in the example above, it may rather be that the quality of the problem has changed:

"How is everything different?"
"Well, it just seems OK now!"
"Do you still feel that such-and-such might happen and you couldn't deal with it?"
"Yes, but now I kind of feel, well, that's life. That's the way it is, you have to accept things like that."
And that is just what he had said to himself over and over again, *without any effect*, before the process in which he focused on the felt meaning and it unfolded! (p. 455)

The third phase of the focusing process is 'global application'. This refers to the fact that when a felt sense has unfolded, the person often experiences a flood of associations with other situations, circumstances and memories, which in spite of their diversity share the same felt sense. 'Oh, and that's also why I can't get up any enthusiasm for this-and-this' or 'Yes, and another thing about it is, this comes in every time somebody tells me what to do or think. I can't say, well, what *I* think is important because, see, this way of making myself wrong comes in there.' Gendlin rejects the view that what is happening here can properly be called 'insight'. The insights which come are the *results* of the process of change which has taken place; for each explicit thought which comes there may be thousands which now could arise from the change which has taken place. The important shift in the person is one which has taken place at a level which is not conceptual, yet in which a multitude of conceptual shifts are implicit.

The fourth phase of focusing is that of 'referent movement'. This is the change which occurs in the experienced 'direct referent' when we focus attention on it, or try to conceptualise it. It may follow immediately from our attending to the direct referent, or may be something we notice after having been through a phase of 'unfolding' and 'global application'. It is the shift in 'how it all feels', a shift in the whole felt sense of the issue, which may be the starting point for another cycle of focusing.

The process which Gendlin is describing here is one that happens naturally when we give direct attention to our experiencing. It is a process in which the links between the steps are not determined by logic or conceptual understanding. What is said at one point may be logically contradicted by what is said next. 'I really don't like him. ... Well, its not that I dislike him, but I don't know how to be with him. ... I could be with him quite OK if Charlie wasn't always there *seeing* how I am with him. ... ' In this process the changes occur in the spaces, in the silences indicated here by ' ...'. In these spaces the person is 'listening inside', referring directly to their own experiencing. If the context is that of a therapy session it is important that the therapist respect these silences, and not distract the client by too many comments or ideas of their own. On the other hand, Gendlin remarks that 'I have also learned that my questions and self-expressions can be useful, provided I always intend what I say to refer to the individual's felt referent and I show that I would like him to continue to focus on it' (*ibid.*, p. 459). The therapist's role is thus that of a facilitator for the feeling-process of the client, which to a large extent is self-propelled, and is 'the essential motor of personality change' (*ibid.*, p. 459).

The question arises of how it is that the presence of a therapist or other listener is facilitative. Rogers' view was that the empathic acceptance of the therapist contributes to the undoing of the client's conditions of worth. Gendlin sees the presence of another person as facilitative in a different way. He draws attention to the fact that there can be a great difference between how we think and feel when alone and how we think and feel when with another person:

> Consider, for example, the type of listener who interrupts with his own concerns and is inclined to be annoyed and critical long before he understands what is said. With him, my manner of experiencing will be quite constricted. ... I will *not* tend to feel deeply, or intensely, or richly. Certain things will never occur to me when I am with him, or if they do occur to me, I will save them for the time when I am alone, and can feel them through without the constricting effects of his responses. ... Similarly there are others (we are fortunate to know one) with whom we feel more intensely and freely whatever we feel. We think of more things, we have the patience and the ability to go more deeply into the details ... If we are sad and dry-eyed alone, then with this person we cry. If we are stopped by our guilt, shame and anxiety, then with this person we come to life again ... (p. 460)

The presence of another person can make a difference to the *manner* of our experiencing. In particular, it can make a difference to what extent our experiencing is 'structure-bound', that is, repetitive, 'frozen', lacking in immediacy, presentness, and openness to fresh detail. To the extent that we are structure-bound we are not really *experiencing* the world at all. Instead we are moving along fixed tracks governed by earlier experiences and generalised notions. We are not dipping into our immediate feelings before making our next step, and hence the process of articulating our feelings cannot take place. Another way of putting this would be to say that to the extent that we are structure-bound the things we say and do cannot *carry forward* what we are feeling. The feelings remain in an implicit form, as in our earlier example of implicit anger. The anger is implied, but its expression or articulation is blocked. For the anger to become explicit the person has to turn their attention to their implicit experiencing. Simply giving attention to the felt sense in the body may be enough for the anger to become explicit. Or it may be that the person will need to ask themself what they are feeling, or to try out various articulations of the feeling, such as 'Maybe I'm a bit hurt?... or irritated?...' In one way or another the person needs to *relate to* their implicit experiencing, so that what was implicit is carried forward into something explicit. Just what will carry forward the implicit experience cannot be known in advance; we have to try out possible expressions such as 'Maybe I'm a bit hurt', and see what happens. Most of the expressions we could try out will do nothing for us; the sense of unease and unfulfilledness simply remains as it was. But then a word or image comes which brings with it a characteristic sense of release – 'Oh, I'm really *angry* with him – that's what it is'. *That* articulation expresses or carries forward the implicit experience, and then things feel different.

The process of carrying-forward requires that we turn our attention to our felt awareness and seek to articulate it. The structure-bound state is one in which we are not doing this in connection with certain aspects of our experience; we are not relating to, not responding to, our felt awareness. Once we respond, we 'come alive' again and the implicit meanings are carried forward. The presence of another person makes a difference because that person can respond to our felt awareness. Then they are doing for us what we cannot, for the moment, do for ourselves. *They* can direct their attention to our felt awareness through saying such things as 'There is something you are feeling there', as we are lost in an account of external events, or in an analysis of why we are the way we are. *They* can say 'Is it exactly hurt that you are feeling', or 'Is hurt all that you feel?' *They* can point towards our felt experiencing without knowing what that experiencing is, and in doing so they can help us to relate again to that experiencing, so that it can be carried forward. Gendlin (1964b/1973, p. 469) writes:

> Personality change is the difference made by *your* responses in *carrying forward my* concrete experiencing. To be myself I need your responses, to the extent to which my own responses fail to *carry* my feelings *forward*. At first, in these respects, I am really myself *only when I am with you*. For a time, the individual can have this fuller *self-process* only in just this *relationship*. That is not dependence. It should not lead one to back away, but to fuller and deeper responses carrying forward the experiencing, which, for the time being, the individual says he can feel "only here".

By the late 1960s it seemed clear to Gendlin and his colleagues that a crucial aspect of effective psychotherapy was the client's ability to direct their attention to their own experiencing. In 1970 Gendlin wrote:

> We have tape-recorded several thousand therapy sessions over the last few years. We asked: what are patients doing when therapy is successful? What are they *not* doing when sessions fail to help them? One finding has emerged consistently from a series of studies: there is indeed a characteristic of patients who improve that is not shared by those who fail. Successful patients are able to work with *felt meanings* ... (Gendlin, 1970, p. 57)

> We are presently engaged in experiments to see whether experiential focusing can be taught. Since research indicates that therapy will fail if it is nonexperiential, can failure-predicted patients learn this focusing procedure? If our teaching turns out to be effective, then possibilities open up for teaching experiential procedures to everyone as a problem-solving skill. This would be a preventive step in mental health, since people could solve more of their own problems and help others to do so. (*ibid.*, p. 59)

There are several ways in which a client can learn to relate to their experiencing. One is through explicit teaching. From time to time therapists interested in Focusing have experimented with giving clients the opportunity to be taught an explicit Focusing procedure. The Focusing teaching has usually been carried out by someone other than the client's own therapist, and after the client has learned how to focus they resume their normal therapy sessions. Most people who know a little about Focusing have come across it as a taught procedure, either through attending a Focusing workshop or through reading Gendlin's popular self-help book *Focusing*.

I will discuss Focusing as a taught procedure in Chapter 4, but there are other ways in which clients can learn to relate better to their experiencing. One way is to introduce the basic focusing ideas to the client as and when they seem appropriate in the session. This seems to have been what Gendlin (1969) did at the time he wrote his first article on focusing.

In this early paper he emphasises three main points. First, that focusing involves a sharp change in one's approach to one's problems. The usual approaches involve such things as telling the story of the problem, lecturing oneself on what one has done wrong, speculating about how the problem has arisen, determining to act differently in the future and so on. By contrast, the focusing approach is to bring one's attention to one's experiencing, as it is bodily felt, gently ask 'What's wrong?' and then *wait*. Then there is the point that one must understand that words can come from a feeling, and can have an experiential effect. 'Sometimes such words are not in themselves very impressive or novel, but just those words have an experiential effect, and no others do. (For example: "I'm scared..." might not be new, but when the words arise *from* one's quietly listening, they often have the effect of: "Yeah, that's what it is all right, (long exhale breath), (shakes head), yeah, boy, I didn't know how true that was"). Yet, perhaps he has been saying for days, among other things, that he was scared.' (Gendlin, 1969, p. 5). Finally, it is important to 'sense a problem as a whole and let what is important come up from that bodily sensing. People rarely let the crux of the problem come freshly to them from their feel of the problem as a whole.' (*ibid.*). Gendlin suggests that the therapist should discuss each of these points with the client, so that the client understands what is involved.

A third way of helping a client to relate to their experiencing is not to *talk* about what is involved in focusing, but to respond in a focusing-oriented way. As we will see in Chapter 5 this way of responding is often little different from the way a classical client-centred therapist responds. It is a matter of responding in a way which 'points' at the client's felt edge of experiencing, and helps the client to relate to that place from which change steps can come.

Chapters 4 and 5 will first introduce Focusing as a taught procedure and then show at greater length how the principles of Focusing can inform therapeutic practice.

4

Focusing as a Taught Procedure

Before introducing the procedure itself it may be helpful to give a summary of Gendlin's basic concepts as they were in the 1970s, when the Focusing procedure was being developed. They can be found in a paper he published in the volume *Current Psychotherapies* (Corsini, 1973).

In this paper Gendlin lists (p. 322) his four basic concepts as (1) *existence*, which is 'preconceptual, internally differentiable and bodily felt'; (2) *encounter*, the principle that people exist only through inter-action with others and with their environment; (3) *authenticity*, which involves acting in a way which carries forward one's experiencing and (4) *value*, the principle that experiencing is purposive or evaluative.

1. *Existence.* It is central to Gendlin's thought that there is a preconceptual aspect to existence and experiencing; there is *that* which can be conceptualised in a variety of ways. But the preconcep-tual is not a blank void; it contains within itself the *possibilities* of distinctions. In therapy this is illustrated by those situations where the client says 'I am aware of something here…but I don't at all know what it is.' The client is referring to *something* but this is a bare reference or 'pointing': *what* is being pointed to has not yet been differentiated or articulated. The client may then try out various possible articulations, which will be framed in concepts with which he or she is familiar. A client familiar with Freudian theory might say that they sense some-thing 'oedipal' about the situation they are in. Someone familiar with Jung might find themself thinking in terms of 'absorption in the Great Mother'. A third person might simply conceptualise their experience in terms of 'lacking assertiveness'. Any of these conceptualisations

could draw out aspects of the situation which were previously undifferentiated, and allow the individual's experiencing to be carried forward. However, there is no way of determining in advance which concepts will prove useful, and there is no finite list of possible conceptual frameworks which we may use to structure our experience. In other words there are no fixed units into which our experiencing must be fitted. Gendlin (1973b, p. 322) writes:

> What are the units of 'this situation' or of 'yesterday' or of 'now' or of 'life'? . . . A small bit of experiencing, like 'now', if articulated, could be seen to include the words written here, the page, the context of the book up to now, the reader's feelings and incipient thoughts about it, and many other present feelings all included in the feeling or experiencing now. There is no way of getting them 'all', nor is there a single definite set of 'all'. There are no definite units, nor a definite number of units – so the smallest bit we called 'now' does not include less in number than what we called 'life'. Both are endlessly differentiable and, as experienced, preconceptual, pre-defined, yet not committed to any one way of defining.

Our existence has the aspects of being preconceptual and differentiable; it also has the aspect of being bodily felt. Throughout his work Gendlin emphasises the importance of the body, but 'body' here does not mean the body as conceptualised in physiology. It is rather the body as 'felt from inside', the bodily sense of situations. One can come into a room, look around and get a sense of the place. From this felt sense words and phrases may arise, but before they do there is the feel of the place, a feel which is sensed in the stomach or chest or some other bodily location. By 'felt from inside' Gendlin does not mean the feel of bodily sensations such as those arising from a tightly fitting shoe or a painful shoulder. It is rather the bodily sense *of* a place, or a situation or a problem.

2. *Encounter.* This is the principle which Gendlin later came to call 'interaction first'. It is the principle that nothing exists except through interaction with other things. In particular, human experiencing is not to be regarded as something purely subjective, but as the experiencing *of* something. Experiences and situations are inseparable. To be jealous is not simply to have a sensation (like having an itch); it is to be involved in an interpersonal situation. In Focusing it can seem as if we are paying attention to something quite 'inner' and private, but this is an illusion. What we are paying attention to is our experiencing-of-a-situation.

3. *Authenticity.*   This is a notion found in much existential philosophy, but Gendlin associates it with his central concept of 'carrying-forward'. The connection may not be obvious, but can be explained as follows. Someone may have the experience of having a 'funny' feeling. What she then says may or may not carry her feeling forward. If she says 'Really, I'm quite OK and ready to get on with my work', that does not carry her forward. In spite of what she cheerfully says the feeling stays as it was. But if she is able to give attention to the feeling and words come such as 'Oh, it has to do with being caught in a situation in which I'm going to appear...sort of unsophisticated' then there may be a felt shift, 'Ah (deeper breath) that's what it is.' Here the feeling has been carried forward by just those words, and now she feels different. *Those* words are for Gendlin the authentic words in the situation. The words 'Really. I'm quite OK' were not authentic. Authentic words and deeds are those which carry us forward.

4. *Value.*   Experiencing has a direction; only certain words or deeds will carry us forward. If we let ourselves sense the whole feel of a situation, a sense of direction emerges. This sense of a direction is distinct from any *concept* of what we ought to do. Concepts of what we ought to do often bring with them a sense of tension or burden, whereas the felt sense of what to do is experienced as a release. Gendlin (*ibid.*, p. 327) emphasises the

> holistic aspect of the direction in experiencing. It is different from giving in to one urge or one intense emotion. It is not a question of just any kind of feeling 'good'. Some people may feel 'good' when they kill someone. To give in to an urge often feels good. The holistic sense of direction in experiencing differs from this. It is not just any release from any pressure, but a *whole* body sense of one's life or specific situation which is used implicitly, without having to separate out all its many facets.

There are clearly important implications for ethics in this view (which I discuss in Appendix A); for the moment it will be enough to appreciate Gendlin's view that our experiencing has a purposive, directed quality to it, which shows up in the fact that some words and actions carry us *forward*, whereas others do not.

Focusing as a taught procedure

Gendlin first gave a set of focusing instructions in his 1969 paper on 'Focusing'. These were instructions which could be introduced to clients in an informal way, or could be used more formally in research projects. They can be summarised as:

- pay attention to that place inside where you usually feel sad, glad or scared;
- see what comes to you when you ask yourself 'How am I now?' 'How do I feel?';
- select a meaningful personal problem to think about;
- try to get a sense of the problem *as a whole*. Let yourself feel *all of that*;
- as you pay attention to the whole feeling of it, you may find that one special feeling comes up. Let yourself pay attention to that one feeling;
- if this one feeling changes, follow it and pay attention to it;
- take what is fresh and new in the feel of it *now*, and try to find some new words or pictures to capture what your present feeling is all about;
- if the words or pictures you now have make some fresh difference, see what that is. Let the words or pictures change until they feel just right in capturing your feelings.

In the same paper he writes that the focusing process is one of

> very intently keeping quiet, zeroing one's attention in, and then – within this deliberately made focus and quiet – only then and there, letting come what comes .... Even though therapists are an introspective lot, I find that I and my colleagues do not do this sharply distinct focusing even in our own introspections, unless we set ourselves to do so specifically. I am as likely to go about in a stew as anyone else, until I specifically bring myself to focusing and say "All right, now. Shut up," and then wait gently as I ask my body sense: What's wrong?". (Gendlin, 1969, p. 7)

Gendlin emphasises that we sense our difficulties in a bodily way:

> How one lives and reacts is a bodily process going on in situations. When someone is about to jump at you, you feel it in your 'gut'. When someone in complicated ways is going to hurt you, again you feel it in your gut. Just as a golfer feels in his body, in the position of his feet, and in the muscular sense of his swing, the whole scene in front of him, so do we bodily experience the complexity of our situations and interactions. (*ibid.*, p. 8)

The body-sense of a problem is pre-verbal and preconceptual.

To attend to it or speak from it is a *further* living and therefore a further structuring, a 'carrying forward' . . . As one acts one perceives one's own acting. This is then a new experiencing which can again lead to an action which is again experienced and leads to another action. This 'zig-zag' between body-sense and visible action is such that each carries the other forward. (p. 8)

In subsequent years Gendlin elaborated and modified the focusing instructions. It seemed clear that they could be used by people as a self-help procedure, and this led to the publication of Gendlin's best-known book, *Focusing*, in 1978/2003. The book has sold nearly half a million copies, and Gendlin still receives notes of thanks from people, sometimes scribbled in pencil on scraps of paper, in which they say that it saved their lives (Hendricks, 2003, p. 69).

The account of Gendlin's instructions which I will now give is not a sufficient guide for practising Focusing. (This is because various difficulties can arise, different for different people, which Gendlin discusses in detail.) In order to learn Focusing the reader should consult the details in the book itself, and preferably attend some Focusing workshops. Although Focusing *can* be learned from the book, most people find it very much easier to learn from a teacher. One can also learn ways of assisting or 'guiding' someone in their Focusing, but that is another topic which is rather outside the scope of the present book.

Gendlin presents the Focusing process in six steps, but he has always insisted that these steps are only a guide, that they do not always happen in the same order, and that not all of them are always present. With those qualifications, the steps are:

1. *Clearing a space.*   Here the focuser takes a few moments to bring their attention into the centre of their body, to the place where we usually feel our emotions, and then notices what comes there when they ask, in a friendly way, 'How is my life going? What is the main thing for me right now?'. Usually there are several concerns which can be felt. The focuser is instructed not to *go into* any of them but just to notice that they are there. 'Clearing a space' has two distinct aspects to it. There is first what Gendlin calls the 'Inventory', that is the listing of the various concerns. This is like making a 'things to do' list; it does not get the jobs done, but it sorts them out and reduces the feeling of being overwhelmed by them all (Gendlin, 1978/2003,

p. 75). The other aspect is that of 'finding the right distance' from the concerns, that is, standing back from them sufficiently for them not to feel threatening or overwhelming, but still being able to feel them. Gendlin (1984a, p. 268) has a whole range of practices to help with this, such as imagining the concerns as packages which can be set down at a distance which feels right. This is often referred to as 'putting things down'. On the other hand, one may sometimes prefer to gently hold or 'be with' a problem.

2. *Felt sense.*   The focuser senses which of their concerns most needs attention. The concern will usually have many aspects, too many to think about explicitly, but they can all be *felt* together. The felt sense is a sense of what *all that problem* feels like.

3. *Handle.*   The focuser now asks whether there is a word or phrase or image which fits the physical felt quality of the problem. Words such as 'heavy', 'jumpy' or 'bubbly' are helpful in catching the physical feel of the problem. The focuser is looking for a word which 'gets a handle on' how the problem is being registered in the body. (For some people the terminology of 'getting a handle on it' feels uncomfortable, but the metaphor is simply that of something – like a suitcase handle – which enables one to hold on to something. Having the word or image allows one to pull the felt sense back if it is lost.)

4. *Resonating.*   The focuser goes back and forth between the felt sense and the handle-word, noticing if the felt sense changes as attention is given to it, or if the handle-word really 'fits'. For instance, is 'jumpy' quite the right word for this, or is it more 'pulled-in'?

5. *Asking.*   Now the focuser can ask, for example, 'What is it about this whole problem that makes it feel so *pulled-in*?'. They then wait until something comes which brings with it a slight shift or release.

6. *Receiving.*   The focuser receives in a friendly way whatever comes in a shift. It is not queried or analysed.

Whatever comes can then be focused on again. If what came from the sense of 'pulled-in' was 'being seen' the focuser could then return to Step 4 and resonate 'being seen' with the felt sense, and then (new Step 5) ask 'What is this *being seen* thing?' and await what might come. Steps 4 and 5 are thus the central ones in the procedure.

The first step, that of 'clearing a space', was not in the original (1969) instructions, but it is something the importance of which

Gendlin has increasingly emphasised. It can be used on its own as a method of stress reduction (Gendlin, 1984a, p. 267):

> One uses just this first movement in the times between one setting and another, that is to say on the bus, or while waiting for the elevator, or while waiting for food in a restaurant. One senses what one's body is just then carrying, puts it down one by one, and feels a physical relief. One works on no problem at all. Just putting them all down enables one to clear oneself of accumulated tension and unease. One is then ready for the next activity. Most people spend every day chronically at maximum tension, so that one more troubled situation does not make any more difference. They never feel the physical easing and reduction of stress which the first movement alone can bring.

Whether used in this way for stress reduction, or as the first movement in Focusing, 'clearing a space' depends crucially on one's ability to sense one's body from the inside. 'Putting down' can be visualised as placing packages on a shelf, for instance, but if when this has been done there is no physical relief, then the problem has *not* been put down. The putting of packages on the shelf is an *image* of the process which is taking place; just what that process is in itself is another matter. Gendlin (1997a, Chapter 8) has important things to say about this in his philosophical work *A Process Model*, and I have said a little about it elsewhere (Purton, 2002).

If a particular form of imagery does not work, then one needs to try something different, such as sitting forward in one's chair, and slowly moving back so that the problem is left where it is. Gendlin (1984a) suggests several things which can be done to get the right distance from a problem, but *whatever* is done, one has to be able to sense in one's body whether there is any release of tension.

People vary a great deal in being able to sense what is going on in their bodies. Responses to the question 'How does this problem feel right now, there in the middle of your body?' can range from 'What do you mean?' or 'Nothing special' to 'There is a wound up feeling in my chest, which sort of needs to be released, but also something, lower down – like a heavy thing – which kind of stands in the way.' Awareness of body feelings is important to the whole Focusing process, so that it may need to be practised as part of learning Focusing. One way is to practise bringing attention first into the toes, then the legs and so on, moving through the body, and ending with the central region of throat, chest, stomach and abdomen, the region in which we mostly register our feelings. It can also help at the start of a Focusing session to make a practice of first bringing one's attention into the body.

Along with putting a greater emphasis on 'clearing a space', Gendlin has, since the *Focusing* book, emphasised the importance of finding a good place (or space, or feeling) *from which* one can work with one's problems. Sometimes we can get to the 'good place' by putting problems down, but the putting down is itself not easy unless there is already a sense of space and the possibility of change. The constricting feelings which we have from our problems cramp our ability to work on the problems. This is a vicious circle, but Gendlin suggests that the way through is first to find a way of experiencing what it would feel like *if* the problem were resolved:

> When have you last felt really wonderful? It would be a long time ago. Many people have to search their memories, way back. But the first movement of focusing (and really, every movement of it) depends on having a good feeling as a background against which the problem is sensed...One asks in effect. "What would it take to feel good? What would be a step toward feeling better?" Or "What is now between me and feeling fine?"...The instruction is now phrased "Suppose *your life* is going just perfectly...you feel glorious...now wait for your body to talk back and give you, how you now *do* feel. Then see, one by one, what that is about, *in your life*...at every step in focusing one really asks "What's in the way of feeling good?" or "What would be a step toward feeling better?" All the while there is an all-good feeling, *from which* one asks about this *whole* problem. (Gendlin, 1984a, p. 271)

Although the problem is not yet resolved, one can feel how it would be if it were resolved, and from that good place it becomes more possible to work towards resolving it.

Other Focusing teachers, such as Ann Weiser Cornell (1993, 1996), Peter Campbell and Edwin McMahon (1985/1997), have their own variants on the Focusing instructions, and in general the development of Focusing as a taught procedure continues to be a lively affair. Kevin Flanagan (1998) provides a useful introduction, but the most thorough practical handbook is Ann Weiser Cornell's and Barbara McGavin's *The Focusing Student's and Companion's Manual* (2002), which is based on many years' Focusing teaching, and is the culmination of several different ways of formulating the Focusing 'steps' (see Cornell, 1993, 1996). I would recommend this work to anyone who wishes seriously to pursue Focusing as a self-help procedure. The authors divide the Focusing process into four stages:

1. 'Coming in', which involves bringing awareness into the body, sensing and inviting what wants one's awareness now, and waiting until something comes.
2. 'Making contact', in which one begins to describe what has come, acknowledges it and finds the kind of contact it would like.
3. 'Deepening contact', which involves settling down with it, keeping it company, sensing in the body, the emergence of symbols, resonating and adjusting, sensing its point of view and letting it know that one has heard it.
4. 'Coming out', which involves sensing for a stopping place, receiving and experiencing what has changed, letting it know that you are willing to come back, thanking it and bringing one's awareness out.

Cornell and McGavin emphasise strongly what they call 'Presence' (McGavin, 2000; Cornell and McGavin, 2002, p. 56). Presence is 'being-with' a felt sense, and what comes from it, in a quiet friendly way. Cornell (2001) quotes Gendlin in this context:

> The client and I, we are going to keep it, in there, company. As you would keep a scared child company. You would not push on it, or argue with it, or pick it up, because it is too sore, too scared or tense. You would just sit there, quietly ... What that edge needs to produce the steps is only some kind of unobtrusive contact or company. If you will go there with your awareness and stay there or return there, that is all it needs; it will do all the rest for you. (Gendlin, 1990, p. 216)

> Focusing is this very deliberate thing where an 'I' is attending to an 'it'. (p. 222)

The state of Presence contrasts with two other states which Cornell and McGavin call 'merged' ('identified') and 'exiled' ('dissociated'). The merged state is what Cornell (1993) earlier called Too Close process, and the exiled state is what was earlier called Too Distant process. The distinction is closely related to Gendlin's early distinction between clients who are caught up in their emotions, and those who distance themselves from their problems by 'externalising' or 'intellectualising'.

Cornell and McGavin (2002) have developed linguistic ways of responding which are designed to help the Focuser 'come into Presence'. These include:

(a) Gendlin's (1996, pp. 46–8) way of using 'something':

> Almost anything can be phrased in a way as to point to something. Let me use as trivial example: "I like that movie." "You can sense a liking there; something in you likes that movie" ... The effect is to point the person's attention inward to something that is directly sensed. The response also turns something that was clearly defined into something that is still unclear and could therefore lead further.

(b) Reflecting 'I' statements such as 'I want to run' in forms such as 'There's a wanting to run', 'Something in you wants to run' or 'Part of you wants to run' (this, and the following examples are taken from Cornell, 2001). I have argued (Purton, 2002) that there can be problems with speaking of 'parts', but this way of talking is much less prominent in Cornell and McGavin's manual than it was in Cornell's (1996) earlier book.

(c) Clarifying 'who' is speaking:

> F: I'm feeling this part of me that's so ... angry, I guess. Like a little kid who hates everyone.
> L: That part of you feels like a little kid who hates everyone.
> F: Just get away from me!
> L: It's like that kid is saying, "Just get away from me!"

(d) Making it explicit that the Focuser is experiencing or sensing something:

> F: This part needs to change quicker.
> L: You're sensing something in you that's needing this part to change quicker.
> F: It's scary.
> L: You're sensing something in you that's feeling scared, and something that finds it scary.

These formulations are designed to help the Focuser (the 'I') relate to a feeling or a 'something' (the 'it'). In Gendlin's terms, they help to create or preserve a space within which the 'I' can relate to the 'it'.

The nature of this 'I', and the nature of the 'space' within which it relates to the 'it' is a theme which needs further exploration. Gendlin (1980, p. 70) writes:

> It is not in the usual image space, nor in the body as usually attended to. There is a new level, a new kind of awareness. One senses a new kind of 'it', that felt sense there. Along with sensing such as 'it', one also senses in a fresh direct way that 'Oh . . . I am not it.' There is a discovery that one is none of these contents. But this is no mere disembodied watcher. Rather, a new flow of energy and a new sense of self-in-touch, makes this new self very concrete and alive, no mere observer. And yet one finds this newly formed 'felt sense' over here, and oneself over here next to it, with a new kind of space in between.

Some further development of Gendlin's thinking about this 'self' and its 'space' can be found in *A Process Model* (Gendlin, 1997a, Chapter 8).

To return to more practical issues, Cornell and McGavin (2002) are concerned with an issue in teaching Focusing. It is not always easy for people to grasp what a felt sense is, and then much time can be spent in wondering whether what one feels really *is* a felt sense. This can lead away from one's experiencing, and the authors seldom use the term 'felt sense', preferring simply to refer to 'something' or 'it'. In Cornell's (1996) earlier book this – to my mind at least (Purton, 2002) – created the impression that the concept of the felt sense was not of great importance. However, in their *Manual*, Cornell and McGavin make it clear that they do not wish to play down the importance of Gendlin's concept (on p. A15 they say 'This is perhaps the central term for Focusing'), but they prefer to introduce it in an implicit way.

They have in other ways modified Gendlin's steps in the light of their experience of teaching Focusing. They prefer not to teach 'clearing a space' as a standard part of the Focusing process, but suggest it as an option where someone is overloaded by many issues. Further, they have found that 'putting things down' can be used as a way to *push away* an exiled part. (Cornell (1995) has for some time emphasised *relating* to feelings rather than *finding the right distance* from them.) They have also come to expand Gendlin's 'Asking' step into a series of stages, since they found that people will often 'ask' too soon, before there is enough of a relationship with the felt sense. In the place of 'Asking' they now have 'Settling down with it', 'Keeping it company' and 'Sensing its point of view'.

In another interesting development Cornell (1990, pp. 69–72) suggests that the felt sense can be approached from different starting points:

> Recently I have been picturing the Full Felt Sense as having four aspects: body sensation, emotional quality, imagery or symbolism, and life connection or story. I have observed that a person usually enters Focusing through one of these four avenues. Then, as the session progresses, the felt sense typically 'fills out' so that more and more of these are present. The person may begin by telling a story about an issue in their life, and then begin feeling an emotion, and then sense something in the body. Or the person may begin with a body sensation, then get an image for it, then sense its emotional tone, then realize what it's about in their life. From this we learn two things. First, that it's legitimate to enter Focusing by any of these four roads. Body sensation is not the only way to begin. Second, if the session gets stuck, the guide might notice which of these four aspects is present, and if any are missing. The missing ones can be invited.

She goes on to give examples of each type of situation, and examples of how to invite missing aspects.

This theme has been taken up by Mia Leijssen (1996, pp. 433–5). She notes that some people begin with an *emotion*, such as fear. They may then become aware of the *physical sensations* involved. An *image* may then arise (in Leijssen's example, 'a creeping fog'), and finally they may connect the image with a *life situation* (in her example, a danger of loss of self in a relationship). There is then in awareness the whole felt sense of the situation, and the fear which it arouses, symbolised by the image of the creeping fog. From this the client carries forward the symbolisation first with 'That is threatening', then with an awareness of the hurt she had sustained in the relationship and finally with 'To lose myself, that is what is painful'.

Another person may describe in detail a *bodily sensation* such as a pain in the arm, which 'nags' and 'pulls'. This leads into *emotions* of anger and sadness, and then into a pervasive *life situation* in which 'she wants to have everything her way, and that life is a big burden like that'.

Often people start with a *situation*. Leijssen's example is of a man having to address a nasty colleague, and expressing this experience with the *image* 'I'm like a rat in a trap'. He becomes aware that he is moving so as to protect himself as he did when, as a child, he was beaten by a tyrannical teacher; there is awareness of *bodily reactions*.

He then notices how an authoritarian man still provokes intense *fear* in him.

> The situation, the symbolisation, the body reactions and the emotions now constitute a complete felt sense which he now words as follows: 'Now, that is what bothers me: I start already by setting myself up as the one who will get beaten so that even the most neutral question on his part becomes threatening!' These words provoke an important shift; he even literally sits up straight and looks securely at the therapist.

Occasionally people start with symbolisation, such as an image, or a sentence from a book. This may then lead to a bodily reaction such as tears, an emotion such as sadness, and then connect with a life situation such as missing a parent.

Leijssen agrees with Cornell that where the Focusing process becomes stuck it may be because one of the four elements (emotion, physical sensation, symbols and life situation) is missing. She writes (*ibid.*, p. 433):

> I do not name these four components...at random. In studying fragments of therapy sessions we have noticed that, regardless of the entry chosen, the felt sense only fully emerges when contact is made with all four components. This model of a complete felt sense is particularly useful at times when clients remain stuck in one or several components and feel that it does not help them to keep exploring those.

In speaking of the 'components' of a felt sense in this way there is perhaps some risk of losing the central notion of the felt sense as the bodily awareness of a situation. Emotions are often there as one element in the awareness of the situation, but I do not think they are not *necessarily* present. The other three aspects *are* essential, but that is because they belong to the *concept* of a felt sense: a felt sense is the *bodily* registering of a *situation* as an implicit whole, which is already specified *symbolically* in some way, even if only by the linguistic symbols 'all that thing'. Nevertheless, Cornell and Leijssen are undoubtedly right that people can begin at different places, that the felt sense can therefore emerge in different ways, and that through giving attention to a missing aspect a stuck process may be freed up.

Further variations and developments of the Focusing procedure include the Interactive Focusing of Janet Klein and Mary McGuire, which is concerned especially to enhance personal relationships; the

Wholebody Focusing of Kevin McEvenue, which integrates Focusing with the Alexander technique; and Barbara McGavin's and Ann Weiser Cornell's Treasure Maps to the Soul, which works with many ways of transforming inner struggles through recognising the value of critical and rebellious parts of ourselves. Details of these developments can be found on the Focusing Institute website.

A final word seems important on the relationship between Focusing and action. Gendlin (1996, p. 237) notes that Focusing can be used as a way of avoiding action:

> Very introspective people resist trying action steps directly. They think it is artificial. They believe that it must be ineffective to act in a way that does not come directly from how they feel. In a difficult situation, instead of attempting an action, they eagerly find some familiar inner conflict. It is as if they said, "What a relief; there is still an inward problem that can be worked on, so it's not yet time for action." But a change in action can alter the whole body, and may bring about just the feeling that is most lacking.

Christiane Bucher (2000), in an article titled 'Why it was crucial for me to quit Focusing, and what came next' writes:

> Where does action come into our Focusing settings? One way would be to stop the "What-is-all-there-and-will-it-shift-and-change-and-get-me closer-to-the-origins-of-my-issue-and-let-it-solve-itself-by-going-pregnant-with-it Focusing" and stay tuned to the signs from within, and just ask, This way? That way? Action-oriented. Life-oriented. Non-psychology oriented. I have a pretty good idea about our tasks in life. Classic Focusing can even distract us from them. It did for me for a while. . . . My body has always been very attentive to the "greater knowledge". Hearing the inner voice has never been difficult for me. It's trusting it and following it which can be so hard.

Focusing should not be seen as a retreat into a subjective world of 'feelings'. Rather it is a practice of felt awareness of one's situation, of how one is – bodily – in interaction with the world.

Having outlined what is involved in Focusing as a procedure, I now turn to how the principles involved can be incorporated into therapy sessions in a person-centred way.

5

Focusing-Oriented Psychotherapy

In this chapter I will explore how the principles of focusing can inform therapeutic practice, without the therapist explicitly teaching the Focusing procedure.

In the first section I will look at how the therapist can help the client to engage more effectively with their experiencing. This is the most important part of the chapter. In the second section I will discuss some things which can prevent the client from relating effectively with their experiencing, and in the third section I will consider what Gendlin calls specific 'avenues' of therapy, such as working with images, emotions, cognition or specific elements of the therapeutic relationship. These are *possible* ways of working, which the focusing-oriented therapist can draw on, depending on the needs and wishes of the client, and on what the therapist feels comfortable with. The Focusing *procedure* could be seen as just one such avenue, as one specific way of proceeding. But each of the avenues needs to be oriented towards what is most characteristic of Focusing, that is, the interaction between experiencing and something that carries the experiencing forward.

Helping the client to relate to their experiencing

In focusing-oriented psychotherapy, as in person-centred therapy generally, the most important thing is to create a receptive atmosphere which will encourage the client to explore what they are experiencing. The therapist's receptive and non-judging attitude is usually crucial to the client feeling safe, and without that sense of safety nothing which the therapist does is likely to be of much use. The maintenance of the sense of a safe, protected place is something to which everything else is secondary. If in the course of the session the therapist senses that the client no longer feels safe, then that must be attended to as the top priority.

Focusing-oriented psychotherapy is client-centred therapy: the client, and the client's frame of reference, is central to whatever the therapist does. This is not to say that the therapist brings nothing of their own to the session. In addition to the crucial fact that they are present as another human being, the therapist may have relevant personal experience of difficulties which are in some ways like the client's difficulties. Or the therapist may have experience of working with other clients with rather similar difficulties. The therapist may know something in general about what can often help in working with this sort of difficulty. Much lies in the background of the therapist's responses to a client; far too much to be set out explicitly. The therapist needs to bring all their experience and knowledge to their work with the client, but not in a way which imposes it on the client, or distances the therapist from the immediate experiencing of the client. Gendlin (1996, p. 286) writes: 'When I expect a client, I put my own feelings and concerns to one side. I don't put them far, because I need to sense when something registers there. I also put aside theories and procedures ... All that is on the side. In front of me the space is free, ready for the other person.'

The therapist responds as a whole person who has considerable resources on which they can draw to help the client. But whether or in what way those resources will be engaged depends on 'where the client is', and on what happens in the relationship with the client. The relationship with the client may draw out ideas and responses in the therapist which are rooted in the therapist's general knowledge and experience, but what is drawn out is something specific to this interaction, something whose precise form could not have been known in advance.

Client-centred therapy is not centred around hypotheses about what a particular client needs. It is centred on the client, and on discovering in the interaction with the client what the client needs. The therapist does not come armed with a theory, but with an open-armed attitude that allows the client to find their own path. Gendlin characterises the essential attitude as one of 'putting nothing between'. On meeting the client the therapist puts aside whatever they have just been engaged with, puts aside their own personal troubles, and puts aside what they know of theory and procedures. Then they are there for the client, but all their past experience and learning is available as an implicit resource upon which they may draw at any time.

Although focusing-oriented psychotherapy is much concerned with clients' experiencing, there is an important sense in which the therapist's attention is centred on the client, rather than on the client's experiencing. It is a central theme of focusing that *we* are not to be identified with our experiencing. We *have* our experiences of anxiety, depression and so forth, but these experiences are not us; they are what we need to relate to and work with. In focusing-oriented psychotherapy the therapist works with the client in helping the client to relate to their experiencing. The experiencing is, in Gendlin's (1984b) phrase, the 'client's client', but the therapist's direct relationship is with the client, not the client's experiencing. If this is forgotten, a client may experience focusing as a technique in which the therapist works with the client's experiencing rather than as a relationship in which the therapist works with the client. In relating to a client we relate to the person, to that which *has* the feelings. We relate to 'the person in there' (Gendlin, 1996, pp. 286–7) who struggles with their feelings.

Given this, the essential question is how the therapist can respond to the client in a way which will help the client to engage with and move forward in their experiencing. There are many things which can get in the way of the client doing this, some of which I will discuss in more detail in the next section. Here I will discuss in a more general way the principles of responding to clients in a focusing-oriented way.

At the heart of focusing-oriented therapy is Rogers' procedure of close listening and reflecting. Even the most literal 'saying-back' of what the client has said can be enormously helpful. It is something the therapist can do when it is unclear what else might help, and it is something that is unlikely to do any harm. Careful reflection maintains the therapist's relationship with the client and helps the client to maintain a relationship with what they are experiencing. As we saw in Chapter 2 ('The client-centred response'), it provides the client with a 'mirror' in which they can see themselves without distortion. It also plays a role in attuning the therapist to the fine details of what the client is experiencing. The words which a client uses may express very subtly and exactly what they are feeling, and in reflecting the words exactly the therapist connects with the intricacy of the client's experiencing. For example, if a client says that someone 'has kind of twisted me round inside so that I can't be straight with myself', it will be better to reflect this word-for-word than to respond with a general sense of the feeling such as 'You feel twisted up' or, even less helpfully,

'He really upset you'. In the same way, if a client says they feel hopelessly lost, it may not be very helpful to reflect this as 'You feel lost'.
The 'hopelessly' was part of what the client said, part of what they
felt. Sometimes clients will correct the therapist when the reflection
is inadequate – 'Not just lost, *hopelessly* lost'. And then it is important
for the therapist to reflect the correction, in a way which makes it
clear that they *value* being corrected.

Of course there needs to be some discrimination in what we
reflect. We are reflecting in order to show that we understand the
meaning that something has for the client, and to help them experience
this meaning. Often clients will tell in detail the story of something
which has happened to them, and it would not be helpful to reflect
the story details. What the events meant to them, how the situation
struck them, may get lost in the convolutions of the story; often clients
simply do not pause enough to get a sense of what they are experiencing. Here it will be necessary to find some way of helping the client
to be more conscious of their own responses, and it can sometimes
help if the therapist simply repeats a word in a reflective way:

T: Can I just interrupt a minute? You were saying that you felt sort of
   embarrassed . . .
C: Yes. It was embarrassing, because, you know, we only met last week,
   and as I was saying, we went along to . . .
T: But it really was . . . sort of . . . embarrassing . . .
C: Yes, made me feel all . . . I don't know . . .
T: There's a sort of feeling there . . . something . . .
C: It really makes me feel quite churned up . . .

Without such interruptions, and the encouragement to pause and
look, the client may be quite unable to relate to their experiencing.
With clients who talk about external events and rarely pause in their
stories, the therapist needs to watch for places where an intervention
could be helpful. These will usually be at points where the client has
been moved or struck by something, where they refer to *their
responses* rather than to the external situation. Gendlin (1980, p. 279)
has the metaphor of watching traffic go past: a car, a car, a car, a car,
a fire engine, a car, a car. We need to respond to the fire engine: here
is a point where the client may be able to connect with their experiencing. If after several sessions no opportunities have arisen, then the
therapist may need to create them, for example, by asking questions
such as 'And how did you react to that?'

In focusing-oriented therapy, as in person-centred therapy generally, we 'respond to feelings', but it needs to be made clear exactly
what that means. It is not so much feelings in the sense of specific
emotions, but the client's feeling-response to their situation. As Rogers
in effect recognised in the early years of client-centred therapy,
'reflection of feelings' needs to be done in a way which points towards
the client's felt sense of a situation rather than simply labelling the
client's experience as a feeling of a particular kind. Rogers wrote
(1951, p. 28):

> Here is a client statement: "I feel as though my mother is always watching
> me and criticizing what I do. It gets me all stirred up inside. I try not to
> let that happen, but you know, there are times when I feel her eagle eye
> on me that I just boil inwardly."
>   A response on the counselor's part might be: "You resent her criti-
> cism." This response may be given empathically, with the tone of voice
> such as would be used if it were worded "If I understand you correctly,
> you feel pretty resentful toward her criticism. Is that right?" If this is the
> attitude and tone which is used, it would probably be experienced by the
> client as aiding him in further expression. Yet we have learned, from the
> fumblings of counsellors-in-training, that "You resent her criticism" may
> be given with the same attitude and tone which would accompany "You
> have the measles" or even "You are sitting on my hat". If the reader will
> repeat the counselor response in some of these varying inflections, he
> may realise that when stated empathically and understandingly, the likely
> attitudinal response on the part of the client is, "Yes, that is the way I
> feel, and I perceive that a little more clearly now that you have put it in
> somewhat different terms."

The counsellor's response needs to be to 'that whole situation' which
the client is experiencing. The counsellor is not trying to fit the client's
experiencing into the counsellor's category of 'resentment' but, in
Rogers' words, 'aiding in further expression'. The counsellor's response
should 'point' towards the felt intricacy of the client's experiencing,
since it is only from that intricacy that change steps can come. In
'reflecting' what the client said, the counsellor is helping the client to
engage in a focusing process.

Two distinct situations can arise here. Where the client is already
engaged in focusing on a felt sense, and trying to find words to articulate
it, it is important for the therapist to reflect these words fairly exactly.
The client is trying out *just that* form of expression, and needs to hear
it back exactly. But often a client will report feelings as if they were

distinct things which are 'just there', and here an exact reflection may be worthless or even irritating to the client:

C: She did it again last night, and I got angry.
T: You got angry.
C: Yes, I just *told* you. And who wouldn't have?

The therapist here needs to find a way of responding not to the simple, packaged way in which the client has expressed their experience, but to what the therapist can imagine as the more intricate situation in which the client is involved. What the client is experiencing cannot possibly be *fully* articulated by 'I got angry'; his experiencing will be of a whole intricate situation involving what exactly she did, maybe the way she did it, the fact that she had done it *again*, perhaps that she had not taken any notice of his earlier complaints, and that he resented that, and how all this reminds him of what someone else used to do and how exasperated he is with himself about getting caught in this pattern again, but he would not be so caught in it if only she would give him a break. The therapist cannot know the intricacies of the client's experiencing, but can still respond in a way which points the client towards that intricacy. For example, the therapist could respond with 'So there it was again last night . . . and her doing it again brought up a real feeling of anger in you . . . there was all that anger and . . . resentment, maybe? . . . something really strong . . .'.

As in the example from Rogers above, much depends on such things as timing and tone of voice. A client might say *in a way that indicated that they were focusing*:

C: She did it again last night, and . . . I got . . . angry . . .
T: You got angry . . .
C: Well, sort of angry . . . but there was a kind of sadness as well . . . I don't know . . .

With a client who is *not* focusing, it may sometimes be possible to respond *as if they were*, to take what they say as if they were in touch with their experiential intricacy. As a result the client may be helped to experience a bit more:

C: She did it again last night, and I got angry.
T: You got . . . *angry* . . .
C: Yes. Yes I really did – *really* angry.

What is hoped for in therapy is usually experiential *change*, not insight. Certainly in person-centred therapy the therapist's aim is not to acquire a deep understanding of the client. Rather, the aim is to interact with the client in a way that will help the client to carry forward their life. The therapist knows in advance that whatever they come up with is unlikely to correspond exactly with the client's experiencing. The 'right' response is not so much the one that 'fits' but the one which facilitates a *client* response in which the client's experiencing moves on:

> C: She did it again last night and I got all worked up.
> T: You were ... angry with her ...
> C: No, not angry ... definitely not angry ... but sort of ... despairing.
>   Yes, despairing ... I hadn't wanted to admit that ...

From that point the session might continue just as effectively as it would have done if the therapist's response had been 'right' in the more obvious way.

When the therapist's response is wrong (in the more obvious way), the important thing for the therapist is to respond to the client's experiential reaction. In the last example the therapist will naturally respond to the 'despairing', but sometimes a 'wrong' reflection may block the client, and then the therapist may need to backtrack:

> C: She did it again last night and I got all worked up.
> T: You were ... angry with her ...
> C: No, not *angry*, not angry at all. Definitely not angry.
> T: You weren't angry at all ... but you *were* all worked up ...

Rather than being 'wrong', the therapist's response may be *irrelevant* to what the client is experiencing. Gendlin writes (1968, p. 213):

> ... if my client's answer to me is "Yes, that *must* be true ... er," I know my response is no good. People say something *must* be true if they have to *infer* it – i.e., when they don't feel it directly. The "er" also indicates that there is nowhere to go with what I said. Now I reply "That sounds sort of right to you, but it isn't what you mainly feel now." And I thus invite him to attend, once more, to what he does feel, so that he won't get hung up on my useless response.

The therapist needs to sense for, and be guided by, those client responses which carry the client forward. 'Forward' here is not a direction which is specified by the therapist, but what Gendlin has called 'the direction of fresh air', that is, a direction specified by whether the client feels less stuck or unhappy or confused. The 'forward' direction is the direction specified by experiential shifts in the client's felt sense. Sometimes a client will talk at length about their issues and their feelings, but at the end of it nothing has shifted, and nothing has been resolved. The felt sense of the problem has not changed. At other times, as the client explores their feelings, there is a sense of something releasing. What the client has come to may not be pleasant in itself, but there is a felt shift. The whole problem now feels just a little different, and now the client may express the problem in a slightly different way. But it is not just a *different* way, it is a way of having the problem which is no longer quite as 'tight' or 'stuck' as it was before.

It is important to notice, and to help the client to register, those places where there *is* experiential release. In the midst of what seems an impossible situation there will also be life-enhancing tendencies. Human problems only arise because of desires, hopes and aspirations which are blocked or conflicted. The client inevitably senses mainly the blocks or conflicts, but may at times also sense the energies out of which the difficulties arise. The notion of 'stuckness' brings with it the notion of 'release'; the sense of stuckness is precisely a sense of a forward energy which has been blocked. The client can get glimpses of that forward energy in the small releasing steps which occur in the process of therapy. At a releasing step the client feels a bit of physical relief; for a short while, at least, the problem does not weigh them down so much, and if the feel of that lightening can be fully registered the client will be in a better state to continue working with the problem.

It is also important for the therapist to be aware of their own emotional reactions to the client. A client's difficulties are often associated with the self-defeating ways in which their fundamentally 'forward-oriented' life energies are expressed. A client's impulse to assert their own rights may emerge as hostility or resentment. An impulse to communicate clearly may come across as stilted or artificial. The need for closeness and affection may emerge as demandingness or clinginess. These ways in which the client expresses their needs and impulses inevitably have an impact on the therapist, who in their own feelings will register something of the self-defeating modes of expression. The therapist, just like anyone else with whom the client interacts, may find themself reacting with anger to the client's hostility, disengaging from the client's artificiality and rejecting the client's clinginess. But simply to respond in these ways to the client, as other people naturally do, will clearly not be helpful. Instead, the therapist needs to be aware of their own emotional reactions, and then to find ways of responding not to the client's distorted self-defeating behaviour as such, but to the positive energies which have become distorted.

For instance, if the client says in a hostile way that the therapy is clearly useless and they are going to stop coming, the therapist's immediate feeling might be something like 'Well, bugger off then. I don't *want* you to keep coming.' This is no doubt the kind of response which the client will have experienced in the outside world. But if the therapist can sense, beyond their immediate reaction, the client's underlying need, they might respond with something like 'You really want to get some help, and are angry that nothing much seems to be happening.' Or in response to a client's continuous talking the therapist may want to put their hands over their ears, or just walk away. No doubt in the outside world people do just make excuses and leave; the client's longing to communicate is defeated by the way in which they express it. The therapist needs to register in themself the feeling of wanting to get away, and then find a way of responding which acknowledges the *whole* of what is going on – perhaps something like 'I can really feel the importance of all this, but I'm finding it difficult to stay with you and respond because there are no spaces to take each bit in . . .'

With some client difficulties it may be especially helpful to work with versions of the difficulties which arise in the interaction between therapist and client. I will discuss in the next section some of the interpersonal difficulties which can interfere with the therapeutic process, and in the following section say more about interpersonal interaction as one specific *avenue* of therapy.

In focusing-oriented psychotherapy the therapist helps the client to articulate what is implicit in the client's whole felt sense of their difficulty, but is at the same time trying to respond from their own felt sense of what will help in the moment. The client needs responses from the therapist which are, as far as possible, responses to 'all that which is right now standing in the way of forward movement'. Such responses cannot be worked out logically, nor are they simply guesses or flashes of 'intuition'. They are responses which come from the therapist's whole felt sense of what is needed.

The therapist's felt sense of what is needed can be informed by their experience of Focusing as a taught procedure. The procedure is not introduced explicitly, but several elements in the procedure may be drawn into play by the needs of particular clients. There is, above all, the basic Focusing attitude of friendliness to whatever comes, an attitude of welcome for, and interest in, whatever the client is feeling. However, more specific elements in the Focusing procedure can also find their place.

For instance, some clients come to a session with a range of pressing concerns, each of which is generating anxiety. The client jumps from one anxiety-provoking situation in their life to another, but is unable to relate effectively to any of them. There is an overall anxiety which is being fed from several different sources. Here it can often help to suggest some version of the Inventory element in 'clearing a space' 'Maybe it would help if we first made a list of all these different things which are troubling you. How would that be?' If the client starts going into one of the anxieties, the therapist can remind them 'We can look properly at all that in a minute, but right now we are just making the list.' Then when the list is complete the therapist invites the client to get a sense of which issue feels most urgent, and to check if it feels all right for the other issues to wait their turn. I think that most clients find this a very natural procedure; they know that it is hopeless to try to sort out everything at once, and just need a little support in staying with one thing at a time.

The other element in 'clearing a space', that of 'putting things down' can also be very helpful to clients who are feeling overwhelmed by their emotions. But here the therapist needs to be sensitive to what kind of imagery, if any, is helpful to the client. A client may not want to 'put down' a very sore and painful issue; they may want to hold it and care for it. Or it may not be possible to put down an issue because it is so closely intertwined with *another* issue which *can't* be put down. Here the therapist's experience in Focusing as a procedure can be very helpful in sensing what might be helpful with particular client difficulties.

Bringing attention into the body can be helpful, especially with clients who have little awareness of their bodily reactions to situations. If the therapist says something like 'How does all that actually make you feel physically?' then this may help to direct the client's attention to their bodily felt sense of the situation. If the client does not understand the question, the therapist can suggest some possibilities: 'Clenched-up? Jittery? Deflated?...How does it feel...?' Then, therapist and client can then stay a bit with the physical feel – 'There's that *jittery* there...it is jittery...is it OK for us just to stay with that for a minute ... that whole jittery feel ...' Often something then emerges from the bodily felt sense, such as a thought, a memory, an image, and the process can carry forward from there.

Gendlin's question 'What stands in the way of me feeling just fine?' is another useful suggestion, especially with clients who have a vague sense of their lives not being satisfactory. It is an invitation to the client to sense what is blocking them, and once the block is made explicit it can itself be given attention.

It may be helpful at this point to reproduce a segment from a focusing-oriented therapy session (adapted from Gendlin, 1980, pp. 290–4) in order to give a better sense of how focusing-oriented responses can fit into a session. Other examples, which are well worth studying, can be found, for example, in Gendlin (1996), Iberg (2001) and Hendricks (2002). In the example which follows, the client is already familiar with focusing. The italicised sentences are those especially characteristic of a focusing-oriented approach.

The client is trying to find a job in her own field, meanwhile working at something she doesn't care about. She says (this excerpt has been altered to make it unrecognisable):

C1: I'm still avoiding those job interviews (in her field). And men too.

T1: *There's something similar* about your avoiding in those two areas.

C2: Yes. I think I'm not willing to take the chance of failing. I go on till there's a real opportunity, and then I run away. I get nervous.

T2: *Nervous is the word that fits it.*

C3: Yes. Uh, well ... I run away.

T3: *Run away is it.*

C4: Yes, being nervous isn't what does it.

T4: The nervous doesn't make the running away.

C5: No.

T5: So we don't know what the wanting to run away feels like, *what it is that wants to run away.*

C6: Well, I think it's that I'm scared to fail and that makes me fail. I'm scared to find out that maybe I won't be any good where I really care about it.

T6: *Can you feel the wanting to run away now, if you imagine going ahead?*

C7: Yeah, I can feel I want to run, but if I decide not to go ahead then I don't need to.

T7: As long as you don't think you'll go ahead, that need to run isn't there. And you suspect it's that you're afraid of finding out you're not really good at it.

C8: Right!

T8: I was also interested in just the feel-quality of it, for a minute *you could feel the wanting to run, just now. Can you still?*

C9: Yeah. I could feel it.

T9: *Let's tap it lightly and see what turns up.*

(silence)

C10: I'm bad, I feel crummy about me.

T10: You feel crummy to yourself.

(silence)

C11: I can feel it right under there, this crummy. It comes and goes. I can feel OK too, and if the crummy comes, I can ignore it and feel OK too, if I want. (laughs)

T11: *The crummy is right there, just underneath, and you don't have to feel it.*

(silence)

T11a: *Let's just be with this crummy, just hear from it, why it feels crummy.*

C12: I used to dance when I was little, just my own way around and round, but they said I was showing off.

T12: They called it something bad.

(silence)

C13: I used to fight with my mother. She would get very upset. She even went to a psychiatrist. One time my father came and said to me "Look what you're doing to your mother!"

T13: He made out you were doing something very bad to her.

C14: I was only going along my way, not fitting in with what she wanted.

T14: You were just going along but it was supposed to be very bad for her.

C15: Like I was hurting them.

T15: Made you feel you were hurting them.

(silence)

C16: It was always like that...

T16: *This part of you experienced that many, many times.*

(silence)

T16a: *Can you now really be glad this part of you came and that it is speaking to us and can you welcome it?*

(silence)

C17: It would rather run away than feel so crummy and bad.

T17: If it has to feel it's bad, it would rather run away.

(silence)

C18: Well. That's sure different than I thought.

Here we can see fairly straightforward client-centred reflecting at T4, T7, T10, T14, T15, T17. T1 is an example of the use of 'something' which I discussed in Chapter 4. There is a 'pointing' at the 'something'; it would not be a focusing-oriented response if the therapist had said 'Avoiding the job interviews is like avoiding men.' At T2 the therapist emphasises the word 'nervous'; this might well have been a place from which changes could come. But the client emphasises instead 'run away', and the therapist (T3) reflects this emphasis. T5 is a focusing-oriented response which again draws attention to a 'something', to 'what it is that wants to run away'. In C6 the client is thinking *about* her feelings, and T6 is the therapist's move to bring out the felt sense. (Imagining going ahead will draw out the wanting to run away, just as imagining that one's life is fine will draw out what is *not* fine.) However the client does not go along with this but comes back to what she was saying in C6. At T7 the therapist responds fully to this and the client (C8) is satisfied. The therapist then tries again to elicit the felt sense (T8, T9), and this time the client, begins to stay with it. *Silences* now begin to appear at places where the client is focusing. T11 and T11a help the client stay with the felt sense, and in C12–C16 something of what is in it begins to unfold. T16 is a move to help the client distinguish between herself and the 'part' which was made to feel bad. T16a is important in helping the client to preserve a friendly attitude to whatever may come.

Many sessions in focusing-oriented therapy would not look like this. This is how it can look when the client has (naturally, or through experience of therapy or training) some feel for the focusing way of proceeding. In other sessions, much of the time will be spent in maintaining good empathic contact with the client, in helping the client to move from 'the story' to how the client felt, in working with difficulties which prevent focusing, and in getting a sense of the client's preferred way of working. In practice, much of a typical focusing-oriented session will involve a kind of orientation towards the possibility of focusing, and the consequent 'moments of movement' which focusing can bring.

I just referred to 'difficulties which prevent focusing' and 'the client's preferred way of working'. This leads us to the next section of this chapter. Focusing-oriented psychotherapy requires the therapist to be sensitive both to the kinds of difficulty which the client has in relating to their experiencing and to the client's preferred modes of working with their difficulties. By 'preferred modes' I mean that some clients prefer to approach their problems through working with images and metaphors, some are oriented more to action and to trying out new forms of behaviour, some need to *understand* what is going on before they can act and some need above all to express feelings which they have never before expressed. Gendlin refers to these different preferred modes as distinct 'avenues' of therapy.

In the next two sections I will discuss first some general kinds of difficulties which clients may have in relating to their experiencing. Then I will consider some of the different 'avenues' along which clients may prefer to work with their difficulties.

Difficulties in relating to experiencing

Analysis of recordings of Rogers' work with clients (Merry, 2000, p. 2) suggests that over 80 per cent of his responses were empathic reflections of what the client had said. Such reflection maintains the empathic attunement with the client, and allows the client to follow a path which they sense is right for them. In focusing-oriented psychotherapy this close empathic following of the client occupies much of the time in most therapy sessions, and in some sessions it may occupy the whole of the time. Where the client is relating to their own experiencing, reflecting on it, processing it and reframing it, all that is required for the therapist is to accompany them in what they are doing. However, there are many things which can prevent the client from working effectively with their experiencing. In this section I have drawn on the work of the process-experiential therapists, as well as that of Gendlin. Much of what is done in process-experiential therapy can be relevant to a focusing-oriented approach, although the philosophy behind the approaches is rather different.

The more we reflect on the different kinds of difficulties which clients may have, the more sensitive we are likely to be in our responses to our clients. But it is sensitisation rather than diagnosis which is important. (I will say more about 'diagnosis' in Chapter 6, which is concerned with possible objections to focusing-oriented psychotherapy.) In none of the sections which follow do I mean to imply that the therapist should 'diagnose a process difficulty' and then adopt a specified response. There is too much in human beings which is subtle, intricate and implicit for this diagnostic approach to be very effective. And yet there *are* general patterns, and the more we are familiar with them the greater our sensitivity can be to the individual difficulty. This point is crucial if focusing-oriented therapy is to retain Rogers' fundamental insight that the client is the authority on what they experience and what they need, while acknowledging that the therapist may have knowledge and experience which may be helpful to the client.

It may be useful here to reflect that in working with a client from another culture it can be very important to know something about that culture. It can be important to read up on the cultural differences because otherwise one will be likely to miss things that are important to the client. For instance, one may not know that in that culture it is seen as disrespectful to sit with one's feet pointing towards someone. Without that bit of knowledge one might not notice the client's discomfort with how one is sitting. But to say that is quite different from saying that one should adopt a rule of sitting in a particular way with all clients who are known to have a particular cultural origin. Obviously, *this* client who appears today may be different. Perhaps they no longer wish to identify with certain of their culture's traditions, or perhaps they belong to a sub-culture which, unknown to the text-book writer, does not have those traditions, or perhaps they do not want people from *our* culture to adapt to them. We do not know for sure how we need to be with this client, but that is not to deny that the more we know about other cultures the better. It is not knowledge of general patterns which is to be disparaged, but the application of such knowledge in a rule-bound way that is insensitive to the subtleties and intricacy of the particular situation.

I think that the same principle applies in connection with our knowledge of the different kinds of difficulty which people can have in relating to their experiencing. Such knowledge can sensitise us to what *may* be difficult for *this* client *now*. It is not a matter of having a set of rules which tell us what to do in each kind of situation, but of developing an awareness of possibilities which will be there for us *in an implicit way* when we open ourselves to the uniqueness of the client, and to what can help that client as they relate to us in the present moment.

For each kind of difficulty which I discuss I will give references to books and papers through which the interested reader can follow up the themes in greater detail. This part of the chapter may need to be read rather differently from the rest of the book, perhaps as a reference section. I will begin with the kind of difficulty in which the client feels so vulnerable that they cannot even begin to explore their feelings.

Client vulnerability and 'fragile process'

Often when a client speaks of a painful or distressing experience it will be helpful for the therapist to reflect what they say, or otherwise help them to 'be with' the experience, to explore it and to 'go into' it. But sometimes the therapist may sense that the experience is so desperately painful that it is not appropriate to encourage such exploration. The client may be feeling that anyone who has done what they have done, or who is feeling what they feel, is totally unacceptable. Consequently, it may be impossible for the client to acknowledge fully what the feeling is, or how intense it is. Having had another child which was not planned, a mother may wish that the child had not been born, and *that is totally unacceptable.* That is something she cannot tell to her closest friend, it is something she can scarcely bear to admit to herself. In attempting to speak about it at all she experiences an intense vulnerability.

Here there is a block to being with the painful feelings, which comes from the sense of the feelings being totally unacceptable. What may be helpful is for the therapist to be sensitive to the 'totally unacceptable', and to respond in ways which show that *they* experience the client's feelings exactly as they are. The mother condemns herself, and expects others to condemn her. Even with the therapist she has deep reservations about whether she is really accepted. The aspect of the client's experiencing which may need to be worked with first is the fear of being condemned. The client needs to know that the therapist both genuinely appreciates what she feels about her child and still respects *her*, the person in there who struggles with these feelings. As the therapist continues to stay with, and affirm the client, the client becomes a little less vulnerable, and then may be able to begin to explore those feelings of which she was so frightened.

The therapist always needs to be sensitive to what the next step might be for a particular client at a particular time. Is it a time for exploring a feeling, or for exploring what makes it difficult to come near the feeling? Does the client need to make changes in their life situation before they can begin to reflect on their feelings? The therapist can only be guided by their felt sense of where the client is, but a background awareness that such choices may need to be made helps in being more open to the client's experiencing.

This theme is closely related to what Margaret Warner (2000b) calls 'fragile process'. Warner discusses recent work which suggests that infants who are securely related to their caregivers are able to modulate their levels of emotional arousal, while less securely attached infants are unable to do this. For the less-secure infants, fear and anger become chronic responses to new situations, with the result that they either cut off from attachment feelings or seek continual contact with a caregiver. A secure relationship with the caregiver involves good empathic responding, and it seems likely that this is what has been missing in clients whose process is 'fragile'. Correspondingly, effective therapy with such clients 'requires high quality listening skills. Clients typically need more than an accepting presence. They need to know that their experience has been understood with exactness and sensitivity as to its emotional vulnerability' (Warner, 2000b, p. 153). There is evidence (Schore, 1994, 2003) that the pattern of moderation of emotion in the presence of an empathic caregiver results in physiological changes in the brain which allow for the toleration of higher emotional arousal, and that similar physiological changes take place through the therapist's empathic relating to the client.

These themes are discussed further in Greenberg *et al.* (1993, Chapter 13) and Warner (2000b).

'Too close' and 'too distant' process

Extreme client vulnerability could be seen as a variety of the more general difficulty that a client may be so close to, so involved with, so caught in their experiencing that they cannot relate to it. There are clients who repetitively express their feelings, but no change results. I think of someone who was repeatedly asked to express his anger in a personal development group. He was encouraged to beat a cushion with a tennis racquet, and this indeed elicited the anger. But the only change, so far as he could tell, was that he was getting blisters on his hands from wielding the racquet! In the same way clients may express their depression and feelings of hopelessness week after week without any changes occurring. Sometimes, of course, a client needs to do this in order to plumb the depths of their despair; to touch the bottom before they can come up. In such cases one can sense the movement even though it is a downward one. But in other cases the sense is one of repetition and of being caught in the depressed mood. If the therapist simply continues to empathise with the client then they may well themselves get caught in the client's depression. To avoid this the therapist clearly needs to get a certain distance from the client's mood, to hold on to themself. But this is also what the *client* needs to do in relation to their mood. The therapist needs to relate to the client – the person in there – rather than the mood, and the standard Focusing moves can help here. For example, the therapist might respond to the client's saying 'I just can't see any point in doing anything' with 'There's something there – like there's no point in doing anything...that's there...would it be OK for us just to stay with that for a bit?' The point of this is to help the client to get a little distance from the feeling and, as Gendlin says, it is often helpful to say something like 'can *we* be with that feeling', since it may be impossible for the client to relate to the feeling on their own.

As we saw in Chapter 4, use of the words such as 'something' or 'that' can be very helpful in relating to what the client is experiencing. They bring attention to what is there without fitting it too quickly into a specific form. Once the client's experience is categorised as 'anger' or 'hurt' it is less easy to sense the *whole* of what is there. Where a client has already specified a feeling as 'hurt', for example, it may help the therapist to 'de-specify' it, for instance by saying something like 'There is that...kind of hurt...all that feeling about him...can you sense how all that is for you right now?' Getting a felt sense of *all that* brings a sense of release; it is as though the whole cloud of painful experiencing condenses into a droplet to which the client can relate. But the droplet is not specifiable as 'hurt' or 'anger'; it contains within it the whole complexity of the situation. Nevertheless, it is a limited emotional whole with which the client can interact. They can now feel '*That* is there; *I'm* here', and this 'separation' from the feeling brings a greater capacity to work *with* the feeling.

As we have seen in earlier chapters there are other ways in which we can lose touch with our own experiencing, and so be unable to work creatively with it. In particular there are the cases in which, far from being caught in our immediate bodily experiencing, we are too distant from it for it to make its proper contribution to what we do. The chief examples of this, as we have seen, are 'externalising' and 'intellectualising'. As in the case of being too close to experiencing, the client may need to spend time in their preferred mode of being. If a client is distant from their experiencing there will be good reasons for this, and it is unlikely to be helpful simply 'to be congruent' and express one's frustration that the client is not expressing their feelings. This would probably mean little to the client, or would be experienced as some sort of criticism.

The appropriate response, for a focusing-oriented therapist, is to watch for those places where the client comes a little closer than usual to their experiencing, and to respond more at those places. If the client tells the story of their week as a series of external events, the therapist notices the place where they say 'I didn't want to go, but I did anyway, and then my mother said she'd come too –' and if necessary interrupts to say something like 'You didn't *want* to go – is that right?' This may help the client to be aware of what they experienced, and may lead to some small discussion of what it was like to go when she did not want to. But if the client responds by saying 'No I didn't, but there it was, and in the end my mother came too, and we went down to see Auntie Flo on the way, because...' then the therapist lets the client continue until there is another opportunity for engagement with the client's experiencing.

Ann Weiser Cornell (1996, Chapter 10) has a useful sequence of therapeutic moves in connection with clients who always narrate events from an external perspective. She suggests first questions of the form 'And how did you feel about that?' or 'What was your reaction to that?' Then once such feeling reactions have been expressed the therapist might elicit feelings in the present through asking questions of the form 'And how is that for you right now?' or 'I wonder if you are feeling that disappointment right now?' Finally, there is the move towards how the feelings are held in the body: 'Can you sense in your body where you're feeling that disappointed?' This may help to bring the client into contact with their felt experiencing.

In focusing-oriented psychotherapy we are helping the client to engage with their experiencing. But 'experiencing', as we have seen, is not the same as 'feeling' or 'emotion'. Helping the client to be more aware of their emotions is an important first step, but the change steps in therapy come not from awareness of emotion as such, but from those places where the client's experiencing is not articulated in terms of familiar emotional categories. For a client who has never acknowledged their disappointment it is important for them to become aware of their disappointed feelings. That is in itself a shift. But deeper therapeutic movement comes from the client staying with 'all that around this disappointment I have now'. Where the client can express some of their emotional reactions the focusing-oriented therapist's task is to help them be with 'all that'. Bringing attention to the emotion in a focusing way can *change* the emotion. It is no longer anger but a sort of bitterness, or it is no longer just anger, but also a sort of being hurt. One of Gendlin's fundamental insights is that when we stay with our experiencing, when we give our attention to it, when we try out our concepts on it, the experiencing changes.

Much of this book has been devoted to explaining this procedure of bringing attention to experiencing, which is the essence of focusing. The therapist can help the client to focus in the session, not by teaching Focusing as a procedure but through responding to the client in a way which encourages the client to give attention to their own experiencing. There is an art to this which is not easy to explain or to put into practice, but is essentially a matter of helping the client to stay with those places where experience is not yet clearly articulated. If a client announces that they are 'angry' or 'depressed', there is as yet little opportunity for change. But the client is not *simply* angry or depressed. They are experiencing a whole aspect of their life which is full of an implicit intricacy. They are angry because of what this particular person did at that time in that way, and also angry with themself because they did not get angry at the time. This anger has a repetitive feel about it – it is almost boring; the client is fed up with being this way, and they are annoyed that they still get like this, though they do not think it helps to criticise themself. This whole wodge of experiencing forms an emotional whole. It could not possibly be articulated fully, but it can be experienced as a whole in the body as a felt sense of 'all that'.

A felt sense of it *forms*. It is from the intricacy of that felt sense that change can come if attention is given to it; if the client (or therapist) asks, for example, 'What's all this really about?' or 'What's the worst of this?' The skill of the therapist here lies in an ability to help the client stay with the vague not-yet-formulated felt sense. The therapist may say things like 'There's something there – can you sense it in your body?' 'Can we just stay with that for a while?' 'There's anger there, but is that all? Can you sense around the anger?' 'How does this anger feel, there in the centre of your body?' or perhaps just keep muttering things like 'Oh yes...that's there...there's that sort of angry thing...there it is...we'll just be with it a bit...'. This is a sort of patter just to keep attention on that place from which the change steps can come.

This theme is discussed further in Leijssen (1993) and Gendlin (1978/2003, Chapter 8).

Difficulties in the client–therapist relationship

What often interferes with our responding to (and from) our own experiencing is the way other people respond to what we say. What we mostly need when we are troubled is a friendly, understanding response which does not add anything of the other person, and which does not try to frame *our* experience in *their* concepts. This client–centred way of responding is at the heart of effective therapy, so that anything in the client–therapist relationship which draws the therapist away from this kind of responding is to be avoided.

More generally, clients cannot relate effectively to their experiencing if they do not feel safe. The classical 'core conditions' are usually the best way of creating the safe place which the client needs. Above all, the client needs to feel that they are not being judged; that whatever the therapist may feel about what they have done, they respect them – the person in there – in their struggles with what they have done. This central theme of client-centred therapy remains central in focusing-oriented psychotherapy.

When there is something not quite right in the relationship with the therapist, the client will be less able to relate to themself. The client's relating to their own experiencing takes place within the framework of their relationship with the therapist. The relationship with the therapist provides a sustaining, holding function which stabilises the client in relation to the difficult feelings which they are encountering. (We can Focus on our own, but it is much more difficult when no one is relating to and affirming *us*, the one in there who is having the feelings. Without a companion we can easily get caught in, or shy away from what we are experiencing.)

So any significant disturbance in the relationship between client and therapist normally needs to be addressed as a top priority. I say 'normally' because there can be exceptions here, as in the case of any other decision about therapeutic procedure. Focusing-oriented psychotherapy emphasises the *felt sense* of situations; it is incompatible with any view which lays down explicit rules about what a therapist should or should not do in a particular kind of situation. Where a client is well able to engage in the focusing process and is doing so effectively, it could be quite inappropriate for the therapist to draw attention to an aspect of the relationship which is troubling the therapist. Focusing does not *always* require the support of another person; where the client is fully engaged in their experiential process it may not matter much *what* the therapist does.

This theme is discussed further in Gendlin (1996, Chapter 23).

Inner critics

Our ability to engage with our experiencing can be interfered with not only by other people's inept or judgemental responses but also by our own self-criticism. It seems to be a universal phenomenon that we have within us a 'voice' (or set of voices) which interrupts and criticises us. For some people the experience is literally that of an inner voice; for others it is more a matter of a vague feeling of being stupid or lazy or wrong. Inner critics may 'say' things like 'You are hopeless, you always mess things up', but some are more subtle and insidious: 'You wouldn't want to do that', 'That wouldn't be you, would it?' The inner critic develops, presumably, from the ways in which we were spoken to as young children. It is an internalised version of what was once external criticism. It is important to distinguish the critic from other 'parts' of ourselves which may have objections to what we are doing. Gendlin identifies the critic with Freud's 'superego' but, unlike Freud, distinguishes it sharply from the voice of conscience or moral sense:

> For example, suppose you have hurt someone. The superego attacks you and grinds you down; it makes you feel guilty. It is all about you and only you. This shows that it is *not* concerned with morality.
>
> Only when the superego attack has subsided, do you become concerned about the other person whom you have hurt. From *you* arises your care for that person; you can now think about what you can do for that person. Rather than constricting you as the superego does, your care and concern causes you to expand. You come forth more; you reach outward. You judge that something should be done. You wonder how you might fix the situation. Should you write? Should you call? Now you want to find out where the event left the other person, and how you might still help. *That* is morality. (Gendlin, 1996, pp. 251–2)

The inner critic can be distinguished from conscience (and from suppressed or split-off parts of the self – see below) largely by its *manner*. It has a destructive or undermining tone, it gives scant attention to the facts of a situation, and its remarks are simplistic and repetitious (e.g. 'You always get it wrong', 'You aren't like that'). The critic comes *at* us, as if from outside. It is like a finger-wagging parent or teacher.

Focusing-oriented therapists have suggested two different procedures for working with the critic (Stinckens *et al.*, 2002). I think that both procedures have their place. The first involves setting the critic aside. We can say to it 'Go away and come back when you have something new to say' or 'I don't have to listen to anybody who talks to me in that tone' (Gendlin, 1978/2003, p. 98). Or we can ask it 'to stay in the waiting room', or provide it with a soundproof cubicle from which it can observe but not interfere. The inner critic often has to be treated like an outer critic who constantly interrupts with disparaging remarks. Such a person first has to be *stopped* .

Once this has been done, and the client is able to regain a sense of their own experiencing, it may be possible to begin to relate to the critic. The energy of the inner critic is energy which we have absorbed from external critics, but it has become part of *our* energy, and may have a positive role to play. The inner critic often attacks us in a misguided, rather than a malicious, way. For example, a client criticises herself for being lazy:

> C: It's like it says 'You didn't get that essay done on time, you always leave it till it's too late'.
> T: How do you respond to that?
> C: But I do need to take some time for my social life, and being a day late doesn't really matter.
> T: You need some time for yourself – it's OK to be a day late. How does *it* feel about that?
> C: It's sort of anxious . . . I want to get a good degree. I don't want to sort of drift through life . . . sort of passive, like my mother.
> T: You don't want just to drift . . . as if it needs a bit of help not to drift . . .
> C: Yes, my father didn't drift – he made sure things got done. No slacking . . . and I kind of admire that . . . But he didn't need to push so *hard* . . .
> T: So there's the not wanting just to drift, and the need for some sort of . . . discipline . . . but not to go at it too hard . . .
> C: I don't need to be *so* hard on myself . . . but I don't want to end up like my mother.

Here the critic which attacks her laziness has her interests at heart but, as is typical of critics, it tries to protect her in a rigid and unhelpful way. When a client is no longer cowed by their critic it often happens that, through relating to the critic, the latter's attitudes soften as the client comes to appreciate that the critic is, in a misguided kind of way, trying to help.

Some focusing-oriented therapists believe that in the end *all* critics have the person's interests at heart, but I am not convinced of this. It seems more likely that some critics are simply introjections of parental attitudes, and in an important sense are not 'parts' of that person at all. A child may, for example, 'absorb' something of their mother's timidity and be afflicted by a 'critic' which says 'You don't want to do that – you are not the sort of person who would push yourself forward.' It may well have been that in their mother this kind of attitude *was* playing a protective role, perhaps protecting her from an unpredictable parent, but the client as a child has taken it in without it having any real function in their life. In these situations, by focusing on the timid feelings, the client may come to sense that they are not their feelings, but their mother's (Purton, 2000b).

However, Barbara McGavin and Ann Weiser Cornell suggest an interesting alternative in this connection. They propose that 'when the criticising part is created, if it is based on a harsh parent, its job is to criticise the person *before* the parent would, to save the person from the parent's criticism...most people are identified with "the critic's victim", and the part that feels criticised feels like "me". So naturally the other part, the critical one, feels "other"' (Cornell, 2003).

In helping a client to work with their critic it is important to try to sense what needs to be addressed first; which bit of the client's experiencing needs attention most immediately? It may be important first to 'wave the critic off' (Gendlin, 1996, p. 254), but sometimes a critic will *not* be waved off, and then it is necessary to relate to it to some extent, to ask if it will at least wait for a while before putting its view and, if that fails, to sit down with *it* first and sense what it really wants. Where this is necessary it will usually be important to come back as soon as possible to what it was that the critic interrupted.

This theme is discussed further in Gendlin (1996, Chapter 19), Cornell and McGavin (2002, pp. 172–81), and Stinckens *et al.* (2002), the bibliography of which provides a number of further references.

Divided experiencing

The inner critic can be seen as one example of a division in experiencing. The client may be divided between wanting to leave their job and the feeling that this is irresponsible. Wanting to leave may have an excited, slightly anxious, but forward-moving feel to it but as soon as this is experienced, a critical voice comes with familiar comments about 'being responsible, being realistic, thinking of others' and so on. This sort of division is the one most emphasised in classical client-centred therapy, where all psychological disturbance is seen as arising from the imposition of 'societal oughts' on 'organismic wants'. However, there has been a growing awareness that this is an oversimplified picture of psychological conflict. Human beings are social creatures from the start, so there cannot be a fundamental conflict between 'the needs of the individual' and 'the requirements of society'. Nevertheless, there is an important distinction to be made here. It is one thing to absorb a way a thinking or responding from other people in a way which carries forward one's own experiencing and allows one to live more fully (think, for example, of learning to play a musical instrument). It is another thing to take in other people's ways of being as 'rules' which do not resonate in oneself, and which block one's own experiencing. The crucial difference is not between what comes from society and what comes from the organism, but between what is experientially valid and what is not.

Focusing is all about finding that which is experientially valid, but often two things seem experientially valid, yet both cannot be lived. A client may deeply experience a sense of responsibility for his family, and equally deeply know that he needs to leave a soul-destroying job. Where there are two or more 'parts' of a person which pull in different directions, it is clear that both 'parts' need to be deeply heard. But they cannot be heard *together*. As in a conflict between two people, each side needs to be given time to express what it feels fully, without the other side interrupting. The therapist may need to check with the client which 'side' needs to be heard first. Often one side is what Perls (1969) calls the Topdog which lectures the other side, the Underdog. Where this is so the therapist may need to intervene to allow the Underdog's point of view to be expressed fully.

The general therapeutic procedure is to work with each side separately, so that the full experiential complexity on each side can begin to emerge. For example, the client does not *simply* want to leave his job, but rather to get away from the confining pressures coming from the way his office is run. But it is not even quite that... there is something about how he cannot withstand these pressures which is a much more general issue... Then on the other side it is not just that he feels responsible for providing for his family, but that there is something about his wife's expectations, which is frightening... he cannot even discuss with her the *possibility* of leaving his job because... it is unthinkable... there is a huge fear... As the two sides are allowed to express themselves, changes often come about. It may be that the client begins to get an increasing sense that the real problem is to do with him not being able to stand up for himself, either with his boss or with his wife. This is in itself a *new* problem, but the getting to it is experienced with a sense of relief – 'Oh, *that's* what it's all about'.

In Gestalt therapy the two sides are often worked with through the two-chair procedure, in which the client role-plays each side while seated first in one chair and then in the other. However, this is not an essential part of working with the two sides in a conflict. What the client does need to do is to get a full sense of first how one side feels, and then the other.

The topic of 'divided experiencing' extends well beyond the kinds of inner conflicts just discussed. Many people experience themselves as being different personalities at different times, or as having different 'parts' which form relatively stable configurations, such as 'my frightened part' or 'my bit that knows I'm always right'. Therapeutic work with such configurations has been discussed at some length by Mearns and Thorne (2000, Chapters 6 and 7), who draw on the family-therapy concept of 'multi-directional partiality', which emphasises the importance of engaging strongly with each family member. This way of working seems to be much the same as that suggested above in the case of conflicts and inner critics.

'Divided experiencing' is a notion which has been developed in different ways in many systems of thought, from Plato's rational, desiring and spirited parts of the soul, through Freud's ego, id and superego, Jung's complexes and archetypes, to the Parent, Adult and Child of Transactional Analysis. From Gendlin's perspective any of these ways of conceptualising divisions in one's experiencing may be helpful; but what is helpful is a matter of how these conceptual forms engage with the individual client's experiencing. It is a matter of which formulation, if any, carries the client forward.

Divided experiencing takes a more extreme form in 'dissociated process' (Warner, 1998, 2000b). In dissociative identity disorder (previously known as multiple personality disorder) there is greater personification, a greater separation between the parts, and some parts may not be aware of the others (Ross, 1999; Mearns and Thorne, 2000). Working with dissociative states requires specialised knowledge, as Margaret Warner (2000b, p. 165) notes: 'In my experience, very few clients come to therapy describing dissociated experiences in ways that are obvious to therapists who are not experienced in working with dissociation.' However, as with other cases of working with divided experiencing, it seems that a crucial element in therapy is that of welcoming *each* part (*ibid.*, pp. 168–9).

Various aspects of the theme of divided experiencing are discussed further in Greenberg *et al.* (1993, Chapter 10), Gendlin (1996, Chapter 13), Mearns and Throne (2000), and Cornell and McGavin (2002, pp. 155–86).

Suppressed experiencing

Often there are parts of us which are not themselves in explicit awareness, though we experience the *impact* of their presence. For instance, we may experience a sense of being confined or controlled, which we may attribute to the way certain people treat us, or to the nature of the society we live in. Through staying with this experience we may come to sense that there is really less external control than we think. We may become aware that the control is exercised by ourselves, that it is we ourselves who do the confining or restricting. Often external people have some role to play, but our extreme sensitivity to their attitudes often comes from something in ourselves.

The reason that one part of us suppresses the expression of another part may be that when, in the past, we *did* express that part, we were criticised or humiliated, and something in us decided that we would never let oneself be hurt in that way again. Or it may be that we need to suppress what we feel simply in order to be able to cope with an intolerably difficult situation. In either case, the suppressing part is not in explicit awareness; rather, we experience what it does to us. We feel squeezed, paralysed, shutdown, suffocated.

Once we realise that this may be so, we can begin to sense what the suppressing bit of us feels and wants. Often the suppressing bit has considerable energy, which it has been directing against us. It has determinedly been keeping us from acting because it is afraid that if we act we will be hurt or criticised. What we experience is the sense of constriction, of not being able to act, but as we become aware of the other bit of ourselves we can begin to sense *its* energy, the feeling of 'I'll make quite sure you don't do anything like that!' Once that is in awareness we can work with the two sides in the same way as with any other division in our experiencing. Both the suppressing bit and the suppressed bit need to be given attention, and allowed to express themselves, and the therapeutic situation is then much the same as in any other conflict.

It seems likely that some of the things we see in dreams are visual representations of the suppressing aspects of ourselves. Someone dreams of being attacked by a murderer, and the experience of this is one of intense fear. But the dreamer can then be asked, as is done in Gestalt therapy, to *be* the murderer, to experience how it is from the murderer's side. *That* experience is not one of fear, but of wanting to kill; perhaps wanting to kill the part of the dreamer who feels vulnerable. If the dreamer is a kind, gentle sort of person, this murderous energy can be indeed disconcerting, but also liberating.

The theme of suppression of experiencing is discussed further in Greenberg *et al.* (1993, Chapter 11) and Gendlin (1996, Chapter 13).

Curtailed experiencing

The natural process of our experiencing can be curtailed in many ways. What would naturally be expressed through crying or shouting can be blocked by a sense of inappropriateness. In cases of trauma, powerful feelings of rage or terror may not be expressed, or not fully expressed. In close relationships, one partner may leave, or die, with the result that the one left behind cannot go through the process of expressing to them what needs to be expressed.

This is the traditional arena of 'unfinished business' and of 'catharsis'. In focusing-oriented psychotherapy we do not push the client into the expression of emotion, or into completing the unfinished business. Only the client can sense when it will be helpful to move into what has been curtailed. But we can be sensitive to expressions of emotion, and welcome them. If the client seems to be sitting tightly on their anger, we can respond to what they say in a light and friendly way so that the client can pick up that it would be perfectly all right to say angry things. Or if the client seems to be holding back their tears, the therapist might explicitly say 'Those tears are welcome if they want to come.'

The signs of there being 'unfinished business' may be more subtle than tearfulness or clenched fists. There may only be a sense of complaining, of resentment, of stuckness, of resignation. In the usual way the focusing-oriented psychotherapist helps the client to stay with and articulate these feelings. But where there is curtailment of experiencing there is the impulse to complete what was not completed. There is something that was not done, yet needs to be done. The client needs to be given the space and safety to do what they were not in the past able to do, to feel the feelings fully.

Where the unfinished business comes from the loss of a significant person it can help if the client can express the feelings as if that person were there. Many therapists will suggest that the client writes a letter to the departed person, and there is no reason why this should not be done in focusing-oriented psychotherapy. Of course, if the client does not like the suggestion it is immediately dropped. Gestalt therapists encourage clients to imagine the departed person in an empty chair, and to say to them what they would like to have said in real life. This again is a perfectly valid option in focusing-oriented psychotherapy, so long as the therapist does not impose it on the client, so long as it does not occupy the whole session, and so long as the client has plenty of opportunities to process what is done and to get a full sense of any changes which have come. The spirit of focusing-oriented psychotherapy is to offer such procedures as *possibilities* which could be helpful, but not to present them to the client as an expert view of 'what needs to be done in this situation'. The therapist never *knows* what is to be done, but at times may have a felt sense that *this* might help. Then it can be tentatively offered.

Post-traumatic stress difficulties seem to involve aspects of curtailment of experiencing, as well as aspects of dissociation. This is a somewhat specialised area of therapy, but the relevance of focusing has been stressed by writers such as Peter Levine (1991, 1997), Ton Coffeng (1996) and the process-experiential theorists (Elliott *et al.*, 1996, 1998). Babette Rothschild (2000) has recently presented an approach to trauma work which is very much in consonance with focusing-oriented principles. A whole issue of *The Folio: A Journal for Focusing and Experiential Therapy* (Volume 17, No. 1, 1998) has been devoted to working with trauma in a focusing-oriented way.

Further discussion of the general theme of curtailment of experiencing can be found in Greenberg *et al.* (1993, Chapter 12), Gendlin (1996, Chapter 16) and Goldman (2002). I will say more about the focusing-oriented way of working with emotion below.

Misconstrued experiencing

There are situations in which we *misconstrue* our experiencing. That is, we construe our experiencing in a way which does not do justice to that experiencing. In Chapter 1 I referred to Laura Rice's notion of 'problematic reaction points', that is, points at which people find themselves reacting in a way which they feel is inappropriate to the situation they are in. Rice's procedure here is that of 'evocative reflection', in which the therapist directs the client back to the details of what they experienced, and this fresh experiencing then corrects the construal. In focusing-oriented terms what is happening here is that the client's experience has become structure-bound; that is, there is a response to the situation which is determined by a general pattern or 'scheme' (Greenberg *et al.*, 1993), rather than by the current experiencing in the situation. What is required is for the client to stay with their experiencing and let that modify the scheme.

A slightly different kind of case is where we misconstrue an emotion as some *other* emotion. We can be mistaken about what we feel, just as we can be mistaken about anything else. An example which I have used before (Purton, 2000a, p. 42) is:

> Emma comes to her adviser in connection with her academic work and it emerges that she is feeling over-pressured in her life. She is thinking of easing this feeling of pressure by ending a relationship which has been

taking a lot of her time and energy. But it is the end of term, and the adviser feels that it is a bit odd to end the relationship now, just when she could reasonably devote more time to it. She remarks upon this to Emma, who agrees that it does seem a strange time to do it; nevertheless she really does feel afraid of the pressure which the relationship brings. She is afraid of letting it continue. The adviser suggests that Emma focuses on the uncomfortable pressured feeling a bit, and encourages her to talk a little about the ideas and thoughts which come to mind in connection with it. It emerges that there have been several little incidents recently in which Emma felt rather insecure in the relationship, moments when she felt jealous, though quite irrationally. She comes to acknowledge that the discomfort she feels involves anxiety about the man ending the relationship, leading to the feeling that she would rather do it first. So while she was correct in construing her feeling as some sort of anxiety, she has misconstrued the nature of the anxiety. It is the sort of anxiety that is involved in jealousy and fear of rejection, rather than the sort that is involved in not having enough time. Having realised this, Emma goes off and talks with her boyfriend about the incidents which gave rise to the jealousy, and they work out ways in which similar misunderstandings can be avoided in future. As a result the emotion which she misconstrued as 'feeling pressured' dissipates, and the relationship improves.

Here Emma herself recognises that there is something 'strange' about her construal, and when she gives her attention to her actual experiencing, the construal changes. The original construal of her feeling as 'over-pressured' was a *mis*construal in the sense that if she had acted on it she would have made all the wrong moves in trying to alleviate her distress; she would probably have ended the relationship, yet that was not what she wanted. One could speculate about why she misconstrued the feeling, but whatever the reason, the important point is that the construal did not arise freshly from her actual experiencing. Once she gave her attention to *that* her feelings (and her situation) changed.

Extreme structure-bound experience

Gendlin (1964b/1973) introduced the term 'structure-bound' to refer to situations where there is a lack of free flow between symbols and immediate experience, and hence little opportunity for either experience or symbolisations to change. Focusing-oriented psychotherapy can be seen as the facilitation of the experiencing process in which experience is put in contact with symbols and symbols with experience. Psychological disturbance is conceptualised in focusing-oriented psychotherapy as a disturbance in the process of relating experience to its symbolic expression.

Such disturbance is a matter of degree. We have already seen something of the factors which can interfere with the experiencing process, and which the therapist can help to alleviate. The therapist can be seen as helping the client to do what they cannot – yet – do on their own. For instance, on their own, the client cannot stand back enough from their emotion in order to relate to it, but with the therapist there to 'hold their hand' they can begin to do this. Or the client is caught in a conflict, and on their own cannot attend to either side of it effectively, but with the help of the therapist they can attend first to one side and then to the other. Or the client on their own distances themself from their emotions, and puts everything in a very abstract way, but with the therapist there they can begin to allow the emotions a little closer and begin to relate to them.

In more severe psychological disturbance, the process of relating to experience is correspondingly more impaired. However, the general principle remains that the therapist's role is to facilitate the client's relating to their experience. We can think in this way about the ground-breaking work of Gary Prouty (1976, 1990, 1998) with schizophrenic clients. Prouty has developed a way of working which centres around making contact with very withdrawn or disturbed clients in a way which facilitates the client's contact with the world. The contact is made through various forms of reflection, such as word-for-word reflections, situational reflections ('There is traffic noise outside') or body reflections ('You are holding your head in your hands'). The therapist is at the same time making contact with the client and helping the client to be in contact with their own experience.

Catatonia is an extreme form of a structure-bound state. Prouty (1998, p. 394) describes a 12-hour-long session with a young man who had withdrawn from his family to live in isolation in the lower part of their farm house in Europe. His family wished him to enter therapy in the United States. A trip there was planned, but the client was in such a withdrawn state that the plan seemed unworkable. Prouty writes that he 'was sitting on a long couch, very rigid, with arms outstretched and even with his shoulders. His eyes were straight ahead, his face was mask-like.' The therapist initially sat at the other end of the couch and over a period of an hour and a half made ten responses such as 'I can hear the children playing', 'I'm sitting with you in the lower level of your house', 'Your body is very rigid.' There was no response from the client. The therapist then brought a chair, sat in front of the client and mirrored his body posture. After about fifteen minutes she said 'I can no longer hold my arms outstretched. My arms are tired.' There was no response from the client and the session continued:

T: Your body is very stiff.

T: Your arms are outstretched.

T: Your body isn't moving.

C: (*Put his hands on his head as if to hold his head, and spoke in a barely audible whisper.*) My head hurts me when my father speaks.

T: My head hurts me when my father speaks.

T: (*Therapist puts her hands as if to hold her head.*)

T: My head hurts when my father speaks.

C: (*Continued to hold head for 2–3 hours.*)

T: It's evening. We are in the lower level of your home.

T: Your body is very rigid.

T: Your hands are holding your head.

T: My head hurts when my father speaks.

C: (*Immediately dropped his hands to his knees and looked directly into therapist's eyes.*)

T: You are looking straight into my eyes.

C: (*Immediately he talked in a barely audible whisper.*) Priests are devils.

T: Priests are devils.

T: Your hands are on your knees.

T: You are looking right into my eyes.

T: Your body is very rigid.

C: (*He talked in a barely audible whisper.*) My brothers can't forgive me.

T: My brothers can't forgive me.

C: (*Sat motionless for approximately an hour.*)

T: It is very quiet.

T: You are in the lower level of the house.

T: It is evening.

T: Your body is very rigid.

C: (*Immediately, in slow motion, put his hand over his heart and talked.*) My heart is wooden.

T: (*In slow motion, put her hand over her heart and talked.*) My heart is wooden.

C: (*Feet started to move.*)

T: Your feet are starting to move.

C: (*More eye movement.*)

The therapist took the client's hand and lifted him to stand. They began to walk. The patient walked with the client around the farm and *in a normal conversational mode* spoke about the different animals. He brought the therapist to newborn puppies and lifted one to hold. The client had good eye contact. The client continued to maintain communicative contact over the next four days and was able to transfer planes and negotiate customs on the way to the United States.

Prouty describes his procedure as 'pre-therapy' because he sees it as a prelude to therapy proper in the form of classical client-centred therapy. Prouty was one of the first to draw attention to the fact that in the client-centred tradition the therapeutic emphasis had been on the three therapist conditions of empathy, acceptance and congruence, to the neglect of the others, and in particular to the neglect of Rogers' first condition that client and the therapist need to be in psychological contact. So if 'therapy' involves work embodying the three therapist conditions, establishing psychological contact can be seen as 'pre-therapy'.

From a focusing-oriented point of view the distinction between 'therapy' and 'pretherapy' seems rather artificial. *All* of focusing-oriented psychotherapy is concerned with facilitating contact between experience and whatever impinges on experience, such as external events, or other people's actions and words. All these things which impact on and change experiencing come in structured symbolic form. With most clients there is already in place some significant relationship between client and therapist, so that with the help of this relationship the client can begin to relate better to their own experiencing. However, with severely disturbed clients who are cut off from relationships with others, the first necessity is to establish some kind of relationship with the therapist. Without the client having a sense of relationship to another person they cannot have any sense of relating to themself. In the young child the relationship with others comes first; only later is the child able to be with themself as other people are with them.

Avenues of therapy

In any effective therapy something new needs to come, which is not part of the client's normal consciousness (Gendlin, 1980, p. 282). Freud had the procedure of asking clients to lie on a couch and free-associate. The procedure opened the client to whatever might come when they were in this unusual frame of mind. Jung worked much with clients' dreams. Dreams are of great therapeutic potential because they bring a perspective on the client's problem which is different from the waking perspective, yet still comes from the client

(Purton, 1989). Even in cognitive-behavioural therapy something similar applies; the client and therapist together work out a programme of action which the client will try out, but then the client has to go out into the world and encounter new situations. Something new has to come in if there is to be change. In classical client-centred therapy what is new is the therapeutic setting in which the therapist listens and reflects in the way Rogers discovered. This encourages a novel mode of experiencing for the client, in which they are open to their own experiencing in a way that is new and different.

In his early work Rogers was interested in psychotherapy *generally*. Given that there were different 'schools' of therapy, including his own newly developed 'non-directive' form of therapy, Rogers wanted to find out what it was that made any form of therapy effective. His conclusion was that it is a matter of whether the therapist's attitude to the client embodies the familiar Conditions. Given that these Conditions are present, it does not matter much what procedures are used or what theoretical views the therapist holds. Rogers was primarily concerned not to set up his own school of therapy, but with how therapy should be conducted irrespective of the particular theories and procedures being used. In the same way, Gendlin sees the different 'schools' as enshrining different theories and different procedures, but believes that almost any theory or procedure can be helpful if it is employed in an experiential way.

Gendlin and Rogers have an approach to therapy which is *radically* different from that found in other schools. In Gendlin's view it does not matter much what theoretical views the therapist has; what matters is whether framing the client's experience in *those* terms is helpful to the client. The important question is not whether the client is suffering from an 'unresolved Oedipus complex', or has 'introjected certain conditions of worth', but whether, when their difficulties are formulated in those terms, there is any shift in the client's experiencing. The only theoretical formulations which are relevant for the client are those with which the client's experiencing 'resonates'. This is not an anti-theoretical stance. Theories are important, but not in the sense of 'corresponding with reality'; they are important in the impact which they can have on clients. The more theories with which the therapist is familiar, the more likely it is that they may find ways of putting things which can resonate with the client's experiencing.

Similarly with procedures. It is not that certain procedures are to be recommended or rejected because they are grounded in 'true' theories. Rather, a procedure is a good procedure for a particular client simply if the procedure is helpful to the client. That should be obvious, but it is often held that adopting certain (or even any!) procedures is not right because 'it is not person-centred'. This strikes me as a curious reversal of what Rogers stood for. Rogers centred therapy on the *client*, not on the theory or practices of therapy, and that principle should be retained even when what is in question is 'person-centred' theories or practices.

Gendlin makes this fundamental principle very explicit. He welcomes the fact that there are many schools of therapy, each with their different theoretical perspectives and favourite procedures. Of course he himself has a theory (which I will discuss further in Chapter 8) but it is a meta-theory, a theory about theories, and about how theories relate to experiencing. He has no first-level theory of therapy beyond the principles which are involved in helping clients to formulate their own 'theories' in a way which will carry forward their experiencing. Similarly he has no theoretically based procedure apart from the 'procedure' of trying to do whatever will help the client to engage with their own experiencing. Gendlin suggests in effect that instead of thinking of different *kinds* of psychotherapy we should think simply of *psychotherapy*, within which many different perspectives are possible and many different procedures can be employed.

Often, what can be expressed in one way from a person-centred perspective can be expressed in a different way from a cognitive-behavioural or psychodynamic perspective. In the main body of one paper, Gendlin (1968) discusses client-centred therapy while in a set of footnotes he suggests how the same things can be expressed in psychoanalytic terms. This is not to say that the client-centred and psychoanalytic concepts are the same; it is rather that a particular point can be formulated in different ways, in terms of different concepts. That there *can be* such points, distinct from their conceptual formulations, is of course Gendlin's most fundamental claim.

To examine the different theoretical perspectives in psychotherapy is beyond the scope of this book, but I will now discuss some of the different procedures, or different ways of helping clients to engage with their experiencing. Gendlin (1996) calls these the different *avenues* of therapy. These avenues can *all* be followed in a person-centred way, and are likely to be effective *only* if followed in that way. In the actual practice of therapy, of course, these 'avenues' cross and merge with each other, but we can nevertheless make some distinctions which may be helpful in thinking about how we might best help a client. A client will inevitably prefer some avenues to others, and the more the avenues with which we are familiar the more likely we are to find a way of working which is right for that client.

Working with imagery

In imagery, in dreams and stories, we can live what we cannot yet live in reality. The image is not – yet – the real thing, but it can bring with it the bodily feel of the real thing. It often seems that if only we could have the confidence that would come from having acted, *then* we could indeed act. But in imagination we can act, and get something of the feeling we need in order to act.

For instance a client always prepares himself carefully for what his day may require. He makes sure that he has all that he needs, so that he will not have to ask anyone's help. But this is associated with a sense of unease and of isolation. An image comes of himself as a snail, which carries its house with it, and therefore has a safe place to retreat to whenever danger looms. He experiences this whole sense of self-sufficiency and isolation in the image of the snail and its shell. Then as he stays with the image, it changes. He sees himself coming out of his shell and feeling more free, although also very vulnerable. He decides that tomorrow he will deliberately leave behind his spare watch, his spare pair of spectacles. If his watch stops he will *ask someone* what time it is, if he breaks his spectacles, well then that will be a whole new experience.

Clients can in this way make spontaneous therapeutic use of imagery. But there can be a tendency to move from one image to another without the images making much impact on the client's experiencing of their situation. This is analogous to the familiar scenario in which a client moves in logical fashion from one thought to another without dipping back into their felt sense of their situation. The client just discussed might have moved from the image of the snail to images of a bird coming to attack the snail, the snail withdrawing into its shell, the bird picking the snail up and flying off with it and so on. Then the client might have returned to talking about other things, and little would have been achieved.

Imagery is therapeutically powerful when it emerges from and is related back to life-situations. Some people conscientiously write down their dreams, and are intrigued by the dream images. But this by itself is unlikely to make much difference to the person's life: the dream can only have an impact if one stays with the felt sense of it, and relates that felt sense to what is going on in the life-world.

For the therapist what this suggests is the importance of helping the client to relate the felt sense of the imagery to their felt sense of their situation. The image needs to be brought up to the life situation, and then something may move. To return to my example above, if the client speaks of his snail image the therapist might say something like 'What is the whole feel of that – of being a snail?', or 'As you see that image, what does it feel like in your body?' The client might then say that he feels sort of snug and safe, but after staying with that experience for a while the felt sense may shift to 'pulled-in' and 'constrained'. The therapist might then ask about this 'pulled-in constrained' feel, and this could lead to what that involves in the client's life, that is, his tendency to live over-cautiously and protect himself from new experiences. In the image of coming out of his shell, feeling vulnerable yet more free, he already experiences something of what he may experience shortly in his life. Something of that increased freedom is already there, and this will help him *really* to become more free.

To a limited extent it can be helpful to ask the client more about the content of the imagery – for instance, 'Where is the snail? What is it doing?' – but with clients for whom imagery comes easily it is unhelpful to encourage the client simply to watch the images as they come.

Working with dreams is a special case of working with imagery. Gendlin has written extensively both on the theory of dreams and on the practice of dreamwork, but because of space limitations I will not try to explain his views here. A summary of the theory, which also constitutes a useful introduction to Gendlin's general theory, can be found in an Appendix to *Let Your Body Interpret Your Dreams* (1986a), and some of Gendlin's thoughts about working with dreams in therapy sessions can be found in Chapter 13 of *Focusing-Oriented Psychotherapy* (1996). See also Hendricks and Cartwright (1978).

Working with emotion

The release of pent-up emotion, or catharsis, is sometimes regarded as the essence of psychotherapy, and as something to be encouraged by the therapist. In the person-centred approach, however, it is a central principle that only the client can sense when such a release of emotion will be helpful. Focusing-oriented psychotherapy takes the same view (Gendlin, 1996, p. 225). The therapist does not aim to elicit catharsis; on the other hand whatever emotions come are welcomed.

Emotions are only one aspect of the felt sense of a situation or, to put it another way, the felt sense always involves far more intricacy than can be captured under the heading of an emotion word such as 'anger'. It may be quite true to say that the feeling is a feeling of anger, but it is *this* person's unique anger here in *this* situation with *that* person, as a result of... When clients use emotion terms to express their feelings this is the beginning rather than the end of the process of relating to their experiencing. The simple reflection of what the client has said will often lead to a further step. Having said that they are angry, the client then goes on to say that it's not *really* anger, or it's not *just* anger, but... It is important for the therapist to stay with the overall sense of what the client is saying, and to respond to this sense. Hence if in response to the therapist's wondering how a client reacted to being ignored, the client says 'Well, I was angry, wasn't I?' and then begins to go on into more details of the events, the therapist might say something like 'You really felt something there...', or 'There was all that angry sort of feeling', in order to point the client towards what they were experiencing. Experiencing which is already packaged-up in terms of familiar emotion terms is not open to change. What the focusing-oriented therapist tries to do is to help the client re-open the package. The client's experiencing is always much richer than the emotion labels which have become attached to it, and it is only from that implicit and more intricate experiencing that change can come.

It is a familiar fact that we can get caught up in our emotions. This is why in earlier times emotions were regarded with suspicion. Gendlin (1973a, 1991a, 1996, p. 223) points out that strong emotions can narrow our experiencing so that we react in a way which is not appropriate to the whole complexity of the situation we are in. The focusing-oriented therapist helps the client to stay in touch with the *whole* of their experiencing, with 'all that' which is 'around' or 'under' the emotion which is being expressed.

In catharsis, emotions from the past are being re-lived. But if there is *only* this re-living of the past then nothing will change. There are therapies in which clients are encouraged to 'let out' their emotions, as in the case I mentioned above of pounding a cushion with a tennis racquet. The first time this is done, there may be a genuine release of feeling and the client feels different. But repeating the process over and over does not lead to much further change. What the initial release may accomplish is the bringing of the past into the present. But the client then needs to relate the newly recovered feelings to their current situation. It is a matter not so much of re-living the past, but of restructuring the past through its relationship to what is present. There is a sense (which I will discuss later in connection with Gendlin's account of time) in which the past is determined by the present as much as vice versa.

The focusing-oriented therapist accepts whatever emotions come but tries to help the client *relate* to their emotions. There are times when pent-up emotions need to be released, and such release will be welcomed. But after there has been such release the therapist will help the client to sense the changes which the release has brought. There is more to the client than their emotions, and the therapist tries to relate to the whole person, the person who *has* the emotions. Where a client remains in an intensely emotional state the therapist will help them to *be with* the emotion, rather than being overwhelmed by it. The Focusing procedures of 'clearing a space' and 'putting things down' provide models of the kind of help which the therapist may be able to provide.

In sum, the situation with regard to working with emotions is similar to that with regard to working with imagery. Both these therapeutic avenues can be valuable, but when imagery or emotion becomes disconnected from the client's wider felt sense of their situation the therapeutic impact is much reduced. The experience of imagery and emotion is not always in itself therapeutic, but becomes so when brought into relation with the client's felt living.

This avenue is discussed further in Gendlin (1991a, 1996, Chapter 16) and McGuire (1991).

Working with thoughts

It is a therapeutic commonplace that intellectual interpretations of a client's troubles have little impact. Nor do the client's own intellectual insights by themselves make much difference. Freud himself made it clear that it is one thing to understand one's conflicts but quite another to face them and work them through. And although Rogers (1942, Chapter 7) did speak of the importance of insight in some of his early writings, he later (Rogers, 1956) remarked that he had long since given up the view that insight is the crucial element in therapy. Gendlin, (1964b/1973, pp. 445–6) wrote, 'An Adlerian therapist some years ago told me: "Of course interpretation is not enough. Of course the person doesn't change only because of the wisdoms which the therapist tells him.... The change comes through some kind of emotional digestion, but then you must admit that none of us understand what *that* is." '

However, from the fact that intellectual insight is not sufficient for therapeutic change we should not conclude that the intellect has no role at all to play in therapy. It seems undeniable that some of the procedures used by cognitive therapists, such as combating negative thoughts or challenging assumptions, can be therapeutically effective. Person-centred therapists, too, may sometimes give their own view of a situation through their wish to be open and genuine in their relationship with the client.

From the perspective of focusing-oriented psychotherapy the important issue is whether what is expressed cognitively 'resonates' with what the client is experiencing. When a therapist reflects what they take to be the essential meaning of what the client has just said (rather than just the words), this is a cognitive act; it is not in principle different from an 'interpretation'. However, such 'person-centred interpretations' arise not from any general theory about how human beings are, but out of the therapist's felt sense of what the client is saying. The client may then find that either the 'interpretation' helps them to move on to further experiencing or it may not help at all. If it does not help, the therapist will immediately drop the idea and come back to what the client now wants to say about their experiencing. Cognitive interventions in focusing-oriented psychotherapy are therefore brief, whether or not they are helpful to the client. If there are many of these interventions in the course of a session, the flow of the client's experiencing is likely to be disrupted, but it is important for many clients to articulate their experiencing in words, and such articulation can actually carry forward their experiencing rather than disrupting it.

Ann Weiser Cornell has suggested to me that thoughts, like emotions, images and body sensations can have felt sense 'edges' around them, and that one can therefore respond to a client's thoughts in a focusing-oriented way. This seems right. For example, if a client remarked that she thinks that her problem is connected with her parents' relationship, then rather than discussing this in a speculative way, or asking the client not to speculate, one could respond with 'There's something in you that says this is to do with your parents' relationship', and the client might then say 'Yes – I feel it here' (pointing to her chest). Thoughts can be a way into the felt sense as much as emotions, images or sensations.

Just as imagery and emotions are not always therapeutically helpful, so thinking and cognitive activity are not always therapeutically harmful. Whether an intervention along one of these avenues is helpful or not is a matter of how it connects with the client's experiencing. Does the intervention bring the client to a more vivid experiencing, and help them to move further, or does it close the client down? That is the important question.

This avenue is discussed further in Gendlin (1996, Chapter 18).

Working with action

Clients often come to therapy because they are unable to live and act in the way they would like. It is then natural to explore the inner forces and conflicts which stand between them and how they would like to live. Through working with what is inside we can begin to be different in our outer behaviour and relationships.

But the relationship between the 'inner' and the 'outer' works both ways. A small act which runs counter to a deeply embedded way of feeling can have a big impact on that way of feeling. A client who is afraid to go into large crowded shops may be able to go into smaller shops, or less-crowded shops. There is still anxiety, but through choosing an outer action which challenges the fear, without evoking so much fear as to make the action impossible, the client becomes different inside. They now experience themself as someone who can go into at least some kinds of shops; they feel physically that bit freer. And then another small step can be taken.

Just as images, emotions and thoughts can have an impact on the whole feel of a situation, so can actions. Just as an image can be checked out for whether it really resonates and helps us to move on, so can an action. The action which is performed is not the action which the client would like to be able to do. *That* action, obviously, is impossible at present. What can be done is something which is sufficiently close to *that* action to cut into the feelings which prevent it.

There are several ways in which an action can be 'sufficiently close'. One involves the kind of 'small steps' I referred to above. Together the client and the therapist may consider what would count as steps of 'the right size'. The client then tries a step out, or finds that they cannot yet carry this step out. Then – if the client wants to continue working in this way – they look together at what might be possible. This of course is related to procedures used in 'behaviour therapy', but I imagine that people have always experimented with such ways of overcoming their fears (De Silva, 1984). Behaviour therapy does not have a monopoly on such procedures.

Another way of getting 'sufficiently close' to *the* action is to attempt the action not 'for real' but, as a client said to me, 'just as an experiment' (Gendlin, 1996, p. 228, calls this 'doing it for practice'). In one session the client announced that he was going to *experiment* with doing the thing he was so afraid to do. He said that if it is an *experiment* it will not matter what the results are. He tried it, and failed. But that was all right, that was like the experimental apparatus blowing up. That was *interesting*. If that happens, he said, then you can try it again with new apparatus.

Other ways of 'practising' actions are through role-play, or through imagining oneself doing the action. These are familiar procedures, but they are sometimes seen as incompatible with a person-centred approach. It will be evident by now that I think that this is a mistake. The person-centred approach does not rule out any particular way of being with the client so long as the client's own experiencing is made central. Such possibilities as role-play are introduced in focusing-oriented psychotherapy as *possibilities* which the client might like to experiment with. The client is never *directed* to do a role-play, and if they show little interest in the possibility then the idea is immediately dropped. Only the client can sense whether a particular procedure might be helpful for them, but without the therapist's suggestion of the procedure they might never even consider something which, in fact, could make all the difference to their progress. The therapist, of course, needs to be sensitive to the matter of whether the client will take up the suggestion simply to please the therapist, or simply because they see the therapist as an 'expert' who must know best. As with any other procedure in focusing-oriented psychotherapy there is no diagnosis of what is needed; rather the therapist relies on their felt sense of what is appropriate in *this* situation. The therapist needs to sense what might help the client, but also whether he or she feels comfortable with the procedure in question.

Therapy is generally a *pause* in the activities of the client. The client often comes to therapy because their actions in the outside world are not working out for them. They are moving from one action to another, but the result is that things are getting worse. What is needed is reflection, certainly. But this does not mean ceasing to act. It means dipping into one's felt sense of the situation before and after acting, to check whether the action carries forward one's felt sense of what is needed. In this way the relation between felt sense and action is like the relation between felt sense and imagery, emotion or thought. When these partial aspects of us become detached from the felt sense and continue autonomously (jumping from one image, emotion, thought or action to another) they do not serve us well. These partial aspects of our lives only fulfil their function as they arise from and drop back into that broader sense of our life as a whole.

This avenue is discussed further in Gendlin (1996, Chapter 17).

Working with personal interaction

One of the most important kinds of impact on our experiencing comes from our relationships with other people, and it is widely acknowledged that the relationship between therapist and client is of crucial importance in therapy.

This is so in several different ways. First, there is the role which the therapist plays in creating a safe atmosphere in which the client can freely explore their feelings. Secondly, there are the moves which the therapist can make to help the client relate to the 'edge' of their experiencing. Thirdly, there may be specific things which arise in the relationship with the therapist, which can be helpful to the client. We have already discussed the first two elements. We have touched on the third in connection with 'difficulties in the client–therapist relationship', but more needs to be said about it.

Psychodynamic therapists place great emphasis on the details of what goes on between client and therapist, and help the client to connect these details with events in the client's earlier life. Through being brought into the present and re-lived, the old feelings begin to lose their power over the client. The focusing-oriented therapist tries to respond to *all* that the client is feeling. For example, the therapist will try to respond both to the client's genuine disappointment with the therapist *and* the disappointment which relates not to the therapist but to significant figures in the client's early life: 'You are disappointed that I can't see you next week. I really understand that. But also I'm wondering if there is more to it . . .' Gendlin (1996, p. 294) notes that clients

> sometimes know that something that we would characterise as transference is involved in the interaction. For example, a client may say "I'm mad at you! Well, not really you, uh, only partly you . . . uh, it's confused . . ." I respond so as to keep both the present and the past open: "You are saying (both at me and at someone else here), that you are really mad at me."

There are many aspects of the client–therapist interaction which may or may not involve transference. For example, there are often issues to do with power and control within the session. If a client tends to be shy and in awe of experts and authority figures, it is important for the therapist not to allow themself to become cast in such a role. Or if a client controls the session by speaking continuously so that the therapist cannot get a word in, the therapist may need to interrupt. Trainee counsellors who are a bit shy often find it difficult to interrupt clients, but such interruption is often important in creating a space in which the client can encounter their experiential edge.

The therapist needs to be able to remain 'solid' within the relationship when the client's emotions threaten to become overwhelming, or when they are directed at the therapist. Gendlin (1996, p. 293) discusses some of the complexities which are involved where the client is angry with the therapist:

> When I reflect a client's anger at me, I firmly stand my ground very solidly, so that the client's anger can come out more. I don't want the client to pull back in guilt for fear of hurting me. I am vividly undamaged when I reflect: 'I think I did all right, but *you* feel I did...' In the implicit concrete interaction we are *both* solid and undefeated.
>
> As a therapist I may be glad the anger came out more. But before I *say* 'I am glad your anger can come out more,' I have to consider what interaction this would be. Some clients might experience such a statement as patronising, that somehow I am out of reach of their anger. I could say this to other clients who share a reflective level with me. I might say it also to a client who feels that by getting angry she will lose me.
>
> 'You and I are now like this,' I sometimes say, bumping my fists together. 'I don't think you're right, but I know *you* feel...' I want the implicit interaction to be one in which there is equality and room for conflict.

The *avenue* of personal interaction is the one used by those person-centred therapists who emphasise 'the use of the self in therapy'. As we saw in Chapter 1, Rogers moved from a non-directive reflective mode of therapy to one which allowed for the spontaneous expression of the therapist's feelings. In Gendlin's terminology these are distinct therapeutic avenues, both of which can be facilitative. Neither of these avenues *constitutes* what person-centred therapy is, and both can be used in ways which are not person-centred, that is, which do not facilitate the client's contact with their own experiencing. Simply 'saying back' *whatever* the client says is unlikely to be helpful; nor is spontaneous expression of *whatever* the therapist feels. When the procedures characteristic of the different avenues become 'techniques' which are employed irrespective of the therapist's felt sense of the client and of the current interaction with the client, they cease to be person-centred procedures.

The avenue of personal interaction is discussed further in Gendlin (1996, Chapter 23).

Working with groups

Each of the avenues provides something that the others cannot provide, and group-work is no exception. For example, only in a group can a client experience the positive regard of many people at once. While in a one-to-one relationship the client may be able to discount what they experience as an anomaly ('Well, *you* may accept me, but then you are a bit peculiar'), with a group this attitude is more difficult to sustain. Again, it is only in a group that a client can encounter and re-live a pattern of personal dynamics which may parallel situations which they encountered as a child. And whereas in personal therapy it is the client who brings what they experience as problems, in a group they may be faced with difficulties that other people have with *them*. Further, groups undoubtedly provide a challenging context for maintaining one's connection with one's own experiencing in the face, sometimes, of a barrage of other people's responses and different ways of seeing things.

Groups can provide an arena for moving back and forth between roles and immediate experiencing, and between explicit task-oriented purposes and personal expression. Such movement between the explicit and the implicit is central to the therapeutic process, and groups provide a distinctive way in which it can be embodied.

Of course, groups can only provide an effective therapeutic avenue if they are set up and facilitated in a way which enables the participants to feel that they belong, that they will be listened to, and that whatever they experience and express will be valued (even if not always liked). The main role of the facilitator is to 'protect the belonging of every member' (Gendlin, 1968, p. 202), and to ensure that no one is ignored or attacked to the extent that their membership of the group seems to come into question.

Group-work thus has its value alongside the other avenues of therapy, but as with all the avenues sustained therapeutic movement is unlikely unless the client can relate their experience of the group to their own edge of experiencing. Group process which does not arise from, and dip back into, the felt senses of the participants is likely to be at best irrelevant and at worst harmful. Group process without the felt sense is as unlikely to be therapeutic as intellectual process, or image process, without the felt sense.

Group-work is discussed from a focusing-oriented perspective in Gendlin (1968) and Gendlin (1978/2003, Chapter 12).

Working with the body

There is a sense in which focusing always involves working with the body. It is in the body that we feel our emotions, and in the body that we have a felt sense of a problem. A shift in the felt sense – what Rogers called a 'moment of movement' – is experienced physically. The shift is a shift in how one's body as a whole is registering the problem. After the shift it is not just that one feels a bit different, but that one *is* a bit different. After the shift one will respond to some aspects of one's life situation just a little differently. Different responses will involve different patterns of physical movement; the muscles and nervous system will be functioning in a slightly different way. The changes that occur in therapy are physical changes, changes which can be physically felt.

Gendlin (1996, Chapter 12) notes that it can be important to let a physically felt change register fully. Sometimes a client may experience a shift (such as 'It feels a bit lighter now') and then move quickly on to something else. It can help the client at this point to ask them to pause for a moment, and really feel the shift, to experience fully the lightening. Letting this energy register in the body will help to consolidate the change, and also help the client to be in a stronger position from which to approach the next issue which faces them. The bodily felt change in a 'moment of movement' always has a freeing quality to it, even if it leads to an awareness of something painful. It is a step in a direction which is experienced as 'forward', a direction that Gendlin calls 'the direction of fresh air'. It is *often* a movement in a direction of 'being oneself' rather than of 'doing what others say', but it does not necessarily take that form. One could feel freed from the necessity of 'having always to find an original way of doing things' and relaxing into 'doing things in the familiar prescribed way'. As always in focusing, the emphasis is on the process, rather than on the content.

Sensitivity to bodily felt changes runs through all of focusing-oriented therapy; the felt sense is something physically felt. However, 'working with the body' can also be understood in another way. There are many different forms of therapy which work directly with body changes, and it seems likely that these procedures will be more effective if used in a focusing-oriented way. Some work is already being done in this area. For example, Hakomi therapy (Kurtz, 1990) is a body-oriented form of therapy which makes explicit use of focusing, Kevin McEvenue (2003) has integrated Alexander Technique with focusing in his Wholebody Focusing, Pam Geggus (2002) refers to focusing in her person-centred approach to Zero Balancing, and Shapiro's (1995) EMDR (Eye Movement Desensitization and Reprocessing) has been used with focusing in the treatment of trauma (Armstrong, 1998).

In this chapter I have outlined the principles of focusing-oriented therapy and have tried to show something of how these principles can be applied in practice. Various difficulties and reservations may have come to the reader's mind, and I will turn now to look at some of the possible objections which can be raised, especially from the point of view of 'standard' person-centred therapy.

6

Objections: Issues of Principle and Empirical Issues

In this chapter I will consider some objections which can be made to Gendlin's focusing-oriented psychotherapy. One important kind of objection is raised by the client-centred therapists to whom I referred in Chapter 2 as 'purists'; namely that focusing-oriented psychotherapy has a directive and diagnostic element which runs counter to the basic principles of client-centred therapy. A second kind of objection is that although focusing may often be therapeutically important, it is not *essential* to therapeutic change. Third, there is the objection that focusing can detract from the relationship between therapist and client, which person-centred therapists see as central to their practice. Finally, there is the objection that the empirical research studies to which Gendlin refers are not as convincing as he suggests.

Issues of principle

Is focusing-oriented therapy diagnostic?

It is central to person-centred therapy that the therapist should work within the client's frame of reference, that the therapist should work with how the situation is, as conceptualised by the client. Unlike other forms of therapy, which bring to bear their own theoretical perspectives on what the client is experiencing, the person-centred approach is concerned with the *client's* perspective.

Now it can seem that focusing-oriented psychotherapy goes against this person-centred principle. The focusing-oriented therapist has a theoretical perspective in which, for example, 'intellectualising', 'externalising' and 'emotional submergence' are seen as being, for the most part, not conducive to therapeutic change. In accordance with this theoretical perspective, the focusing-oriented therapist will do things which help to release the client from these ways of being which cut them off from engagement with their own experiencing. But if the therapist is to do this, he or she must in some sense make a 'diagnosis' of what the problem is; for example, a judgement about whether the client is distancing themselves from their experiencing through talking about it in an intellectual way, or whether they are too caught up in their emotion to be able to relate to it.

Now in practice, of course, a therapist is unlikely to experience the making of such a judgement as a 'diagnosis'. As I suggested in Chapter 5, it is rather that the therapist is sensitive to the different ways in which a client can be, and responds to the differences in an appropriate way. This is not different in principle from the fact that when a client turns up in tears we respond differently from the way in which we usually respond. It may be objected that the latter case is a spontaneous difference in response which has nothing to do with theoretical knowledge, but that would be to draw an implausibly sharp line between responses that are based on theoretical knowledge and those which are not. Our theoretical knowledge (we hope!) becomes part of us, and comes to *inform* our responses.

It seems to me that there are two kinds of situation which contribute to person-centred doubts about the value of 'diagnosis'. One is where the therapist imposes on the client's experiencing a set of concepts which are not the client's concepts. For example, if a therapist says to a client who does not think in terms of Freudian concepts 'This situation seems to re-activate your Oedipal complex', that will be of no use to the client at all. The client cannot do anything useful with this, it does not connect with their experiencing, and they are likely to be *distracted* from their experiencing by this sort of intervention. (However, it is different if the client *does* find it natural to think in Freudian terms; then the therapist's concepts may engage with the client's experiencing, and the client's experiencing may be carried forward by what the therapist says.)

The second kind of situation is that where having conceptualised a client's difficulty in some way the therapist (or the client) moves forward along a purely conceptual track, without checking whether what they *now* say is experientially valid. Gendlin (1964b/1973, p. 463) calls this 'process skipping'. For instance, having correctly sensed that a client is feeling bereaved, the therapist (or the client) might then deduce from what they have read about bereavement that the client must be angry, even if the client does not feel it, and that if the client really is angry she had better not do such-and-such, but rather... What is wrong here is not necessarily the general principle, but how it is being applied in this case. Having got to the sense of being bereaved, the therapist's (or client's) background knowledge may sensitise them to the possibility of anger being present. It may help them to see what they might otherwise not have seen. But they need to look, to check. Whether they are angry is a matter of what they are now experiencing, not of what the books say.

These two objections which person-centred theory has to 'diagnosis' are valid ones. But the objections are not objections to the use of general concepts and principles in therapy. They are objections to two kinds of *misuse* of general concepts and principles. Gendlin's (1962/1997) theory is grounded precisely in this issue of how concepts can effectively relate to experiencing. In finding a way forward in any difficulty which we have, we need concepts to specify and formulate the difficulty, but equally we need to relate the concepts back to our experiencing. When we formulate our experiencing in concepts, the experiencing changes; but it is also true that our concepts change through being brought into contact with our experiencing. That is what happens in focusing. Where things go wrong is where we follow a purely conceptual track without periodically dipping back into the relevant experiencing.

Is focusing-oriented therapy directive?

Probably the most persistent critic of Gendlin's focusing-oriented psychotherapy has been Barbara Brodley. In a paper presented at the University of Chicago Counselling Center as early as 1966 she 'tried to clarify the non-directive nature of client-centred work in order to counter Gene Gendlin's influence which was stimulating some junior staff and students at the Center to think of themselves as client-centered while pursuing the goal of helping their clients to raise their levels of experiencing as they talked in therapy' (Brodley, 1991, p. 1).

Brodley sees the essence of client-centred theory in the actualising tendency. The role of the therapist is to 'foster the optimal functioning of the inherent growth tendencies in the person' (Brodley, 1990, p. 88) through embodying and communicating the therapist conditions of empathy, acceptance and congruence. The therapist does not in any way direct the course of therapy, but simply provides an environment in which the client's actualising tendency will find its own way forward. 'The non-directive attitude results in the therapist's surrender of control . . . to the client' (pp. 88–9). Brodley's fundamental objection to focusing-oriented psychotherapy is that the latter does not fully surrender control to the client, but instead directs the client's attention towards their own experiencing. Although focusing-orientated therapists do not see themselves as authorities on how their clients should live, or on how clients should see the world, they do have a view on what is therapeutically effective; and associated with this view there is an element of authority, and of direction of the client towards a goal that the therapist sees as valuable.

I think there are two things which can be said in response to this. One is that the kind of directivity involved is a very special one. The focusing-oriented psychotherapist is encouraging the client to listen to their *own* experiencing. It is as if he or she is saying 'Don't listen to anyone else for a moment, just listen to *yourself*.' This instruction has an element of paradox to it, since in following it (doing what the therapist suggests) the client could be said to be listening to the therapist and not themself! In reality, of course, the therapist is simply suggesting to the client that it may be helpful to them to focus on their own experiencing, and if the client did not want to do this, the therapist would of course back off. Directing the client to listen to and trust their own experiencing is clearly a unique kind of directivity which should not be put on a level with other kinds of directivity. There is perhaps an analogy with the familiar paradox of tolerance: one should tolerate everything except intolerance. The intolerance of intolerance is a quite special case which should not be allowed to cast doubt over whether tolerance is a good thing.

The other reply would be to turn Brodley's argument back on herself – for, Brodley, like any person-centred purist, has her own theoretical position on what makes for effective therapy. It is the view that clients should be exposed to the therapist conditions without anything else being done in a systematic way. Such a view can be argued for – as Bozarth (1998) argues for it – through appeal to Rogers' Conditions of Worth Theory (see Chapter 1). The purist adopts a way of being with the client which derives not from the client's wishes but from a theory about what is helpful to people. Clients, as any person-centred therapist knows, do not always welcome the non-directive attitude; they get treated non-directively because the therapist thinks that is what is best for them. Purist person-centred therapists, like any other therapists, cannot avoid the responsibility of responding to clients in ways which the therapist thinks will be helpful. Clients normally come for *help*; not just for theoretical understanding, and also not just for acceptance and empathy. The purist honestly thinks that the client will be best helped simply by an offering of the therapist conditions; the focusing-oriented therapist honestly thinks that the client will be best helped through being encouraged to relate better to their own experiencing. In practice, the issue is much less stark than this, since the purist welcomes focusing which arises spontaneously, and the focusing-oriented therapist sees the therapist conditions as providing the context for focusing. What does seem clear is that the purist cannot reasonably criticise the focusing-oriented therapist on the grounds that the latter is guided by theoretical assumptions while the former is not.

On the issue of directivity, focusing-oriented therapy diverges to some extent from the process-experiential approach. As we saw in Chapter 1, the slogan of the latter approach is 'direct the process but not the content'. The focusing-oriented therapist does not *direct* the client's process; the directivity is limited to the attempt to direct the client towards their own experiencing. As we have seen, the focusing-oriented therapist may have important general knowledge about 'process difficulties' and such knowledge may sensitise them to what might help in the immediate situation with the client. But the attitude of the therapist will not be one of diagnosing process difficulties and directing the client accordingly. It will be one of trying to sense what would be facilitative for the client in the present moment, sometimes suggesting a particular move, then checking how the client responds to the suggestion, and getting a sense of where the client needs to go next. For instance, one bit of 'process knowledge' which the therapist has could be that of the value of Making a List: where we are overwhelmed with many problems it often helps to separate them and so create the space to deal with each one individually. Nevertheless, with this new client, who complains of being overwhelmed by all their problems, the therapist may sense that the client really needs to *stay with* that sense of being overwhelmed; that the client's most urgent problem is not *any* of the specific issues, but their difficulty in standing firm in relation to problems, and what gets in the way of doing *that*.

I am not convinced that the process/content distinction is very useful in connection with the issues of diagnosis and directivity. It is central to person-centred thinking that the therapist is not in a position to *direct* clients effectively, whether in regard to content *or* process. At the same time, *interaction* with the therapist may constructively influence both process *and* content. I have discussed at some length some of the ways in which the interaction can make a difference to how the client processes their experiencing, but I do not think that there is anything in person-centred principles which rules out interactions which influence content. For example, Gendlin (1996, p. 267) remarks that on occasion he will say to a client 'Every child should be cared about' as an expression of the content of his own values. He continues:

> Another person's statement can have a carrying-forward effect, or it can engender blockage and difficulties. Therefore, if my statement gets in the way, I drop it. I might quietly reaffirm it once, but if there is no carrying-forward step, I go back to reflecting the client's side.

As an example of a case where there *is* a carrying-forward step, Gendlin (*ibid.*) gives the following:

> C: It's so hard to reconcile that she [his wife] might die [of cancer].
> T: (*Listens for a long while.*) This shouldn't be happening. A person in their forties with a small child – that's not the right time to die. That shouldn't be happening. It's not right. (*He stares at me, and then a huge amount of relief shows in his face and body. Tears come. He sits a long while, just exhaling long breaths. I did not know why, until he explained.*)
> C: I was trying to feel that it was a *right* thing to happen.

> What I said so briefly had connected to and carried forward something inside him that had been pushed down and silenced.

Similarly, when a therapist tentatively formulates their sense of what the client is saying, that may well help the client to find a formulation which carries them forward. In the pre-Wisconsin phase of client-centred therapy the making of 'interpretations' was banned; but post-Wisconsin it was realised that the important question is not whether the therapist behaves in any particular way, but whether the therapist's behaviour carries the client forward. Dave Mearns' example, in Chapter 1, of a therapist telling their client that they should take the job is another illustration of this principle.

I think it is important to see that such therapist responses cannot be justified simplistically in terms of 'congruence'. However strongly the therapist may feel that children should be cared for (or that mothers should not die while their children are young, or that the client should take the job), the point of expressing the views is not that the therapist holds them and that therefore they must be expressed, but that in the moment the therapist feels that such expression *might be facilitative for the client*. If it is not then the therapist needs to notice this, and to return to what the client is experiencing. Gendlin (1996, p. 267) gives the following example:

C: I could never give my mother what she needed emotionally.

T: You felt her need, but you could never give her enough of what she needed.

C: And that always made me feel insufficient, inadequate; I ought to be able to do better and I can't.

T: This shouldn't have been that way – you shouldn't have had to try to give her what she needed. *She* should have tried to give *you* what you needed. A little child should be mothered. The mother shouldn't mostly need to be mothered.

C: Oh well. It sure wasn't like that.

T: But you *do* know that you should not have had to meet her needs and feel insufficient?

C: Well, not really, I don't know it. It sounds good. But I still feel the same way. I have to try, and I'm always insufficient.

T: Can we touch where that boy you were *still* feels he should have been able to do it? Can we tell him he shouldn't have had to?

C: (*Silence*) Sort of. (*Silence*) There's a hopeless feeling. I can never do it right.

My assertion has moved nothing at all. Therefore I now pursue the feeling he finds there, the one he tried to express at the outset:

T: It feels hopeless to you. It's a feeling of "You can never do it right."

Does focusing detract from the depth of the therapeutic relationship?

While some person-centred counsellors object to focusing in any form, due to what they see as its diagnostic and directive elements, others are more open to it so long as it is practised *within* a close relationship with the client. For example Mearns (2003) writes:

> these variants of a focusing response will only carry an impact if the counsellor is close to the client's experiencing and the client perceives that closeness. It is useless to endeavour to mimic these responses as a technique

There may also be concern about whether focusing may actually militate against entering into a relationship of 'relational depth' with the client (Thorne, 2002, p. 7); that it could help the client to be in touch with their experiencing, but draw them away from relationship with the external world. However, Gendlin (1990, pp. 205–6) himself has always emphasised that the use of focusing in therapy takes place *within* a personal relationship:

I want to start with the most important thing I have to say: the essence of working with another person is to be present as a living being...Do not let focusing, or reflecting, or anything else, get in between....the first thing we need to do is to communicate that attitude. That is so necessary in a field that is becoming more and more "professional", which is to say useless and expensive.

Other therapists within the broad experiential tradition also emphasise the importance of not separating focusing as a procedure from the therapeutic bond with the client. For instance, one conclusion from a research project on focusing carried out by Claudia Clark (1990, p. 153) is that 'Therapists using a heavily task-oriented form of therapy must be particularly careful to pay attention to the bond aspect of the therapeutic alliance.' Similarly, Leijssen (1997) urges the need for a balance between therapeutic relationship and experiencing process.

Gendlin emphasises that although there is sense in which we turn 'inwards' when we focus, what we are turning our attention to is actually our awareness of our *situation*. Feelings and situations go together; a felt sense is a felt sense *of* a situation. And when our feelings change, our *situation* is no longer the same. In focusing we are not retreating into an inner subjective realm, but bringing our awareness to the intricacy of what we are living. I will return to this point when we look at Gendlin's theory of psychotherapy in Chapter 8.

There is a further dimension to the question about whether focusing could detract from the depth of relational experiencing. Brian Thorne (2002) argues that person-centred therapy has a mystical dimension. He draws on some remarks which Carl Rogers (1986b, p. 198) made towards the end of his life:

I find that when I am closest to my inner, intuitive self, when I am somehow in touch with the unknown in me, when perhaps I am in a slightly altered state of consciousness in the relationship, then whatever I do seems to be full of healing....At those moments it seems that my inner spirit has reached out and touched the inner spirit of the other. Our relationship transcends itself and becomes a part of something larger. Profound growth and healing and energy are present.

Thorne (2002, p. 7) does not doubt the effectiveness of focusing, but he wonders whether

the move into focusing can be a flight for the therapist from the challenge of entering into the kind of relational depth where greater spiritual truth can be encountered . . . Could it be that the client ends up in touch with his or her body, attuned to the inner flow of experience, emotionally literate and yet still alone and existentially bereft of meaning?

I think that part of the answer to this is that there are indeed ways of doing Focusing which are open to Thorne's objection. If the therapist is not relating to the client in a way which makes the client feel safe and at home with the therapist, then suggestions that the client might turn their attention towards their inner experiencing can make the client feel very alone. Focusing can only work effectively in a context in which the client feels safe enough to explore their experiencing. Sometimes we can feel safe enough on our own, at other times the presence of another person is crucial, and where another person *is* required it is essential that the person should 'receive' the focuser in the warm, respectful way which is central to person-centred therapy. Often in Focusing it helps if the therapist (or other listener) says something like 'Maybe *you and I* can spend a bit of time with this hurt bit . . . not probe it, just sort of keep it company . . . would that feel OK?' Gendlin sometimes uses phrases like 'Can we sit down with it . . . pitch a tent beside it.' The therapist is deeply with the client in these moments, accompanying the client in being with their painful experiencing. In Focusing, the therapist *stays with the client* as the client engages with their experiencing.

I think that Thorne has two related concerns: one is that Focusing might isolate the client from the therapist and from relationship with the world in general; the other is that it might isolate the client from 'the greater spiritual truth'. Thorne writes from a point of view which takes for granted that there *is* a greater spiritual truth, and that this 'mystical reality' forms a deeply important backdrop to the whole endeavour of counselling and psychotherapy. I share his view, and I think that there is much in Gendlin's philosophical position which can be used to articulate such a view. I will return briefly to this point in Appendix A, along with some brief discussion of the relationship between the 'spiritual' and the 'paranormal', but it may be worth just saying at this point that Gendlin thinks in terms of an order of reality which has an intricacy and responsiveness which can be expressed, but not exhaustively expressed, in many different ways. We bring our symbols (our concepts and theories) up to the infinite intricacy of the world, and the world responds to them. It responds in different ways to different approaches, and Gendlin takes this in a radical way. It is not just that we might approach a client with the alternative perspectives of, say, Freud, Jung or cognitive theory, but that *all* our concepts, including our most basic concepts of space and time, are just possible ways of approaching the world. Certain 'paranormal' experiences, such as Jung's (1983, pp. 159–60) experience of a thud in his head at the time a client shot himself, suggest that our current notions of human beings as essentially separate in space and time are not always useful concepts. There may be ways of thinking which better accommodate the sphere of the 'paranormal', and Gendlin's philosophy, far from cutting us off from this sphere, may begin to provide a way of thinking about it more effectively.

Is focusing necessary for therapeutic change?

We have seen that focusing-oriented therapists do not hold that explicit teaching of focusing is necessary for effective therapy. Nor is it held that large portions of therapy sessions should involve focused experiencing. Gendlin has always asserted that focusing is simply one important element in therapy, while maintaining that procedures which are carried out in non-experiential ways are unlikely to be effective.

So far as the debate between purist person-centred and focusing-oriented therapy is concerned, the question arises of whether there are typical therapeutic changes which take place in purist person-centred therapy, which are not in any significant way related to experiential focusing. Brodley (1991, p. 5) says explicitly that 'focusing...is not necessary for therapeutic change in client-centered therapy'. She goes on (p. 10) to list some 'change processes occurring in successful, helpful client-centered work *other than focusing*'.

1. There is first the kind of case where a client seems to become increasingly self-confident through being understood and valued by the therapist. There seems here to be a direct impact on the client of the therapist's empathic acceptance. Rogers always emphasised the impact of being understood by another human being: such understanding can make us feel that, after all, we belong to the human race. Wilhelm Dilthey held that 'nothing human can fail to be understood', from which we may derive the rather alarming corollary that if we cannot be understood we are not human. The therapeutic importance of being understood seems undeniable, but there is nothing in this which contradicts Gendlin's view of psychotherapy. If we feel that

our experience does not make any sense, we will be unlikely to put much trust in it. Nor will we be inclined to reveal what seems to be confused nonsense to anyone else. Hence there will be both a block to any full awareness of our experiencing, and a block to anyone else's attempts to carry our experiencing forward. Being misunderstood alienates us from others and from ourselves; correspondingly, empathic understanding helps to put us back in touch with ourselves and with others.

2. Brodley writes: 'Another non-focusing involved process that I have observed is the gradual shift from self-hating feelings towards self-acceptance as a direct result of the client receiving the therapist's acceptance in the context of the client's confessions' (p. 10). This is of course a common phenomenon, but it has a clear and indeed central place in focusing-oriented psychotherapy: if we do not accept our feelings we are unlikely to spend much time with them. Self-hatred is a powerful block to looking patiently at what is 'in' our feelings. Hence the experience of the therapist's acceptance can encourage our own acceptance of our experience, and from there therapeutic movement can take place. However, it seems unlikely that such movement would take place if, in spite of the therapist's acceptance, the client did not become themselves more accepting of their own experience.

Both the above change processes can be illuminated by Gendlin's (1984b, p. 83) conception of 'the client's client':

> The felt sense is the client inside us. Our usual conscious self is the therapist, often a crudely directive one who gets in the way of our inward client all the time. That therapist frequently attacks in a hostile way or at least wants to use all the old information, claims to be smarter than their client, talks all the time, interrupts, takes up time with distant inferences and interpretations, and hardly notices that 'the client' is prevented from speaking. That 'directive therapist' hardly knows the client is there...
>
> Research shows that those clients succeed who are client-centered with their felt sense...
>
> But it would be imprecise to call it being client-centred 'with oneself'. Rather, one needs the distinction between the usual self and the felt sense. The latter is exactly that part to which client-centered responses are directed.
>
> From Plato to Freud people have distinguished different parts of the psyche. Here now arises a distinction that is best delineated in client-centered terms.

Just as with an external client, the felt sense responds to an attitude which is accepting and understanding. The therapist's embodiment of these attitudes can encourage the client to take the same sort of attitude towards their felt sense; it is when *that* shift takes place that therapeutic change is likely to follow.

The two change processes just discussed (changes resulting from therapist empathy and acceptance) can thus be seen to be closely connected with the client's need to engage with their own experiencing – they are not 'processes other than focusing' but processes which are involved in, and which facilitate, focusing.

3. Brodley says 'Another non-focusing process I have observed involves the supportive impact of the relationship resulting in actions taken outside of the therapy that raise the client's confidence or involve new learnings about the self.' This comment usefully draws attention to an aspect of focusing-oriented therapy which can easily be missed. The point of focusing is not to gain insight but to facilitate change. The therapist's task is to be with the client in a way that frees the client up, so that what is implicit in the client can be expressed and lived. It is often true that a change in how one experiences things can spontaneously lead to new forms of action, but at other times one must act first, and then the experience will be different. As I have discussed in Chapter 5, focusing-oriented psychotherapy can and does work through the avenue of action.

Nevertheless, it would be quite wrong to say that *all* therapeutic change results from the client relating to their experiencing in a focusing-oriented way. Mia Leijssen, in a study (in Bozarth, 1998, p. 281) of what clients found most helpful in their focusing sessions, found that some of the helpful things were not to do with focusing at all. One female client reported that the most important thing had been the experience of being treated respectfully by a *man*. Here is something specific to the client, and which happened (presumably) just by good fortune. In a comment on Gendlin's philosophical work, Hatab (1997, p. 245) says 'I can imagine anxiety being resolved by uncovering early childhood traumas, by bootstrapping or coping skills, by the grace of Jesus, by Buddhist emptiness, or even by some success or a little good news.'

To this Gendlin (1997b, p. 251) responds 'I love Hatab's list of what might alleviate anxiety, including "a little bit of good news". Yes, we also play without a . . . , and we can do mathematics where the answer is prefigured.' By 'without a ...' Gendlin means without the felt sense (I will explain the (...) device further in Chapter 8): while focusing-induced therapeutic change results from a restructuring of experience that comes out of a '...', there can be significant emotional changes which happen in a more direct way. It may be true that some phobias can be deconditioned without proceeding via a felt sense, and it is certainly true that good news can alleviate depression, that finding out that you were not responsible for some bad result can alleviate guilt and so on. Life changes can give more relief than any therapy, but such changes cannot often be arranged in order. Some direct therapeutic interventions may also bring change (the intuitive therapist just happens to hit on the right image; the charismatic therapist inspires; the Zen master hits you over the head). All this is undeniable: focusing is not the only source of help there is, but it is one of the few resources which are available, however impoverished, or lacking in grace, the external world may at times seem to be.

Empirical issues

The empirical testing of theories in psychotherapy raises a whole range of complex issues. Carl Rogers himself was the first to take the possibility of such testing seriously, and client-centred therapy probably remains the form of therapy on which the most empirical research has been done.

Regarding the Therapeutic Conditions Hypothesis, Neill Watson (1984), after a thorough review of the evidence, concluded that the hypothesis has never been effectively tested. This has been partly because the presence of the three therapist conditions has often been assessed by external judges rather than by how the Conditions have been perceived by the client, partly because in those cases where client perceptions have been used, not all of the six therapeutic conditions have been included, and partly because not enough has been done to establish whether the sometimes-observed correlation between the Conditions and therapeutic change is a matter of the conditions *causing* the change in the client. (As we saw in Chapter 3, even Rogers himself at one time wondered if it might not be the other way round: that the way the *client* is determines which attitudes are called forth in the therapist.)

Yet while Rogers' Therapeutic Conditions Hypothesis has not been satisfactorily tested, there have been many general tests of the view that the client-centred counselling (at least as much as other forms of counselling) is correlated with therapeutic improvement. In Britain there has recently been a commonly accepted view, at least in the medical profession, that cognitive-behavioural therapy is more effective than client-centred therapy, but a recent large-scale study on depression by King *et al.* (2000) showed that while psychological therapy had a greater impact than normal medical care alone, there was no difference between the effectiveness of cognitive-behavioural and client-centred therapy. This, and many other studies, indicate that counselling and psychotherapy do contribute to therapeutic change, but there is little evidence that any particular form of therapy is better than any other (Smith and Glass, 1977; Stiles *et al.*, 1986; Lambert and Bergin, 1994).

This conclusion is consistent with Gendlin's view, which is that all the major forms of therapy are likely to be effective if conducted in a way which encourages the client to be more in touch with their own experiencing. As we have seen, for Gendlin the different forms of therapy are best regarded not as different *therapies* but as different avenues along which therapy can be conducted. What is important is not which avenue is used (whether dreamwork, Gestalt procedures, reflection of feeling, psycho-analytical interpretation and so on) but whether what is done is done in a client-centred way, that is, a way which continually refers back to the client's own experiencing. If Gendlin is right, one would expect studies of any therapeutic approach to indicate that sometimes the approach works well, and sometimes not, depending on whether it was conducted in a client-centred way. What one would not expect would be any overall difference in the effectiveness of the different approaches.

The negative aspect of this prediction − that there should be no significant differences between the effectiveness of the different approaches − seems well confirmed. We can turn then to the positive aspect of the prediction − that Focusing should be therapeutically effective, and that therapeutic procedures which are focusing-oriented should be more effective than those which are not so oriented.

Gendlin's empirical evidence for the efficacy of Focusing goes back to the time of the Wisconsin schizophrenia project. Gendlin and his colleagues had initially expected that exposure of the client to the therapist conditions would result in a gradual increase in experiencing level, which would be correlated with therapeutic progress. In fact the results seemed to show that the impact of the Conditions was not very great, and that the clients who made progress were often those who, *from the start*, had higher experiencing levels. Through the years Gendlin has referred to a number of studies which appear to support this view. Klein *et al.* wrote in 1969:

> The most powerful and consistent finding in the early studies (Gendlin and Tomlinson, 1967; Gendlin, Beebe, Cassens, Klein and Oberlander, 1968) is that successful therapy patients start, continue, and end therapy at a higher level of experiencing or process than do less successful patients.

Gendlin (1986c, p. 133) wrote:

> We had predicted that success cases would increase on the Experiencing Scale. Instead we found (Gendlin, Beebe, Cassens, Klein and Oberlander, 1968) and continue to find (Mathieu-Coughlan & Klein, 1984; Klein, Mathieu-Coughlan & Kiesler, 1986) that scores on the Experiencing Scale are significantly higher also in the first period of successful therapy ... The challenge ... was to get failure-predicted people to do what we found success-predicted clients doing.

Brodley (1988) surveyed the evidence provided by these studies and others, finding a total of forty-eight articles, monographs or chapters in books 'which were mentioned by Gendlin and others as providing support for the generalization that early-in-therapy experiential level predicts therapy outcome' (p. 6). However, only seventeen of these were original empirical studies of the relation between early-in-therapy experiential level and outcome; the other thirty-one were theoretical studies, or studies relating experiencing to variables other than outcome, or reports which repeated the findings of the seventeen relevant studies. Of these seventeen, eight studies seemed to confirm Gendlin's hypothesis, while the other nine did not. Brodley then went through each of the eight 'confirmatory' studies, and suggested various reasons why in each case the research procedure was inadequate. Typical reasons were lack of a high correlation between the ratings made by the process raters, and the possibility that even in very early sessions therapist conditions might be affecting experiencing level.

Brodley concludes (p. 12) that '[t]here is not sufficient scientific evidence for believing that there is a positive relation between early-in-therapy experiencing level and outcome at this point in time. Therefore the generalization, though often stated, cannot be a reason to be led away from client-centred therapy.'

The view that high experiencing level is *essential* for therapeutic success has been widely doubted even by many who are otherwise enthusiastic about Focusing. Mia Leijssen, who has been involved in research in Focusing since 1981, writes (Leijssen, 1997):

> Fifteen years of intensive process research make me conclude that the capacity to move smoothly along an experiential continuum, and to shift the attention from inside to outside and back, may be a better indicator of healthy functioning than the one-sided fixation about one particular experiencing level.... A balanced theory of therapy which leaves room for internal and external dialogue, in which following and steering are allowed to alternate, in which the two vital components, i.e. relationship and experiencing process, remain in interaction is the most fruitful combination for a client to grow in.

Gendlin himself said in the early days (Gendlin *et al.*, 1968, pp. 227, 228)

> We can conclude that less than one third of those who start low are successful, but still, it is incorrect to conclude that this never occurs!... there is a fairly strong relationship between initial EXP level and case outcome, but there are enough exceptions to warrant consideration... There may be two patterns. In some people, effective therapy behavior is present all along. In others, a good outcome occurs because they do develop their experiencing capacity as therapy proceeds.

And in connection with a recent study in which clients were trained in Focusing and their experiencing levels recorded in the two sessions before and the two sessions after the training, Gendlin remarks (Durak *et al.*, 1997, p. 14):

> The findings show that while the focusing process contributes substantially to successful outcomes, it is not impossible to succeed in therapy without focusing ability. One client of the seventeen succeeded despite not being effectively trained, and beginning and remaining low on the EXP scale.

The reason for this is presumably that, as discussed above, there are a range of non-focusing processes which have therapeutic effects. Gendlin has never claimed that focusing constitutes the whole of therapy, only that it has a substantial contribution to make.

Marion Hendricks (2002) has provided a comprehensive review of the empirical evidence in support of focusing-oriented psychotherapy. She lists twenty-six studies showing that higher experiencing levels correlate with successful outcome in therapy. (However, thirteen of these are studies which Brodley maintains are open to criticism.) One sophisticated recent study (Goldman, 1997), showing higher Experiencing in session two to be correlated with greater reduction in depressive symptoms over the course of therapy, may be especially worthy of study.

Hendricks (2002, pp. 231–3) notes twenty-three studies in which Focusing, measured by instruments other than the Experiencing Scale, is correlated with successful outcome, including studies with prison inmates, psychotic patients and patients with health-related issues. She also cites a number of studies which provide empirical evidence that focusing training can increase experiencing level, and lead to increased therapeutic success.

Orlinsky *et al.* (1994), in an extensive review of process research based on a literature search from 1985 to 1992, provide some incidental support for Gendlin's general position. Amongst their conclusions are that the therapeutic relationship is almost always important (p. 308), that it is not *what* clients talk about but *how they talk about* it which is significantly associated with outcome (p. 296), and that client's self-relatedness (in Gendlin's terms, 'experiencing level') is very significant (p. 339).

Not all research into focusing and focusing-oriented psychotherapy is directly concerned with therapeutic outcome. The 'evidence' in favour of a theory is not confined to deducing its consequences and testing them against experience. In addition there is the question of whether the theory is fruitful in uncovering new relationships between phenomena, or in showing that what was expected does not in fact occur, or in generating new concepts and new lines of research. In this connection it will be worth looking briefly at some studies which indicate the potential of the focusing-oriented approach.

There is an interesting series of studies by Rainer Sachse (1990a,b) on the effects of therapist responses on the 'depth' of client experiencing. Sachse introduces a scale of processing ranging from 'shallow' to 'deep'. At the shallow extreme the client does not process their experience at all. Then there are successively deeper modes of processing, the later ones being focusing processes:

(1) *intellectualising* (using knowledge without reference to own feelings or personal data);
(2) *report* (concrete descriptions without explicit reference to opinions, evaluations and feelings);

(3) *assessment/evaluation* (assessment labelling such as 'A is stupid'; the assessment is seen as a characteristic of the content);
(4) *personal assessment* (recognition that the assessment is part of the client's own frame of reference);
(5) *personal meaning* (the client senses a felt meaning about the content and says so explicitly);
(6) *explication of relevant structures of meaning* (the client verbalises aspects of meaning which the content has for them);
(7) *integration* (making connections between the verbalised meanings and other meanings).

The therapist's responses can be assessed by a similar scale, and then for each therapist response it can be noted whether the therapist matches the client's level of processing (e.g. the client speaks at the level of reporting events, and the therapist comments on those events), or whether the therapist exceeds the client's processing level (e.g. the therapist stimulates personal assessment when the client is still on the level of reporting events) or whether the therapist keeps at a lower level of processing than the client (e.g. the therapist asks about the events when the client is at the level of personal assessment). Sachse (1990b, p. 325) gives the following illustration:

> A client says, "Yesterday, I had again a terrible quarrel with my husband." This statement is of a purely reporting nature. What the therapist can do now is to encourage the client to continue with her report (the therapist offers a level-maintaining proposal, e.g., by saying, "You have had quarrels like that quite frequently", or by asking "Have you had quarrels like that often?") On the other hand, the therapist could make a proposal that encourages the client to attend to emotional aspects of the comment (in this case, a deepening proposal is offered that raises the level from 3 to 6) for example by commenting, "This must have been a terrible experience for you," or asking "What did you feel at that moment?". However the therapist may also flatten the level by prompting the client to speculate about her husband's motives (this will bring the process to the intellectualizing level), for example, asking a question like "What do you think causes your husband to get involved in such a quarrel?"

Sachse found (Hendricks, 2002, p. 232) that 'depth' of client experiencing is related to therapeutic success as measured by personality tests and therapist estimates of success. He also showed that the therapists of successful clients tended to make more 'deepening processing proposals' than the therapists of less-successful clients.

A study by McMullin (1972) suggested that client-experiencing level could be increased by Focusing instructions, even when therapist empathy and positive regard were kept deliberately low. This suggests that there *can* be circumstances in which clients can feel safe enough to engage in Focusing without the presence of those conditions which usually create the necessary safety.

From a process-experiential perspective, Claudia Clark (1990) has investigated in detail what takes place when clients engage in focusing in the course of experiential therapy. Her method involved the use of Robert Elliott's (1989) Comprehensive Process Analysis (CPA), which is a way of describing significant therapy events in context. The context includes such things as general client background (conflicts, style, symptoms), therapist background (orientation, level of experience), recent extra-therapy events, client task (what the client is trying to do), therapist task (what the therapist is trying to do), client actions and style in the session, therapist action and style in the session, impact on client of the therapeutic event and effectiveness of the event as assessed psychometrically. The CPA framework analyses the 'pathways' of significant therapy events in terms of what contributes to them and what flows from them. Amongst Clark's conclusions (pp. 138–53) are (1) that focusing may be of value to unassertive clients where their inability to assert themselves comes from their difficulty in knowing what their experience is; (2) that focusing is interrupted not so much by strong emotion as by the intrusion of the 'inner critic'; (3) that the impact of problematical affect can be ameliorated through helping the client to be aware of the positive aspects of painful experiencing (for instance that although it is painful, the client really wants to work through it); (4) that trainees can be helped to use focusing with clients through focusing being presented as a 'natural' attitude of receptivity towards internal processes rather than as a prescribed set of six 'movements'; (5) that therapists using focusing need to give attention to the 'bond' as well as the 'task' aspect of the therapeutic alliance.

James Iberg (2002) has developed scales for measuring the extent to which focusing has taken place in a session. The scales incorporate subscales which assess how clients relate to their experiencing (to what extent they have the friendly, curious, patient focusing attitude), to what extent feelings 'open' in the session (to what extent a felt sense forms) and to what extent there is release or 'carrying-forward'. One scale (the *Focusing-oriented Session Report*) is based on a questionnaire which the client completes after the session; the other (the *Therapist*

Ratings of Client Focusing Activity) is based on a questionnaire which the therapist completes. Iberg reports good correlations between client and therapist ratings on each subscale, and also good correlation between the level of focusing present and the level of client satisfaction with the session.

Part of the evidential basis for focusing-oriented psychotherapy lies in its potential for generating creative research. Indications that this potential exists can be seen not only in works such as that of Sachse, Clarke and Iberg within the broad client-centred tradition but also (Gendlin, 1969) in research into experientially oriented versions of procedures used in other schools of therapy, such as Gestalt (Greenberg, 1979), desensitisation procedures (Weitzman, 1967, pp. 311–12) and work with post-traumatic stress disorder (Levine, 1997; Rothschild, 2000).

So far as coherence with other knowledge is concerned, views which we hold in psychotherapy generally have connections with, and implications for, fields such as ethics, education, psychology, sociology, biology, linguistics, art, spirituality and philosophy. A plausible theory of psychotherapy needs to maintain its place in relation to all these fields, and the extent to which it can do so will be part of its evidential basis. In Appendix A, I will explore how Gendlin's view of psychotherapy fares in this regard, but I hope in this chapter to have given reasons for thinking that even if we take the simple-minded view of evidential support which unfortunately is current in many contemporary discussions, focusing-oriented psychotherapy has as good an evidential basis as any other form of therapy.

I will discuss the theoretical foundation of focusing-oriented therapy further in Chapter 8, but before doing that will discuss briefly the question of how the general principles and practice of focusing-oriented therapy can be incorporated into counselling and psychotherapy training courses. There are as yet rather few such courses, so that Chapter 7 has the character of a preliminary reconnaissance.

7

Training and Supervision

We have seen that in Gendlin's view focusing-oriented psychotherapy is not so much another 'school' of therapy as an 'experientialising' of the procedures of any school. There could therefore be training courses grounded in the procedures of, say, cognitive-behavioural or psychodynamic therapy, which would differ from the standard courses only insofar as they explicitly incorporated focusing-oriented principles. Although the *procedures* of the specific schools (such as desensitisation, free association or dreamwork) would be retained, there would be a fundamental re-orientation towards the primacy of the client's experiencing. Whether such courses will be developed is an open question.

The relationship of focusing-oriented to person-centred therapy is a special one, as we have seen. In standard person-centred training courses there are characteristic procedures which are already closely connected with focusing principles, especially active listening, reflection and the provision of safety through the therapist conditions. In addition, as the person-centred approach has developed, there has been a growing emphasis on the presence of the therapist, and on the therapist's need for self-awareness and self-acceptance. Person-centred training courses already incorporate much that is focusing-oriented, at least so long as listening, reflection and the presence of the therapist are taught with a view to helping trainees to help clients to engage with their own experiencing.

Training at diploma level

The institutional structures for counselling and psychotherapy training vary widely from one country to another. In this section I will refer mainly to the situation in Britain, where the award of a diploma typically follows a two-year part-time, or one-year full-time course. Such training is usually preceded by a one-year certificate course in counselling skills, and is followed by a period of at least three years in which sufficient hours of supervised clinical practice are built up in order for the practitioner to apply for registration as an Accredited Counsellor.

Gendlin's work, and experiential therapy generally, is much less familiar in Britain than the 'standard' person-centred therapy which I outlined in Chapter 1. Standard person-centred training books such as Mearns (1997) or Mearns and Thorne (1988) include short sections on focusing and on basic focusing-oriented concepts such as the 'felt sense'. Some person-centred training courses include a brief introduction to focusing, and so do some integrative courses. The full-time diploma course in counselling on which I teach at the University of East Anglia has for a number of years included one or two sessions on Focusing. Beginning in the 2003–2004 academic year we have added a focusing-oriented component to the course which runs through most of the year, and trainees also work regularly in individual focusing partnerships.

The University of East Anglia course can provide an illustration of how focusing-oriented principles can be integrated in a person-centred training course. The main components of the course currently are:

- twice-weekly meetings of the student community along with two tutors;
- weekly skills training groups;
- fortnightly group supervision;
- weekly individual supervision;
- weekly personal development groups;
- theory sessions;
- fortnightly listening/focusing groups;
- focusing partnerships.

These course components, which largely follow the pattern described in Mearns' (1997) book on person-centred counselling training, can be seen slightly differently from the perspectives of 'standard' person-centred and of focusing-oriented therapy. I will sketch how the components of the course look from a focusing-oriented point of view, which can be compared with the 'standard' view presented in Mearns' book. On this course some of the tutors are more 'focusing-oriented' than others, but this does not seem to create any difficulties.

From a focusing-oriented point of view the different components of the course provide a range of opportunities for trainees to experience interaction with other individuals, with different groups, with various procedures, with different theoretical viewpoints and, crucially, with themselves. Out of these interactions come changes and developments in the trainees' experiencing which should enable them to interact with clients in an increasingly therapeutic way. The learning process is not seen as a matter of learning discrete skills which are then applied to specifiable client problems. Rather, each learning experience is seen as deepening the resources which the trainee has available to them when working with a client. Just how those resources will be deployed in the moment will be a matter of the trainee's felt sense of what is needed at that moment in the relationship with that client.

As with any other training process, much depends on the general ethos and atmosphere in which the training takes place. It is central to person-centred and focusing-oriented thinking that counselling education is a drawing-out of what is already a potential in the trainee. The training should facilitate the trainee becoming the kind of therapist which *they* can become. It sometimes happens that trainees coming on to a person-centred training course feel that they must jettison all their old ways of being with people and take on the new 'person-centred' way. But this can involve simply the adoption of a new set of conditions of worth, which may cause more trouble than the set which was jettisoned! A person-centred training course needs not only to introduce notions such as the therapist conditions and conditions of worth, but also to encourage the trainee to explore what these concepts can mean for *them*. Person-centred concepts, like any concepts, can be adopted in a 'structure-bound' way which skips over the trainee's lived experiencing.

Being 'person-centred' cannot be pinned down to any specific forms of behaviour, or even any specific attitudes; it is a matter of whatever, in the circumstances, encourages the client's ongoing interaction with their own experiencing. However, only certain kinds of interaction will, at any particular moment, carry the individual forward. Hence a counselling training course needs to provide a wide range of learning opportunities which can be taken up by trainees. The different components of the course provide different opportunities for interaction, analogous to the different 'avenues' of therapy which I discussed in Chapter 5.

Community group

The community group fulfils several functions on the course. As well as having an administrative function, it provides an opportunity for the trainees to feel connected with the course as a whole. It tends to draw out certain kinds of personal difficulties, especially those related to conflicts between the need to belong and the fear of being rejected (Draper, 2002, p. 46). It also provides a place in which to practise being empathic, accepting and genuine.

Mearns (2003) sees the community group as above all an arena for the development of congruence, and this remains the case if we consider the community group from a focusing-oriented perspective. If counsellors are to help clients relate to their own experiencing they need to be able to do this effectively themselves, even in difficult circumstances which can sometimes arise in the client–therapist interaction. For many people, the setting of the large group provides genuinely difficult circumstances for speaking authentically from one's own immediate experiencing. This is true both for the shy trainee who finds it difficult to stay in touch with their own experiencing, in the midst of the fear which the group situation arouses, and also for the trainee who is used to relating to people in groups in a more superficial kind of way, but not used to speaking from the level of their own felt sense.

The community group also provides experience of a situation in which one almost *has* to work from the level of the felt sense. The interactions which go on in a group of twenty or more people often cannot be understood in terms of *any* familiar concepts or patterns. Nevertheless people can still speak and act.

Personal development group

The function of the personal development group centres around the issue that trainees need to work through their own personal difficulties sufficiently for those difficulties not to interfere significantly with their client work. Counsellors need to be able to provide a safe, yet stimulating, environment for their clients, and personal issues which interfere with this requirement need to be worked on. Examples would be trainee tendencies to push their own views on to clients, or not really listen, or over-intellectualise, or get caught in clients' projections, or get lured into clients' games, or not be aware of their own 'sore spots'.

Personal development groups, as distinct from individual therapy, are important here because some of the things which can interfere with a counsellor's effectiveness may not constitute a problem from the trainee's point of view; they may be unaware that there *is* a problem for other people. Clearly there is an overlap of function between the community group and the personal development group, but there is undoubtedly a difference in the quality of the group experience which has to do simply with the difference in numbers. (On the UEA course there are normally twenty trainees in the community group and ten in the personal development group.) In the personal development group there is more time for a trainee to work uninterruptedly with an issue, in the kind of way they might do in individual therapy, whereas in the community group there will seldom be the opportunity for sustained attention to the individual's experiencing. The community group *can* give sustained support to a trainee, which can be the more powerful because of the number of people involved, but what the community group primarily provides is the opportunity to hold on to one's own experiencing in the face of interruptions, challenges and the competing needs of others. The question of why, beyond a certain size of around seven to ten people, the group experience is different, is an interesting question in its own right (Mountford, 2001).

There is one difference between 'standard' person-centred view and the focusing-oriented view on the question of personal development. The standard view is that trainees should above all develop their ability to manifest the therapist conditions, since it is the ability to offer the conditions which is the healing element in therapy. From a focusing-oriented point of view the therapist conditions remain important in providing a safe place in which the client can engage with their experiencing, but the most important thing is simply that the therapist be present as a human being. From a focusing-oriented point of view the therapist does not have to be anything approaching a 'fully-functioning person'; they simply have to be *present*, and to be able to set aside their own personal difficulties for the duration of the session. The most important things are (a) *to be there* and (b) *not to obstruct the client's process*. This difference in theoretical viewpoint makes no difference to the work in the personal development group, but I think that the focusing-oriented position can make it easier for trainees who become over-anxious about whether they have achieved sufficient 'levels' of the therapist conditions.

Skills group

In the skills group trainees work on all the standard counselling skills, such as listening, reflecting, building the therapeutic alliance, issues surrounding beginnings and endings, and finding ways of responding which are right for the individual trainee. The more specifically focusing-oriented skills are worked with in a separate group.

Listening/focusing group

The listening/focusing group deepens the trainees' listening ability, gives plenty of time to develop awareness of what happens when we are listened to carefully, gives experience of the 'self-propelled process' which can be initiated by exact reflection, gives experience of the difference between responses which reflect content, or emotion, or 'point to' the edge of awareness. It is also a place where trainees can begin to develop the crucial quality of self-acceptance, as they learn to be with their own experiencing in a friendly way.

In this part of the course Focusing is also introduced as a procedure which trainees can learn in order to develop their own ability to recognise and stay with a felt sense. It is a place to learn experientially about what can interfere with the process of experiencing, and it can provide some experience of working with dreams, with 'inner critics', 'problematic reactions', 'inner splits' and 'unfinished business'.

Focusing partnerships

The focusing partnerships provide a place on the course where trainees have a regular weekly opportunity to be listened to with undivided attention for a period of twenty minutes or so each way. It is entirely up to the focuser how much they wish to reveal of the content of their experience; the listener is there simply to encourage and assist with the process. These partnerships are designed to show experientially how deeply therapeutic listening and focusing can be. They also go some way towards satisfying the British Association for Counselling and Psychotherapy (BACP) requirement that trainees should have some experience of being in the client position. It has always been the person-centred view that no one should be *required* to engage in counselling, and the BACP has respected this position by allowing, as an option to individual therapy, that trainees must engage in personal development work which provides an equivalent to such therapy. The vagueness of this has led to some difficulties in deciding what can count as an equivalent, but regular one-to-one listening/focusing partnerships come as close as anything can to satisfying the requirement.

Theory sessions

These introduce the basic person-centred theory and the central focusing concepts, and also provide introductions to other major theoretical positions such as the psychodynamic and the cognitive-behavioural. In addition, they introduce ways of thinking about specific kinds of difficulties, such as anxiety, depression, bereavement, and the effects of trauma and abuse. They also introduce issues such as spirituality, gender and sexuality, race and culture, which impinge on the work of therapists.

Grappling with the intellectual issues involved in therapy is to be encouraged, but this 'avenue', the avenue of interaction with ideas, will be of more importance to some trainees than others. Those from a more academic background may find themselves giving more attention to other avenues of learning of which they have little experience, while those with considerable experience of helping relationships, but little theoretical knowledge, may find in the theory sessions exciting new worlds to explore. As always, only the individual trainee can sense – often with the help of others – what it is that they most need at *this* point in their development.

Supervision

I will discuss focusing-oriented supervision more generally later, but on any counselling course supervision provides the opportunity for the trainee to reflect on their practice with the help of an experienced counsellor. It is important that the supervision session should provide a safe enough place for the trainee to bring what is *really* troubling them in their work. For this reason it is best for the individual supervisor to have no other role on the training course, and especially not to be involved in any assessment procedures.

In addition to weekly individual supervision, the supervision *group* provides opportunities for trainees to role-play clients and to get a whole range of different responses to their work. The role-playing of a client is also, of course, a good method of getting a felt sense of what it may be like to be that client, and following a role-play trainees may find themselves interacting rather differently with the client. Role-plays can be recorded and replayed, so that the trainee can go back and examine, for example, just what it was which made them feel awkward when the 'client' said *that*.

Focusing-oriented psychotherapy training

Again I will discuss training primarily in the British context. Because of the developing interest in focusing and experiential therapy there seems to be a place for courses which will enable qualified therapists to experience an in-depth training in the theory and practice of focusing-oriented therapy. The main interest in such a course (in Britain) will undoubtedly come from person-centred therapists who wish to develop their understanding of focusing-oriented therapy, which they would see as part of the person-centred approach. However, it may also be that qualified practitioners in other approaches will be interested in seeing what focusing can add to the way in which they normally work.

Training of this kind is new in Britain, but it may be of interest to give a brief outline of a course which we are introducing at the University of East Anglia. The course is a one-year full-time diploma in Focusing and Experiential Psychotherapy, which with the addition of a research methods module and a dissertation can be taken as a master's degree.

The objectives of the diploma course are:

- To provide sufficient experience and theoretical understanding of the focusing-oriented approach to enable therapists to incorporate this approach into their clinical work.
- To provide an appreciation of the philosophical grounding of focusing-oriented therapy.
- To explore the ways in which focusing-oriented therapy is related to 'standard' person-centred therapy.
- To enable students to make use of Focusing in their own personal and professional development.
- To provide an historical understanding of the development of the focusing-oriented approach.
- To develop an awareness of how the experiential approach can inform other approaches to therapy.
- To develop an awareness of how Focusing can contribute to creative activity in general.
- To introduce students to issues involved at the interface between psychotherapy and spirituality.

The sessions on general focusing theory and its philosophical grounding will include:

- the historical relationships between client-centred therapy, experiential therapy and focusing;
- the basic concepts of the 'felt sense' and the ways in which it is distinguished from emotions, imagery and ordinary physical sensations;
- process difficulties such as intellectualising, externalising and 'overwhelm';
- therapist procedures for engendering process steps – the concepts of 'implying', 'carrying-forward', 'handle-words' and 'clearing a space';
- Gendlin's 'six steps' and Focusing as a taught procedure;
- bringing focusing into therapy sessions;
- the philosophical background in existentialism, phenomenology and pragmatism;
- the theory of the relationship between experiencing and concepts;
- the theory of specific process blocks such as conflicts and the suppression of experiencing;
- theoretical approaches to the 'inner critic';
- experientialising of other approaches to therapy, such as Gestalt and cognitive-behavioural;
- the experiential theory of dreams;
- the relationship between Focusing and meditation;
- experiential theories of personality change: Gendlin, Greenberg, Rice and Elliott;
- the self and 'parts' of the self. 'Disidentification';
- introduction to Gendlin's *A Process Model*;
- objections to focusing-oriented psychotherapy;
- the research and evidential basis for focusing-oriented psychotherapy.

The experiential part of the course will include:

- experiential work in listening and reflection;
- work in Focusing partnerships;
- work with finding a felt sense;
- looking at how process steps come;
- learning to be aware of the body-sense;
- learning to 'be with' a felt sense;
- practice in using Gendlin's six focusing steps;

- practice in role-play;
- working with the 'inner critic';
- working with conflicts and experiential suppression;
- experientialised versions of the empty-chair and two-chair techniques;
- experientialised working with cognitive-behavioural procedures;
- working with dreams;
- experimenting with the differential effects of meditation instructions compared with Focusing instructions.

Courses similar to this would seem to be appropriate in countries in which psychotherapy training is undertaken at postgraduate level following completion of a psychology degree.

Training in teaching Focusing as a procedure

The Focusing Institute in New York has developed a structure for the training of Focusing teachers. It is emphasised that such training is not a training in psychotherapy. Rather it trains people to teach Focusing to anyone who wishes to use the procedure for their own benefit. There is an international network of 'Focusing co-ordinators' who are responsible for setting up courses which train Focusing teachers. There are progressive levels of training and a process of certification for the different levels. In the same way, there are the beginnings of a network of trainers in 'Thinking at the Edge' which applies Focusing principles to creative thinking. Different countries may in addition have their own training programmes. The British Focusing Teachers' Association, for example, has courses and provides its own certification.

Supervision

Focusing-oriented principles would encourage the counsellor to speak from their felt sense of clients, to notice subtle feelings which they may have in connection with a client, perhaps a sense of unease or excitement, and then to gently approach this felt sense and enquire what is 'in' it. The counsellor can also be encouraged to ask themself questions such as 'What would I *really* like to say here?' or 'What stops me?' and wait to see what comes. At the same time the focusing-oriented supervisor will want to stay with their own felt sense of what the counsellor is doing, and of what might be happening for the client. The intricacy of the supervision situation far exceeds what can be expressed in words, so that only responses which come from the supervisor's whole felt sense are likely to be helpful.

Lambers (2000, p. 187) writes that person-centred supervision is a matter of facilitating congruence. The role of the supervisor is not to judge the counsellor's work from some outside perspective, but 'to facilitate the therapist's ability to be open to her experience so that she can become fully present and engaged in the relationship with the client'. Focusing can be used in an explicit way in helping the therapist to be open to their experience, as shown in the following extract from a supervision session (Baljon, 2002, p. 320–1). The therapist already knows how to focus.

Jill, the therapist, begins by saying that her problem is that the problems of her client *seem so understandable to her*. The supervisor is intrigued by this remark, and asks what she means by 'understandable'. Jill says that the client is unfit for work and that he is worried about making his mortgage repayments. The supervisor still does not understand Jill's problem and asks what this means to *her*. Jill says that she has a feeling that she should be able to solve these problems for the client, although she realises that this is impossible. The supervisor recognises here a difficulty with which Jill often struggles, and says

> S3: Yes, that is a field of tension in this profession. You empathise with how someone gets in a fix through practical circumstances and you cannot do anything about it. But what do you feel, when you think about it for a minute, when you realise what the client is going through?
>
> J4: Of course, this is my doctor-attitude again, my desire to help find a practical solution.
>
> S4: Yes, but think about what you feel inside yourself for a minute when you consider the financial situation of your client, now that he has to live on a disability insurance.
>
> (*Jill starts to focus.*)
>
> J5: Some sort of tension.
>
> S5: Where do you experience this tension?
>
> (*Jill imagines how it would be to be the client and focuses on what emotions this evokes in her.*)
>
> J6: Here on my breast, as if a stone is weighing me down.
>
> S6: As if you bear a burden?
>
> J7: No, not like that, it doesn't weigh down on my back. I think it is extra difficult for me because there are children involved.
>
> (*The next intervention sprang forth from my perception of Jill's facial expression.*)
>
> S7: You seem to feel something like sorrow now as well.

J8: Yes...now I remember, that is what the client needs, that he can express his emotions about this, that these emotions are allowed to exist.

....

J10: Now a sort of heavy feeling rises to my head.

S10: Can you breathe towards that feeling?

J11: What do you mean?

S11: You know, let the feeling be there and breathe calmly.

J12: It is still as if it is not allowed, as if that is not my job, as a therapist, being occupied with my own feelings that way...

S12: How does it feel to realise that these messages keep emerging inside of you, saying that you should be rational?

J13: I feel something like...not exactly sad.

S13: It moves you.

J14: More a feeling as of a child that is not allowed to do something, a bit of, a bit of...yes, sadness after all.

The supervisor then worked for a bit with the therapist on how she could deal with the inner critical voice which tells her that she should not, as a therapist, be occupied with her own feelings. Much later, Jill recalled that this supervision session had been a turning point in her personal development. While imagining herself to be the client

she had had an intense sensation in her breast, which had given greater depth to her experience. For the first time she had understood what a 'felt sense' was... She had experienced how she could be in touch with herself and with the client at the same time, without losing sight of the distinction between her own feelings and those of the client. She no longer saw that many mental images when focusing now, but made contact with her physical experience instead. She emphasised that time had been a very important factor for her in the supervision. She had been enabled to discover what was meant by congruence in her own time. (*ibid.*, p. 322)

8

Towards a Theory of Psychotherapy

In this chapter I will outline some of the central themes in Gendlin's account of psychotherapy. Gendlin's views are not easy to summarise, and his major work *A Process Model* (1997a) has not yet been formally published, although a draft of it has been available for some time from the Focusing Institute in New York. Rather more accessible introductions can be found in Gendlin (1962/1997, 1964b/1973, 1990, 1991b, 1996). It could be some years before his work is thoroughly discussed and understood, but in the meantime even a partial understanding of it may contribute much to our understanding of what psychotherapy involves. In what follows I have tried to sketch my own present understanding of psychotherapy as it has developed through a study of Gendlin's writings. I have tried to convey what I take to be Gendlin's central ideas, but have to some limited extent presented them in my own way. Gendlin's view is that in reading we 'cross' what we read with our own understandings (I will discuss 'crossing' shortly) and that through this we are carried forward. This book, and especially this chapter, comes from the crossing of Gendlin's writings with my own thought and experience. In the reader there will then be a further crossing which I hope will be fruitful.

The implicit (...)

There is an implicit background of feeling to all we do and say. We can turn our attention to what we are feeling, and refer to aspects of it. There is then an *interaction* between the continuing feeling-process and the attention we bring to it. The interaction generates a specifiable feeling, a 'this'. We may recognise the feeling as of a particular sort

175

(jealous, excited, hurt, for example), or we may not. If not, we can still refer to 'this feeling'. The feeling can be quite recognisable and distinctive even if we have no ready-made category into which to fit it. Gendlin calls that to which we can directly refer in this way, a 'direct referent'. A direct referent may be a specified feeling or a felt sense which is in the process of being specified.

We can say that we *find* the felt sense when we turn our attention to what we feel. However, before we focussed our attention, there was not this *specified* feeling. It only emerges as something specific, as a 'this', through the impact of our attention. So we could also say that the felt sense is *made* in the interaction between our feeling-process and our attending to that process. It is impossible to draw a sharp line between 'finding' and 'making' here, but this is so wherever we are concerned with creativity. The sculptor 'finds' the form in the rock as much as they 'make' it. The psychotherapy client makes a new life for themselves as much as finding it.

We can bring our attention to our implicit feeling-process and then find (create) specific feelings. This is an important and distinctively human activity, though a relatively uncommon one. Most of the time our feeling-process is interacting not with our attention but with what we are doing or saying.

When we are engaged in practical activity our feeling-process informs what we are doing. Each movement we make registers with us and how it registers makes a difference to our next move. There are degrees to which our feeling-process is engaged as we act; when acting habitually there is less of immediate feeling and more of the structure of habit coming from the past. But when we are doing something important for the first time then our feeling-process is vividly present as we act.

Further, when we act, our feel for our *environment* informs what we do. In a familiar environment the things we see and hear connect smoothly and implicitly with our feeling-process. But when we encounter something unexpected the smooth ongoing interaction between feeling-process and environment is interrupted. We stop and give our attention to the environmental event – 'What on earth is *that*?'

When we read, the written words connect with our feeling-process. They draw out felt meanings. We do not normally give explicit attention to the meaning of each word, but each word's meaning functions implicitly as we read. When we come to a place where a word or phrase does not connect with our feeling-process the reading process (the interaction between symbols and feeling-process) comes to a halt. Then we give more attention to the words which are blocking us, and try to get a sense of what they could mean here.

When we write, the relation between words and symbols is reversed. We start to write or type the words as they emerge from what we want to say, as they emerge from that feeling-process. When we come to a place where our feeling-process is not being expressed by the words which are available to us, the writing process comes to a halt. Then we give more attention to the feeling which is not getting expressed, and try to get a sense of what would express it.

A real difficulty in thinking about experiencing is that in our experiencing there is an element, what I have been calling a 'feeling-process', which never exists by itself, independently of its interaction with other things such as external events or symbols. Gendlin often refers to this 'feeling-process' by the device (. . .), 'dot, dot, dot'. (. . .) points to that element in experience which is not conceptual, but which interacts with symbols to form concepts. Experiencing is always one aspect of a relationship between (. . .) and something which relates to it. But the (. . .) is something real; we can refer directly to it, although when we do that the (. . .) takes the specific form of a direct referent, a 'this'. The (. . .) *in itself* cannot be expressed in words; but 'it' can lead to words, and words can have an impact on 'it'. With the (. . .) we are right at the limits of what can intelligibly be said. For while in a way it is right to say that the (. . .) in itself cannot be expressed in words, it is equally true to say that *it* is exactly what *is* expressed in words. What else could words articulate? The (. . .) is the implicit, what has not yet been made explicit. The implicit *cannot be said*, because saying it makes it explicit; but also, the implicit *is said* precisely in making something explicit.

The (. . .) is not a blank, a nothing. It functions in specific ways in our experiencing. As mentioned above, it functions in the formation of a direct referent. When we bring our attention to the (. . .) and ask 'What's this?' something may form. That is the formation of a felt sense. The formation of a felt sense requires our attention, but it also requires the (. . .). Again, as mentioned, the (. . .) functions in our activities generally, and can be seen to be fulfilling specific functions in reading and writing (also, of course, in listening and speaking). We can read only if the marks on the paper connect with a (. . .), only if a felt meaning is generated for us. When we write we start with a (. . .), and then seek words whose (. . .) expresses our (. . .). When we find such words there is the sort of release which we experience in therapy – 'Ah, *that* says it!'. Of course it is often true that we cannot find words whose (...) is our (...); we cannot find words to say what we mean. Then we cast around for words which can be *made* to mean what we want to say. This is the realm of metaphor and simile. We have our (...) and we bring up to it words which have their own (...). The lover says his girl's eyes are bright as diamonds. Now 'bright as' has a meaning in connection with comparisons of lights (is this star as bright as that one? is the sun shining as brightly today as it was yesterday?). But the lover is not of course thinking in terms of photometric comparisons of the reflectivity of his girl's eyes with the reflectivity of diamonds. The existing (...) of 'bright as diamonds' contains more than this, and other than this. Once the image has been used we can see certain aspects of this 'more' and 'other': her eyes *sparkle*, they express something of intense and intrinsic value, there is something beautiful, and something that is a 'hard' independent reality. The use of the image was not *based on* these similarities; rather something in the (...) of 'bright diamonds' draws out something in the (...) of the lover's experience of his girl, and the similarities are created in the interaction (Gendlin, 1962/ 1997, pp. 113–17, 140–4).

Any two words with their respective (...)s can be, in Gendlin's terminology, 'crossed', and then new aspects emerge (Gendlin, 1991b, pp. 96–9; 1997a, pp. 51–7). Suppose we are thinking about clocks and time, of 'living by the clock'. We select something apparently quite unrelated, such as *jellyfish*. We bring the word 'jellyfish' up to our felt sense – our (...) – of clocks. What can 'jellyfish' draw out from our (...) of clocks? Well, jellyfish do not move around spontaneously, and this draws out the lack of spontaneity of clock time. Jellyfish stay attached to the rock, as the tide washes in and out, and we see that there is a similar passivity of the clock world, a world of routine, which goes round and round. The jellyfish's life is peaceful, comfortable, not proactive, and that is what clock time is like. But also, if we get too close to a jellyfish we may get paralysed by its sting, and is not that what can happen to us if we live too much by the clock? A student in a workshop I taught on Gendlin's *Experiencing and the Creation of Meaning* was initially sceptical about the idea of 'crossing'. How could it possibly help, for example, to cross *her partner* with *a tin of sardines*? But then she found herself thinking...it is quite hard to open up the tin...what is inside is good and nourishing...when you think you have got to the end there is always that little bit more ....

Anything can be crossed with anything, but only some crossings are fertile. What 'just comes' to us when we stay with something arises out of the whole intricacy of our experiencing, which includes 'all that' surrounding the thing we are staying with. If we select two words at random from the dictionary, their senses *can* be crossed, but if we let two words 'just come' to us then they will already have their interconnections. It is not just chance that we choose 'clocks' and 'jellyfish', or 'my partner' and 'a tin of sardines'. And even if we cross words taken at random from the dictionary, *how* they cross will undoubtedly be a function of who does the crossing.

We are here in the realm of the creation of metaphor. Gendlin argues that metaphors are not formed through the noticing of like-nesses; rather, the likenesses are created by crossing the (. . .) of one thing with the (. . .) of another thing. The metaphor is *formed through the interaction*. This happens frequently in psychotherapy. A client cannot find words to express what she is experiencing. She stays with the felt sense of her experiencing and the image comes to her of an empty box. She says with a sigh, '*That's* it, my life is an empty box.' There is already some release in this, but then she goes on to explore what is in the image. What is an empty box? Well, empty boxes were once full, but no longer are, they are things which are put aside, thrown away; they are far less important than what they contained, they have no value in themselves. How then is *she* an empty box? Now the image begins to unfold: she had a family but her husband left her and her children have now grown up and moved away. She provided a protective container for them which was her sole function in life. She did it well, but now she has no role any more. She is a discarded, empty box. She explores all the pain of this, and tries to sense whether the empty box image is still alive for her. Perhaps not, perhaps its function was simply to crystallise out what her felt situation is. But anything can cross with anything, and when an image comes it may have in it not only the problem but a hint of a way forward. She stays with the metaphor of the box. She feels, there is nothing *wrong* with a cardboard box that has fulfilled its function. Does it just have to be thrown away? No, it can be recycled, or it can be used for an indefinite range of other things. It can have many functions. Its life can continue in quite new ways, maybe no longer as a box at all. Something may emerge for her from this.

Metaphor has a widely acknowledged place in psychotherapy, but without the concept of felt experiencing, of (. . .), metaphor is unintelligible. For metaphor to be possible old words have to work in new ways. One has to let go (a bit) of the familiar ways in which the words work and dip down into the (. . .) out of which they emerge. This is what happens in focusing.

In Gendlin's view, experiencing is always an interaction between a (. . .) and words, actions or events which function to draw something forth from the (. . .). In focusing, what interacts with the (. . .) is first the attention which we bring to it. Giving attention to a (. . .) constellates it as a 'this'. The (. . .) is now a 'something'; there is already a change. Such a change may not be negligible; often a client feels real relief at getting to the point of sensing that '*there is something wrong here*, I can really feel the shape of it now, it's something that has been there a long time'. Once there is the sense of a 'something' (i.e. a felt sense has formed), words and images can be brought up to the 'something'. The client can ask 'What is this?' and wait for what comes. When a word or image comes they can then try to sense whether it 'fits' the felt sense. If it does, then there is a further releasing step: 'So that's what it is, I'm jealous. Well, if *that's* what it is I can see a bit more what I need to do.' If no words come which carry the client on, then more waiting and sensing is required, until something, often a metaphor, comes. Then from the metaphor there can be further steps, as we saw above.

The (. . .) is a feeling-*process* rather than a state. Our feeling-process is ongoing, it has a momentum. We might even say it has a direction, except that 'direction' here does not refer to something that can be specified as a goal. The momentum of the feeling-process can be seen in the steps that occur in therapy. The client feels something disturbing, then seeks for a way of articulating it. A word or image comes, the disturbing feeling shifts a bit, and then further words or images come. There is an ongoing process here in which the need for something further is felt, then something comes which at least partially satisfies the need, and then there is a new need. At each point the feeling-process 'implies' something further. The client (or the therapist, or the client's life situation) interacts with this 'implying' and one of three things can then happen. (1) The interaction may simply leave the implying unchanged. For instance, the client senses the discomfort of their situation, which they have just characterised as 'being irritated'. The therapist says 'I think you are angry with me'. This does not connect with the client's experiencing. The sense of 'being irritated' is still there, unchanged. The therapist's response has not helped in carrying the client forward. (2) The interaction may distract the client from what they are experiencing. For instance, the therapist says 'I wonder if this is the same sort of irritation as you said your father used to feel for your mother?', and the client's experiencing of his irritation is lost, as he turns his attention to the therapist's question. (3) The interaction may provide just what is needed for the client to move on. For instance, the therapist simply reflects the client's irritation, and the client then says 'Well, it's not really irritation, it's more like feeling trapped'. When this happens the gnawing feeling of 'I'm irritated, but I don't know what this is all about' vanishes. What the therapist did has resulted in *that* implying no longer being there. There is now something new, the sense of being trapped, but the irritation has gone; it has carried forward into something else. This is quite different from the case where the therapist's response gets rid of the implying by diverting the client to something else. In that case the implying disappears because it has been knocked on the head, as it were, whereas in the other case the implying disappears because that which was implied (in this instance, the sense of being trapped) has now *occurred*. In Gendlin's terminology the therapist's reflection *carried* the client *forward*. In general, when something is implied (in this sense) there can be events which remove the implying, not by destroying it, but by carrying it forward.

Implying and carrying-forward

'Implying', as it is used here, is one of Gendlin's key concepts (Gendlin, 1997a, pp. 9–11). In any human process there is an implicit implying of what is to come next. What is implied is not *explicit*, that is, there is no specifiable event which must occur if the implying is to be 'satisfied'. Gendlin's 'implying' is not like logical implication, where the premises of an argument logically determine its conclusion. It is more like the earlier lines of a poem 'implying' what will complete it. The concluding line is not logically or physically determined by the lines which have already been written, but it is implied in the sense that *something is required to complete the poem*, and when that comes the sense of 'something needed' will vanish. It is possible that the poem could be completed in more than one way, and it is also possible that no final line can be found. Gendlin's concept of implying does not entail either that there *will* be something that will 'carry forward', or that only *one* thing can do so. This concept of implying is also distinctive in that once the implied event has occurred, what led to it may have to be revised. The coming of the final line of the poem may lead the poet to revise some of the earlier lines. This means of course that it is impossible to get from the beginning to the end by logical deduction; if there is logic here it is a peculiar logic in which the conclusion of an argument alters the premises!

Interaffecting ('interaction first')

We are in all this thinking of systems which are not analysable into distinct parts which retain their form independently of their place in the whole. Each element in the whole is affected by all the other elements, but these in turn have been affected by the first element, so that they affect the first element not as they are independently, but as *already affected* by the first element. Gendlin holds that human beings, and biological organisms generally, can be thought of as systems of this kind, as interaffecting wholes, within which everything is affected by everything else.

Gendlin (1997a, p. 41) tells this story to illustrate the notion of interaffecting:

> When I was in the Navy, I learned to repair and tune the radio receivers of that time. They had several parts called "IFcans" (Intermediate Frequency), each of which had a screw on top. I had to turn the screw on the first one to the point where the signal is loudest. Further turning diminishes the signal again. Then I would turn the screw on the second to its maximum. But this would make a difference to the first. I would turn the screw on the first to what was now the loudest point. But this would affect the second, so it had to be turned to its loudest again. Now this altered the first again, but only a little. After going back and forth a number of times, both are at their loudest. Now came the third, and then each time going between the second and the first again, second and first, second and first, between every turning of the third. And so with the fourth, where one must retune third, second and first, second and first between every two tunings of the fourth. Eventually all differences all of them can make to each other, and to all the differences that makes to all the differences, and so on, is taken account of.

This 'Ifcans' story is only a machine analogy for the notion of interaffecting. It differs from interaffecting in that (a) the adjustments are made in sequence, whereas in interaffecting everything is there in one time instant and (b) the adjustments are made from outside the system in accordance with a human goal, whereas in interaffecting the 'goal' is simply what the system as a whole implies.

Interaffecting is an interaction process in which the elements in the process are what they are *through* being in interaction with the other elements. This notion runs through all of Gendlin's thought. We are who we are in and through our interactions with others. Psychotherapy can be seen as an interaction between client and therapist in which both participants are changed. It is also an interaction between the client's experiencing and whatever is brought up to that experiencing along the specific avenue of therapy which is being pursued. Solitary reflection is an interaction between our experiencing and the words and images we bring up to our experiencing. In that interaction our experiencing changes, but so may the meanings which the words have for us. Our bodies can be thought of as interaffecting systems in which each organ functions in interaction with all the other organs, and is fully itself only through that interaction.

There are many different kinds of interaction, and Gendlin's *Process Model* lays out some of this complexity. Running through all of the Model is the theme of 'interaffecting', but Gendlin then develops more specific concepts for thinking about the kinds of interaction which characterise plants, animals and human beings respectively.

Organism and environment

In Gendlin's view it is important that human beings (and organisms generally) can be seen not only as interaffecting wholes, but as existing in similar interaffecting relationships with their environments. 'Organism' and 'environment' are correlative terms: an organism's environment is not usefully describable in purely physical terms, but in terms of how it relates to the organism's needs. Just as in specifying the parts of an organism it is necessary to think in terms of function (the eye of a fly is *physically* quite different from the eye of a mammal), so things in the environment which are *physically* various count, for this organism, as 'food' or 'shelter'. Organism and environment need to be thought of as a single interaffecting system (Gendlin, 1997a, pp. 1–6, 38–46).

Organisms, from this perspective, are interaffecting systems which imply their own continuation. Their continuing depends critically on their environment. If certain events occur in the relationship between organism and environment then the organism's life will be carried forward. If these events do not occur then the organism will remain in a state of 'implying', and this will usually result in particular sorts of behaviour. For example, if no prey appears an animal will prowl around, or wait very quietly, or do other things which will increase the likelihood of encountering prey. The animal's life continues in this different way, during the period when the prey-catching behaviour is blocked. Prey-catching is still *implied* however, and this implying is manifested in the searching or waiting behaviour. When prey does appear then *this* implying ceases. The appearance of prey carries the animal forward.

Levels of life

In what follows it is important to realise that Gendlin is not engaged in developing a scientific theory. Rather, he is developing new kinds of concepts which will allow us to think about organisms, behaviour, language and focusing in ways which *begin with* process and interaction. In the standard way of thinking, one begins with individual things (entities, atoms) and *then* develops principles of change and of inter-connection. Within that way of thinking the problem is how to explain change and interdependence within a basic framework in which the 'atoms' stay the same and are separate from each other. In Gendlin's model the problem is the opposite: we need to be able to account for stability (lack of change) and for individual entities, within a framework in which everything is in flux, and everything depends on everything else.

Gendlin has developed a set of concepts for thinking about organic life in which there are several levels of implying and carrying-forward. There is the level of plant life, which already involves intricate implyings arising from interaffecting processes within the organism, and between the organism and its environment. A seed implies the emergence of shoots and roots. This implying can be blocked, for example by a stone which the shoot encounters. Instead of continuing upwards the shoot now behaves in a new way: it turns along the base of the stone until it can resume its upward course. If the stone is removed, then the upward movement carries forward without the need for a detour.

On the level of animal life the implyings, carryings-forward and blocks which characterise plant life are all still there, but with animals there is in addition the whole new dimension of perception and behaviour. Gendlin (1997a, Chapter 6) has an intriguing account (which I am greatly oversimplifying here) of how this new level of organisation involves and builds upon the previous level. The new level brings the notion of an aspect of organic process which *registers* the organism's other processes. The organism then interacts not only with its environment but with that environment as registered within itself. The previous bodily processes still continue of course, but they now embody a new kind of process, that of sentient behaviour. Behaviour, for Gendlin, is seen as a new way of carrying-forward what was stopped. As the animal prowls, eating is still stopped and still implied, but the prowling behaviour carries the animal forward in a new way.

Then just as bodily process may be blocked and behaviour arise, so behaviour may be blocked and symboling arise. Gendlin uses as an illustration of two monkeys who cannot actually fight (perhaps because they are on opposite sides of a chasm), and who then begin to gesture at each other. The gesturing is a kind of behaviour, but it is a new development in behaviour. The fighting behaviour, which is blocked, *begins* to occur (the monkey raises an arm and snarls) but it is not carried through. Instead the movements and sounds convey to the other monkey something of the first monkey's state, and the second monkey gestures back. Here is the beginning of communication, and also of symbolisation. Gesturing, and symboling in general, can be seen as a new kind of carrying-forward which arises when non-symbolic behaviour does *not* carry forward. From gesturing to the full development of language involves several more stages of development, the outlines of which Gendlin delineates in Chapter 7 of *A Process Model*.

In Gendlin's scheme, focusing and other processes of creative change arise out of paused symboling in the same kind of way as symboling arises out of paused behaviour and behaviour arises out of paused body-process. Symboling is paused when we cannot find the word (image, gesture and so on) which will carry us forward. As in the other cases of stopped process, the first part of the usual process occurs – we try out first one word or image, then another. Thus far we are on the symbolic level. But we are also beginning to do something new here. We are sensing into 'all that which we can't yet express', and awaiting what comes. There is still symboling going on, but it is going on in a new way, just as in gesturing behaviour is still going on, but going on in a new way.

Let me now try to explain what I think Gendlin is saying in a slightly different way.

An animal's prey-catching behaviour can be blocked by the non-appearance of prey, but it can also be blocked by such things as misperception. Animals have far more resources than plants, but along with their extra capacities go new ways in which their lives can be blocked. What is new and different about animals is that they interact with their environment via how they *register* that environment. But along with all the advantages of perception come new kinds of problem. If the animal's registry is not functioning properly then the animal will respond to the environment not as it *is* but as how it is being registered. For instance, if the animal's temperature registry is defective it may register a warm environment as cold, and hence behave inappropriately.

Then the human level brings all that is there at the animal level, but also the dimension of language and a social form of life which allow us to act through knowledge of general principles rather than only through our particular experience. For example, a human being lost at sea may become desperately thirsty. Their body accurately registers their need to drink, but they know that to drink *salt* water will make things worse. Here the human being does not relate directly to their organic awareness, which impels them to drink. Instead they relate to their general knowledge of the situation, which tells them *not* to drink. Human beings have, in addition to their needs (which plants have) and their registering of their needs (which animals have), a further awareness of what is true or false *in general*. This knowledge of general principles is closely tied up both with linguistic ability, and the ability to reflect on what one is registering. Both of these abilities are aspects of the social nature of human beings; a human being does not simply respond to what they register but to what *kind* of situation this is. An animal sees the food, registers hunger and proceeds to eat. A human being sees this *as* food (as of the general kind: 'food'), and the situation as one in which it would be appropriate (or not) to pick it up and eat it. Whether the human being *will* eat this food depends crucially on the social situation and on whether *this* is generally seen as food. (In some cultures, but not in others, dogs are seen as food.)

Human beings live in and respond to what is sometimes called a socially constructed reality. Of course, societies do not entirely construct their reality – we cannot eat just anything – but the social form of human life transforms animal consciousness in a radical way. The human form of consciousness brings with it huge advantages – it prevents us from drinking salt water, and in general it gives us the resources of general knowledge that have been acquired by others and formulated in terms of the language and traditions of our community. Most of what we know comes not from our own individual experience but from what we have been told, from what we have read, from what we have picked up from people with more experience than ourselves. Human beings are educated, and initiated, into the ways of seeing the world which characterise the society they live in. Our modern society has peculiar features, which I will come to shortly, but in most human societies (and still in ours to a large extent), what is learned is how *we* do things, how *we* see things. If someone does not know what to do in a situation then they consult someone who does know. There is a tradition of knowing and doing which provides the means for individuals to find out what they, in their specific situation, need to do.

Now just as the development of animal awareness, which involves the registering of the environment, can in spite of all its advantages, lead to new kinds of problem, so too the development of human awareness and tradition can lead to a new kind of problem. Just as an animal's awareness may not always further its needs, so human cultural forms may not always further either awareness or needs. With the human form of life come general truths, such as the truth that drinking salt water is harmful, but where there can be truth there can also be what is false or misleading. In the animal world there is no issue about what is the true thing to say or the right thing to do; that only comes with human society and human agreement about how we see things. Only where there are standards of judgement can there be any sense of what is 'correct', and standards are essentially social in nature. Yet these standards do not arise in a vacuum; they arise in relation to awareness of needs. In general the standards are there, and are passed down as the tradition, because they enable people to live together and to flourish. A tradition which went fundamentally against human awareness of need would not be propagated for long. Yet traditions can, to some extent, become alienated from the needs of the people who live them. Traditions tend to be self-perpetuating whether or not they still satisfy any need.

Traditions, social forms and ways of seeing the world do change. This has always been so, but it is only in recent times that the possibility of whole alternative traditions has become widely accepted. With this acceptance has come the widespread postmodernist scepticism about the very possibility of truth and knowledge. But I think that this concern is unfounded. Truth and knowledge are notions that belong *within* traditions. In the traditional Aristotelean view of the world objects composed largely of the earth element seek their natural place at the centre of the world, while things containing much of fire seek their natural place in the heavens. Sparks from a bonfire rise into the sky. If we ask, *within this scheme of things*, whether it is true that these sparks, which we are observing tonight, are seeking their natural place in the heavens, then the answer is yes. But if we are thinking within the scheme of modern science, we cannot ask that question. There are no *concepts* of 'fire element' or 'natural place' in the scheme of modern physics. We can ask whether these sparks are composed of particles of carbon which are in the process of combining with oxygen, and within the modern scheme the answer is yes. In Aristotle's scheme it is not that the answer is no; it is rather that neither the question nor the answer has a place.

Questions of truth and knowledge arise *within* traditions. It does not make sense to ask whether these traditions are themselves true. A tradition is not the sort of thing which can be true or false; it is there. As Wittgenstein put it, 'This game is played.' But that is not to say that traditions cannot be challenged or cannot change. The Aristotelean tradition in physical science is no longer one which we can live within. It does not relate sufficiently to all that has happened since Aristotle; it is no longer something through which we can orient ourselves in our thinking about the physical world. The explanation of why this is so can only be given through a detailed laying out of the subsequent history of physical science. It is a long, complex, human story with many aspects: intellectual, personal, social, religious. It is not that from some impossible position outside of all traditions we can look and judge that Aristotle was wrong; rather, as a result of a myriad of factors, we can no longer live within the Aristotelean tradition.

Within a tradition there are standards for assessing what is true and what is right; those standards indeed make the tradition what it is. But traditions themselves can be queried, and this can make it seem that, in spite of what I have said, there must be *some* sense in which one tradition can be 'better' or more 'true' than another. But 'better' and 'true' must have a new sense here; otherwise they would presuppose a further tradition in terms of which we could make such judgements. What we might say is that a 'better' tradition is one which *helps us more*, which works for us, which allows us to move forward, which enables us to live more fully. There can be changes in a tradition, but whether the changes are for the 'better' can only be assessed in terms of whether they 'make things better for us'. And whether that is so is not a matter to be judged by the standards of any tradition but in terms of whether we can live better. It is something to be felt rather than thought.

In the end what is right about a tradition has to refer back to what is right in our felt awareness of our lives. This is not to say that the rightness of a tradition is simply determined by the felt needs of its adherents, because to some extent their involvement in the tradition *changes* their felt needs. The tradition and the felt needs are enmeshed with each other; in Gendlin's term they *interaffect* each other. Nevertheless, if the question is one of whether the tradition needs to change, the place to seek the change is in the felt need. From the practices and assumptions of the tradition we have to drop back into our *experiencing* of our situation. We have to bring our attention to 'all that' which always far exceeds what can be expressed explicitly in cultural forms. It may help to bring up to our experiencing *other* cultural forms, and see what happens in our experiencing when we look at things through the lens of a quite different tradition. The aim here is not to take on the forms of that other tradition, but to see what they might elicit for us. Something new may come.

Psychotherapy

The difficulties that arise in connection with postmodernism and cultural relativism are the *same sort* of difficulties which face psychotherapy clients, and I think that this is not just a coincidence. It is only in our modern world that the tradition of psychotherapy has arisen. In traditional cultures there is neither the need for nor the possibility of psychotherapy. In such cultures, if someone encounters a personal problem that cannot be sorted out within the family, they will consult someone who plays the role of an elder within the culture, someone who knows the traditions of the culture very deeply. The elder will then advise, and the troubled person learns something about how such situations are to be handled. They may then be able to pass on something of this wisdom to others.

This pattern of dealing with personal troubles only begins to break down where traditions begin to be questioned. Once we become aware that there are alternative traditions and that, for all we know, our tradition may not be the best, the role of the 'elder' becomes equally questionable. All that an elder can do is to advise from their deep knowledge of *a* tradition, and that no longer satisfies us. If that is how it is, then we are thrown back on ourselves. Yet the difficulties in question are just those which we have not been able to resolve on our own. That is precisely why there was the need to turn to an 'elder' in the first place.

Something new is needed here. In turning to a (person-centred) psychotherapist we turn to someone who is not an expert (an 'elder') in any tradition, *except that tradition which encourages the person to go beneath the surface of traditions and await what comes from the intricacy of their own experiencing of their situation.* Like anyone else, the person-centred therapist *does* speak from within a tradition, but it is a tradition which works on a different level, a peculiar sort of tradition which could be seen as a way of dealing with traditions.

Clients approach therapists because they are some way troubled. Their normal ways of coping with difficulties have failed. They have in some sense 'got stuck', for example they are 'caught' in the tangle of some dilemma, or in some state of anxiety or depression. This is the starting point in therapy. Successful therapy involves the client being able to move forward again in their life. It is not a matter of the problems having been 'solved', but of the client being able to move freely again.

When we are 'stuck' we try various things. We may tell ourselves to snap out of it, we may distract ourselves from the problem by reading a book, we may take a holiday, listen to inspirational music, talk to a friend, dig the garden and so on. Any of these procedures may help, or they may not. Where something does help we are, in Gendlin's terminology, 'carried forward' by that procedure. The blocked state is released.

Prior to the carrying-forward we are in a state of tension. Something is *implied* which is not yet there. It is like the case of hunger, where the animal moves about restlessly, seeking for food. Here eating has not yet happened; instead there is the implying of eating. That is hunger. The implying continues until an event occurs – sight of food – which carries the animal forward into eating. Then *that* implying ceases.

When we are stuck we feel the implying of something, but we may not know what would carry us forward. Even in the hunger example it may not be clear in advance what will carry the implying forward. We know we are hungry, but neither chocolate, nor biscuits will do. The gnawing is still there, until we go to the fridge and find the Stilton cheese. And something *completely* different, such as an intravenous drip, can also carry hunger forward.

The carrying-forward which occurs in psychotherapy is a particular kind of carrying-forward which can only occur in human beings. As we have seen, there are other kinds which occur in the organic and animal realms, though also in us insofar as we too belong to these realms. Gendlin's model in general emphasises *processes* rather than states. Even in the physical world there is continuous process. A moving body not only has a specifiable position and direction of motion, it also has *momentum*. A body's momentum is something it can be said to have at a particular moment, but momentum is also about where the body is going to be in the *next* moment. The body's present momentum tells us something about what is to come next. As physical beings we ourselves have momentum – when the car brakes suddenly we are physically carried forward just as much as anything else.

What can stop or block physical movement (such as a stone in the way) need not block a plant (it can grow round the stone). What can stop or block a plant (such as a large change in temperature) need not block an animal (it registers the change and seeks shelter). What can stop or block an animal (such as illness) need not stop a human being (they recognise the symptoms and consult a doctor). Human problems are often sorted out by reference to general principles, whether these are enshrined in 'common sense' or in the specialist knowledge of experts, or in books or other reference sources. The more a human being knows about the general principles of things the greater is their ability to deal with problems as they arise.

Yet general principles never fully apply to individual cases. Even in the 'hard' sciences there are always exceptional circumstances. There is a general principle that salt dissolves in water, but not if the water is frozen, or already saturated with salt, or the salt grains have an insoluble coating, or... There is no exhaustive specification for what the 'exceptional circumstances' are; all we can say is that *normally* salt dissolves in water. The working scientist has to develop a feel for 'normal circumstances', for what can reasonably be taken for granted in setting up an experiment, and what cannot. This 'tacit dimension' of science has been explored in depth in the writings of the scientist and philosopher Michael Polanyi (1958, 1967).

Science, and human life generally, requires general principles, but these always operate against a tacit (what Gendlin calls an 'implicit') background. The creative scientist has an ability not only to work with the principles (with the logical and mathematical formulations) but also to dip into the tacit background out of which the formulations arise. It has become increasingly recognised that science is a creative activity rather than a purely logical one. The scientist creates pictures or models and goes back and forth between these and the experimental data. Then the model may need to be modified, or different data may emerge from the application of the model. In science, and in other creative activities, there is a zigzag between concepts and experience. A creative writer (see Appendix A), as much as a scientist, *tries out* various formulations; these then modify the felt sense of what he or she is trying to express, and lead to a new formulation.

Creative people have always worked like this, but in traditional societies there is by definition little need for creativity. The general principles of the tradition are sufficient, and in both art and practical affairs there is little need for innovation. The need for creativity arises only when the tradition is called into question. Then we cannot simply proceed with the established forms. It is not a matter of abandoning them, but of reconnecting them with immediate experiencing, so that they become open to modification.

The relationship between traditional forms and creative innovation lies at the heart of Gendlin's (1964b/1973, 1997a) account of psychotherapy. Very briefly, Gendlin's view is that psychological disturbance arises from our becoming 'structure-bound', that is, caught in specific forms of thought and emotion which are not open to modification by our immediate lived experiencing. Our experience has become 'frozen' into specific forms, so that in certain areas of our lives the creative interplay between form and feeling has ceased.

The re-establishment of the interplay is one crucial function of psychotherapy. The therapist looks for the places where the interplay is still possible, the places where the client pauses, feels a bit uncertain, does not quite know how to go on. At those points, the blurry places (the '...' places on the transcript), there are the possibilities for creative change. It is possible to notice or seek such places by oneself, but it is very much easier if we have someone with us who can say 'Could you just stay with that a while?' or 'What is in that?' or 'What is the crux of all that?'

However, making such moves is not the only thing, or even the most important thing, in re-establishing the interplay. The most important thing is simply for someone to be there with us. This is because our experiencing is different when we are with another person. On our own we tend to go round in the same old circles, or drift away into dreamy states. If we say the *same* things that we say to ourselves to another person the effect is different. Even if they say nothing in reply we know that they have heard, that there is someone there who is receiving what we have said. And that reception by another person encourages *us* to receive what we have said. Our relation to the other person changes our relation to ourself. If the therapist does more than simply listen then there is the potential for the interaction to be better *or worse*. It will probably be worse if the therapist comes in with criticism, advice, accounts of their own experiences and so on. Responses like that tend to close us down.

Where a client is already engaging with their experiencing all that is required from the therapist is the listening which enables the client to stay on their own experiential track. Here it is simply the presence of the therapist which facilitates the client's carrying-forward. Anything more than listening or minimal reflection is likely to be distracting.

However, further intervention by the therapist is needed where the client is not on an experiential track at all. In these circumstances the art of the therapist lies in finding places where the client *can* still interact with their experiencing, even though at present they are not doing so. Then, once the interplay of form and feeling is facilitated in these places the consequent changes in the client's experiencing may allow the 'unfreezing' of those aspects of their experience which are currently structure-bound.

We can now consider further what is involved in relating in a creative way with one's experiencing. It can easily seem that focusing is a matter of turning our attention inward and 'working with our feelings', but this is a misleading way of putting it. What we turn our attention to in Focusing is our *situation*. Certainly we look into ourselves, but this 'looking into' is more like 'looking into what went wrong with last year's business plan' than looking into a private room which no one else can see into. In focusing we get a felt sense of 'all that' about our situation, but the feel of 'all that' is not separate from the situation. Our feelings and our situations come together; something is a situation for us only if it has an impact on us, if it involves what we want and feel. And our feelings are always tied up with situations. A specific feeling, such as guilt, is tied up with a situation in which we think we have done something wrong; a feeling of hope is embedded in a situation in which we believe, but are not sure, that something good is going to happen. Specific feelings or emotions such as these are not just internal goings-on, like itches; they are how our bodies are responding in specific kinds of situations.

It can help us in thinking about human emotions if we compare them with the emotions which animals can have. Animal emotions are more limited than ours in two ways. First, there are situations which only human beings can get into. Perhaps a dog can hope that he will soon be taken for a walk, but he cannot hope that his master will return next Tuesday. Nor can he be concerned about having broken a promise. Animals cannot have feelings which are embedded in situations which are distinctively human. Secondly, as we saw in Chapter 3, animal feelings are feelings-in-behaviour (Gendlin, 1997a, pp. 95, 218). The fighting monkey is angry, the tail-wagging dog is pleased, the cowering dog is frightened. Animal feelings are there in the flow of the animal's behaviour. What an animal *does not* do is to sit down and reflect on its feelings. It cannot say to itself 'I was really angry about that', or 'I have that feeling of fear again'. This is not just because of the lack of language. It is because such reflection requires a social form of life in which others respond to our feelings in a way which leads to our being able to respond to our feelings ourselves. The mother conveys to the child (not necessarily in language) that she experiences the child as upset, and the child then acquires a sense of 'me upset' which he or she can retain even when mother is no longer there. Human beings not only experience emotions-in-behaviour but emotions as inner states. We can bring our attention to our emotions, and in the emotion we find the structure of the situation to which the emotion is the body's response.

Now just as there is a way our body gets when we feel specific emotions such as guilt or hope, so there is a way our body gets in relation to the *whole* situation which we are in (Gendlin, 1973a). As I said in Chapter 3, the body-sense of a whole situation is usually less obvious than the body-sense of a specific aspect, such as the fear associated with being attacked. In any culture certain common situation-aspects are recognised and the corresponding emotions are given names (Purton, 2000a), such as fear (corresponding to a kind of situation where there is danger), pride (corresponding to a kind of situation where I have done something, and I feel good about it) or regret (corresponding to a situation where I did something and I wish I had not). These kinds of situations are familiar, and the emotions associated with them are easily recognised. Other kinds of situation can arise for which the corresponding emotions do not have names, and then we have to find a circumlocution which will allow us to refer to the emotion (for example, that feeling you get when you know that you are being cheated but you cannot see how).

But in addition to responding with emotion to *kinds* of situation, we also respond to *this* particular situation which we now are in. Our response to this situation may involve feeling-in-behaviour in the situation, but we can also turn our attention to the *feel of the situation*. This is not something which people normally do, and there was no word in the language for 'the feel of this whole situation' until Gendlin introduced the term 'felt sense'. (Gendlin's other phrase, 'direct referent', more properly covers any inner state to which we can directly refer in our experiencing, and so covers both emotions and felt senses.) Thus the felt sense is how the body is registering 'this whole thing', while an emotion is how the body is registering a *kind* of situation.

From this we can begin to see how it is that through giving our attention to a felt sense of a situation we can change. Through giving our attention to a felt sense we bring it into focus and articulate some aspect of it. The physical feel of a situation may be describable initially as, for instance, 'jumpy', 'tight' or 'pulled-in'. Words like this give us a grip on the felt sense – there it is, *all pulled-in*. This feel of 'pulled-in' is how our body is registering the situation as a whole. But in that bodily reaction is an intricacy corresponding to the intricacy of the situation. The bodily reaction is the physical 'focaling' (Gendlin, 1997a, pp. 46–7) of one's engagement with the situation; for instance, feelings of fear in connection with what someone has said they will do, but also an irritation with oneself for being afraid, a sense that one has not changed in this way in all these years, a tiredness with having to deal with this again, memories of what happened last time (and all those other times) it was like this, doubts about whether it can be different...*All of that*, which clearly could never be exhaustively articulated, is there in the felt sense, in the 'pulled-in'.

To give attention to the felt sense already makes a difference to it. What was a vague amorphous feeling comes into focus – 'that's there', that whole pulled-in thing. There will no doubt be other troubles in one's life, but one can now sense the emotional unity of this one. It is distinct from the other difficulties which are around; its unity cannot be spelled out in words, but it can be distinctly felt. That in itself makes for a certain release. It is as if a whole cloud of vague apprehension has condensed into a droplet of precise feeling. One's body feels a little easier. This is the effect of bringing up to one's experiencing something external to it, namely *attention* and the specifying of the experiencing as a 'this'.

Having got the formed felt sense as a 'this' one can then seek to articulate it. One is now bringing other things up to the felt sense, such as the question 'What is all this?', 'What is the crux of this?' or 'What does this need?' These verbal forms interact with the felt sense. They begin to draw out aspects of it which were previously only implicit. From the felt sense new verbal (or imaginal) forms arise. They are checked with the felt sense, one notices whether they 'resonate', whether there is a felt shift. Where a felt shift occurs this is registered and welcomed. Now the felt sense is different, and this means that the feel of one's situation is different. But feelings are not distinct from situations – *after the felt shift one's situation is different*. It may or may not be possible to express the change in words. Sometimes one says things like 'I was scared and saw her as threatening, but now its more like I see her as just going along her own track, and I can go along mine too.' At other times it is *just that things are different*. Gendlin (1964b/1973, p. 455) writes:

> A whole vast multiplicity of implicit aspects in the person's functioning and dysfunctioning is always involved. For, when a direct referent of experiencing "opens up", much more change has occurred than the cognitive recollection of this or that ...
> "How is everything different?"
> "Well, it just seems OK now!"
> "Do you still feel that such-and-such might happen and you couldn't deal with it?"
> "Yes, but now I kind of feel, well, that's life. That's the way it is, you have to accept things like that."

Like Rogers (1956), Gendlin holds that it is not insight which lies behind therapeutic change. Insight often comes as part of the change, but is an effect of the change rather than a cause. The cause of the change is the bringing of something (attention, words, actions, personal interactions) up to one's experiencing so that there is an interaction. From the interaction new things emerge from the implicit depths of the feeling-process. Those new things were not already there 'in the unconscious'; they are formed (given a form, made explicit) through the interaction.

The different avenues of therapy, which we looked at in Chapter 5, involve bringing up different things to our experiencing. The Focusing procedure in which we encourage a felt sense to form and then bring to the felt sense questions such as 'What is this?', 'What does this need?' is just one avenue. Psychodynamic therapists bring interpretations up to the client's experiencing, behavioural therapists encourage interaction between experiencing and behaviour, some person-centred therapists bring the emotional responses of the therapist. The important matter is not so much which of these procedures is used, but whether they are used in such a way that they connect with the client's experiencing and carry it forward. Any of the standard therapeutic procedures can in this way be 'experientialised' or conducted in a 'focusing-oriented' way.

Rethinking some person-centred concepts

In addition to giving us a new perspective on psychotherapy generally, Gendlin's work can be seen as leading to a reformulation of some of Rogers' concepts.

The actualising tendency

It seems clear that what corresponds, in Gendlin's thinking, to Rogers' 'actualising tendency' is the carrying-forward of the life of the organism as a whole. The multifarious organic processes do not just go on side-by-side; they interaffect each other and the behaviour of the organism arises from the implicit 'totaling' and 'focaling' of all the processes in interaction with all the others. In the same way human behaviour arises from the totaling of everything that is within us, in interaction with our current environment. The full complexity of what moves us to action cannot be fully articulated, but nevertheless when the time comes to act we are often able to do so. Our actions cannot be arrived at by logical calculations; they arise from what we feel implicitly, from how our situations are registered in our bodies. Logic, calculation and other explicit forms of experience may form part of what moves us to act, but there is always far more that is implicit.

This applies even to a simple action such as crossing a crowded room to talk to someone. There lies behind the action all kind of considerations of why we are going to talk to this person, why *now*, how we are to navigate through the press of the other people, how we are going to greet this person, how friendly our smile will be and so on, without limit. All of this is implicit in the action which we take. We may be able, if we give attention to what is going on in us, to make explicit some of the factors involved, but many more will remain implicit. Yet the fact that we cannot *work it out* does not prevent us from acting. Even though 'we' (as intellectual calculator) cannot work it out, our 'body' knows what to do. Gendlin often refers to 'the body' as that to which we give our attention in focusing. 'The body' here is not the body as conceptualised by anatomy and physiology, but the living body as felt from inside, the body in which we are aware of a felt sense, and from which change steps come.

What corresponds to Rogers' 'actualising tendency' is what Gendlin (1996, Chapter 20) calls the 'life-forward' direction: the 'direction' in which we are carried forward by our current state of implying. This is a 'direction' not in the sense of an explicit goal (though it may include explicit goals), but a direction sensed with the whole of our being. In therapy the explicit direction in which the client is going may change from session to session, or even from moment to moment (they are going to leave their job...well, not leave immediately...not actually leave, but make some changes...or rather make some changes in how they relate to their job...but the job paralyses them, so actually they do have to leave . . .). We know that a process is going on here, which has its own kind of 'direction'. Gendlin uses in this connection the analogy of a winding road: sometimes we are going north, sometimes south. In a superficial sense we keep changing our direction, but in a deeper sense we are going in the same direction all the time. It is this deep, implicit direction which in Gendlin's thought corresponds to the actualising tendency in Rogers' theory.

Unconditional positive regard

Rogers held that the client's perception of the therapist's acceptance, or UPR, was a crucial factor in dissolving conditions of worth, which are themselves the source of psychological disturbance. One problem with this is that the more a client is enmeshed in conditions of worth the less able they will be to appreciate the therapist's acceptance of them. It follows that the more disturbed a client is the less effective person-centred therapy should be, but that is not obviously the case.

Gendlin's view is that it is not the client's perception of the therapist's acceptance that is crucial, but whether the therapist can help the client to relate to their own experiencing in the way I have previously discussed. Gendlin (1964b/1973, pp. 468–9) acknowledges that rejecting attitudes on the part of the therapist are likely to be untherapeutic, but he thinks that this is because when we feel that our experiences are not being accepted we find it difficult to stay with the implicit meanings of those experiences. The non-accepting therapist's 'pushing away' of our feelings tends to distance *us* from them, while an accepting attitude on the part of the therapist encourages us to stay with and articulate the feelings. Gendlin holds that even if the client is unable to appreciate the therapist's acceptance, therapeutic progress can still be made. For the therapist can still *respond* to the client's experiencing in a way that may encourage the client to do the same. Acceptance, in Gendlin's view is therapeutically facilitative, and rejection is therapeutically destructive, but it is not that the degree of therapeutic change depends in any simple way on the level of therapist acceptance. So long as the client feels safe *enough* to engage with their experiencing, and so long as the therapist encourages such engagement, therapeutic movement can take place.

I do not think that Gendlin's alternative view of the therapeutic effect of acceptance should be seen as denying the possibility of the dynamic which Rogers postulated. Where psychological disturbance *does* originate from the introjection of conditions of worth, it seems plausible to suppose that the consistent acceptance of the therapist may well play a role in undermining those conditions. This dynamic is not very much different from that involved in desenitisation therapy – the client initially expects that the therapist will condemn them for having their feelings, but as time goes on and no condemnation takes place, the client gradually feels it is possible to acknowledge and reveal the feelings. Even so, of course, the client may suspect that the therapist is not being genuine, or that the therapist can accept the client's feelings 'only because you are a counsellor – you are trained to do this'.

The 'desensitisation dynamic' is one example of a therapeutic process which does not involve anything like focusing. It is important to see that Gendlin does not deny that such non-focusing therapeutic processes exist. Focusing is a centrally important element in therapy, but it is not the only element. Focusing works with what is implicit in experience but not yet articulated, but some therapeutic processes take place in the realm of what is explicit, as I discussed in Chapter 6.

Since our positive regard for things or people is usually conditional on what those things or people are like UPR has often been seen as a paradoxical notion. It can seem that no one could *genuinely* have positive regard for a client irrespective of what the client is like, yet genuineness of course is one of the crucial therapist conditions. From Gendlin's perspective, there are several things which can be said about this. First, there is the point that the client is not to be identified with their feelings or attitudes. In focusing we distinguish the feelings from the person who is struggling with the feelings. Gendlin (1996, p. 287) writes 'There is often so much unlovely stuff in a client, which cannot genuinely be regarded positively. But I see no contradiction, because, as I formulate it, unconditional positive regard is for the embattled person in there, not for the stuff.'

However, it seems clear that a person cannot entirely be separated from their feelings, attitudes and personal qualities in general. It is true that the *person* struggles with their feelings, but their feelings are *their* feelings, feelings which have in part arisen from the life which they have led, and choices which they have made in the past. Struggling with one's feelings is different from struggling with something external to oneself. I am not clear how this relationship between the person and their feelings should be explicated, and I am not convinced that Gendlin has given a satisfactory account of the matter. On the other hand, I think that in his theory we can find hints of the way forward.

For Gendlin, all organic events 'imply' other events. For instance hunger 'implies' eating, eating 'implies' digestion and so on. Hunger goes on implying eating until the animal encounters food, and then the implying of eating stops. In Gendlin's terminology the appearance of food 'carries forward' the implying which is hunger. In the psychological realm, anger implies attack, fear implies withdrawal and so on. Even the most difficult, painful and entangling feelings imply events that would carry them forward. Each difficult thing carries within itself the implication of what it requires in order for it to no longer imply what it does. The things that are 'wrong' or 'bad' in our lives imply what is needed for our lives to be better. As Mary Hendricks (2001, p. 135) puts it in an interesting study of UPR from a focusing-oriented perspective: 'What is twisted, stuck, painful has implicit movement. There is even a sense in which the twisted gives rise to untwisting. Untwisting inheres in twistedness.' It is for this reason that in therapy we need to accept unconditionally what is there; what is there, if we can stay with it, can show us what it needs in order to move forward. But this is difficult to do on one's own. It requires turning *towards* that which is painful, and experiencing its meaning. The therapist can help the client by adopting towards the client just that unconditional acceptance which the client needs to adopt towards their own experiencing. And the therapist can do this *genuinely* because he or she sees whatever is there in the client as an element in the client's moving forward. What the client feels and expresses may, taken in itself, be self-defeating or ugly or unethical, but the therapist knows that it is but an aspect of the process which is unfolding.

Gendlin (1997a, Chapter 4) has a way of thinking about time which is relevant here. Sometimes, when a suicidal client has recovered, they look back and say that they never really would have done it, they love life too much. From where they are now, this is a true account of how it was when they were feeling suicidal. But they may also *remember* how they felt at the time, which is quite different. There is a difference between how things were (we now see) and how we experienced them at the time. There is a sense in which, as time goes on, the past changes. In looking at a client with unconditional positive regard we are looking at them as if from that future point at which it will be clear that the 'bad' things contribute to the greater good. The therapist does not have to know how it is possible for the ugly things to be 'redeemed'; it is enough to have the attitude that everything has its place in the ongoing process of the client's life. There are clearly implications for ethics and spirituality here, some of which I have discussed elsewhere (Purton, 1998). I say a little more about Gendlin's view of time in Appendix A.

I have been suggesting how the 'standard' person-centred view of UPR can be reformulated in terms of Gendlin's approach. We could also consider how, conversely, Gendlin's view could be reformulated in terms of the standard account. I think that the reformulation would go something like this:

From the perspective of the standard account it is the therapist conditions which are central. However, these conditions can be embodied either superficially or in what Mearns (1997) calls 'relational depth'. A superficial embodiment of UPR is one in which the counsellor accepts the client in the sense of being warm, supportive, accepting, sympathetic and non-judging. This kind of UPR embodiment is very appropriate in many kinds of helping relationships, such as welfare work or citizens advice. It also provides a good *foundation* for counselling work. However, UPR in its full embodiment involves 'being able to meet the client at sufficient depth to work at the existential level of the client's experiencing. . . .When I am working with my client at the existential level of his experiencing it means that he is giving me access to his innermost feelings and thoughts about his Self and his very existence' (Mearns, 1997, p. 16). The 'acceptance' here is not simply of the client, but of the client's existential experiencing. Trainee counsellors often provide support for, and acceptance of, their clients through giving helpful suggestions, or reassurance which *distracts* the client from what they are experiencing. They manifest 'acceptance' in the sense of being kindly disposed towards the client and trying to ease the client's pain. This is not accepting the client at relational depth; it leaves out the full experiential aspect of UPR. From this perspective Gendlin's view does not *add* anything to the standard account of UPR but rather explicates and emphasises the existential, experiential and relational-depth aspect of the notion.

Empathy

Rogers' (1959, pp. 210–11) classical definition of 'empathy' was:

> [B]eing empathic, is to perceive the internal frame of reference of another with accuracy and with the emotional components and meanings which pertain thereto as if one were the person, but without losing the 'as if' condition. Thus it means to sense the hurt or the pleasure of another as he senses it and to perceive the causes thereof as he perceives them, but

without ever losing the recognition that it is *as if* I were hurt or pleased or so forth.

According to Rogers the reason that empathy is crucial is that the client needs to feel understood if the conditions of worth are to be dissolved. The therapist's unconditional positive regard would clearly be ineffective if the client felt that the therapist were not seeing them as they saw themself. The client would feel 'Of course you can accept me if you see me like *that*, but I'm not like that, I'm like this, and no-one could accept a person like *this*.'

For Rogers, then, what is crucial is that the therapist should understand the client and that the client should experience this understanding (along with the therapist's acceptance). One important way of checking that the therapist has understood is through reflecting back to the client what the therapist thinks the client meant. Reflection can thus be understood as a procedure for checking on the accuracy of the therapist's empathy, but it needs to be distinguished from empathy itself. There are other ways in which the therapist may show that they have understood the client, some of which may be quite idiosyncratic to the situation (Bozarth, 1984).

For Gendlin, what is crucial is that the therapist should facilitate the client's carrying-forward of their experiencing. An important aspect of doing this is through the therapist reflecting back to the client the therapist's articulation of the client's experiencing. The client can then check whether what the therapist has said does articulate their experiencing. Often it does not, but this lack of understanding by the therapist is not *necessarily* a bad thing. Though being *mis*understood we can come to appreciate what we really do feel. (I think here of Jung who at one stage of his life used to tell his dreams to his gardener. The gardener always made utterly inappropriate interpretations which allowed Jung to arrive at helpful interpretations through thinking 'Well, it's certainly not *that*!'.)

On the other hand, as in the case of unconditional positive regard, empathy usually *helps* the client to go further into their own experiencing. Lack of empathy may make the client feel that their experiencing is not understandable and hence not worth staying with. More important, if the client is at present unable to articulate their experience, articulation by the therapist becomes crucial. In Gendlin's (1964b/ 1973, p. 469) words 'To be myself I need your responses, to the extent to which my own responses fail to *carry* my feelings *forward*. At first, in these respects, I am "really myself" *only when I am with you*.'

But to be able to articulate the client's experiencing the therapist must be empathically in tune with the client. Empathy, in the sense of being in tune with the client's experiencing, so that client and therapist can together refer to 'this feeling' or 'what you are sensing here', is often central to the therapeutic process. But *only* often – clients sometimes find it impossible to believe that the therapist could understand them, but the change process takes place in spite of this. (Gendlin (1990, p. 213) remarks that he himself was such a client.) In such cases therapy can still be effective because what it depends on is not *primarily* whether the client feels understood, but on the process of articulation of what is implicit. Whether the client feels understood or not, the therapist's responses can serve the function of drawing the client's attention to the 'edge' of their experiencing, and of encouraging the client to carry that experiencing forward.

As with UPR we might reformulate Gendlin's view in terms of the 'standard' view of empathy. Again the central point would be that there are forms of empathy which are relatively superficial (such as being aware that the client is angry, or sad, or jealous, ...), but also the kind of empathy where the therapist is engaging with the client at an experiential level where at first neither may be able to articulate the client's experiencing, yet the therapist accurately senses or tunes in to that experiencing. Gendlin's perspective could thus be characterised as one which emphasises the experiential and relational depths of empathy.

Congruence

As we saw in Chapter 2, there are serious difficulties in Rogers' notion of congruence. Rogers seems to have thought that these difficulties could be resolved by the development of new kinds of measurement, but I suggested that the difficulty is a conceptual one. The phenomenon of incongruence is something that we can recognise when we come across it; we do not need the development of new tools of measurement to establish whether a person is incongruent or not.

From Gendlin's perspective incongruence is a matter of a person not adequately symbolising their experiencing, where 'experiencing' (unlike Rogers' 'experience') refers to what is going on in that person's awareness. To pick up on Rogers' example in Chapter 2, someone says that he feels admiration for his father, then on further reflection and discussion says that nevertheless he does find his father irritating sometimes ... in fact quite a lot of the time ... there are even aspects of his father's personality that he does not like...and even hates. This process of differentiation and symbolisation of one's experiencing is precisely what goes on in therapy, and after several months of therapy, perhaps, the man may one day say, with vehemence, that he hates his father. He may then add that he has always hated him.

Here (where Rogers would say that the man has indeed always hated his father, though up to now this experience has been denied to awareness) Gendlin (1959, 1964b/1973, 1999) has a novel perspective, which I referred to briefly in Chapter 3. His view is that at the earlier time the man was in a state of implicit hatred. That is, he was in a state which would naturally have emerged as hatred had the hatred not been blocked. What happens in therapy is that the block is released and the hatred is expressed in words and/or behaviour. Gendlin holds that the hatred was not just there, waiting. What was there was a whole intricate situation with the father, one aspect of which was being expressed as admiration, while another aspect was blocked aggression, expressed perhaps in bad moods and depression. There was something wrong, but there was no hatred, only that which would lead to aggression given the circumstances which would release it. Gendlin compares such situations with the experience of hunger: hunger is a state which naturally leads to eating. Eating, we could say, is the expression of hunger, but we cannot say – except quaintly and metaphorically – that the eating was there, waiting to appear. At the earlier time the person *was not eating*, but they were in a state which, in Gendlin's terminology, 'implies' eating. Similarly, we can say that our man's anger is an expression of his relation to his father, but we should not say – except quaintly and metaphorically – that the anger was there, waiting to appear. At the earlier time the man *was not angry*, but he was in a state which 'implied' anger.

For Gendlin, this earlier state, like all states, is indefinitely intricate. It is the resultant of a myriad of events and influences: the man's early childhood experiences, what had happened to him at school, his experience of how his parents related to each other, the effect of an illness when he was a teenager and how his father had reacted to that, and so on. His present state carries the implications of all this, implications which cannot be neatly parcelled out, but which form an intricate whole to which, in therapy, for example, he can give his attention. As he focuses on 'all that about me and my father', words and images may arise which give expression to 'all that'. It is 'heavy', 'paralysing', but in that 'paralysed' thing there is ...something... irritation...yes, but an energy in it...anger, yes hatred, but also pain and . . . pity? To say he is 'now aware of the anger he had not felt before' is a very crude and misleading description of the situation. The reality is that an indefinitely intricate situation has been carried forward in a particular way which expresses some new aspects of what had up to now been only implicit. The saying 'I am angry' is not a matching of symbols to experience but an expression of his experiencing (which might instead have been expressed by striking his father). In Gendlin's view therapy does not succeed through people coming 'to know what they really feel', but through the changes in them which come about through expressing what was implicit, but blocked.

Gendlin's notion of 'implying', that is, of implicit states later being articulated in explicit statements and behaviour, enables him to think about incongruence in a new way. Incongruence is no longer a matter of a mismatch between symbols (such as saying 'I'm not angry') and a state of mind (being angry), but an incomplete expression of one's experiencing. From Gendlin's perspective we are congruent (authentic) when what we say flows from the totality of our experiencing, when it formulates and expresses that experiencing. We are incongruent (inauthentic) when what we say comes from some other source, for example, from what we think should be said in such situations, from what we would theoretically expect, from habit, from what we have felt about similar situations in the past, from just one conceptualised bit of our experiencing or from what we would *like* to be true. Inauthentic expression is expression which does not come freshly from our current experiencing, but from some kind of conceptual structure which bypasses that experiencing. In Gendlin's terminology we are incongruent when we are structure-bound.

It may be worth adding that the difference between Rogers' and Gendlin's accounts of congruence is closely related to different philosophical perspectives on how language relates to the world. The traditional picture has been that language *represents* the world. The world is just there, with its complex structures. Words then symbolise different elements in the structures, and the structures of sentences mirror the structures in the world. This kind of view, often referred to as the 'picture' theory of language can be found in philosophy from Augustine to the early Wittgenstein. However, in the twentieth century, the difficulties in such a view of language became increasingly evident. In the later Wittgenstein, in postmodernism and in Gendlin's thinking, language is seen as *creating* meanings rather than as acquiring its meanings through 'corresponding to', 'reflecting' or 'being congruent with' a non-linguistic reality. In this more recent philosophy symbol-isation is no longer seen as involving congruence between 'symbols' and 'world', and this suggests that Rogers' notion of congruence does need to be reformulated. The geometrical metaphor of congruence (a matching of one thing to another) will itself need to be dropped, but this does not mean that authenticity will be any less significant a notion in psychotherapy. It is only the philosophical picture of authenticity as a 'matching' which needs to be set aside.

In Gendlin's account the essential structure of Rogers' thinking is retained. It remains true that the broad aim of therapy is to enable clients 'to become themselves', or to live authentically in whatever way is right for them. It also remains true that it is important for the therapist to respond to the client in an authentic way, that is, from the whole felt sense of their experiencing, rather than from the standpoint of a specific theoretical framework, or in any other way that imposes some specific form on the client which is not the *client's* form. The therapist needs to respond from *their* felt experiencing if the client is to be helped to do the same.

Conclusion

What I have tried to do in this book is to look at person-centred therapy from Gendlin's focusing-oriented perspective. This perspective itself originates in a way of thinking which sees concepts and theories as possible ways of relating to and carrying-forward our experiencing. It holds that there is something beyond the concepts, something which nevertheless responds, in different ways, to different conceptual formulations. Gendlin's perspective joins naturally with that of Rogers, in which the emphasis is not on the therapist's concepts but on the client and on the client's experiential frame of reference.

Gendlin's perspective allows space for there to be many different conceptual formulations of the nature of human personality, of psychological disturbance and of psychotherapy. It also allows for there to be many different therapeutic procedures. Amongst such procedures we find Rogers' procedure of reflection, Gendlin's Focusing procedure, the person-centred 'use of the self' procedure and also many other procedures which are characteristic of other schools of therapy. Any of these procedures may be helpful for a client, but it is crucial to Rogers' and Gendlin's thinking that there is also something which is not a matter of 'procedures' at all. This 'something' is the experiencing process of the client which is facilitated by the presence of the therapist. The mere presence of another person can be facilitative, so long as they are present in the receptive way which Rogers articulated. Then within that facilitative presence a variety of procedures can be used.

Focusing-oriented therapy as a 'school' of therapy involves the general background conditions of genuineness, respect and empathy, together with the reflective and focusing procedures characteristic of Rogers' and Gendlin's ways of working. However, the way of thinking behind focusing-oriented therapy points to a reformulation of how we might think about 'schools of therapy'. Gendlin's view, which is quite strongly confirmed by empirical research, is that most of the specific concepts and procedures which are characteristic of the different schools make little overall difference when it comes to therapeutic effectiveness. What does make a significant overall difference is the quality of the relationship between client and therapist, and the ability of the client to engage with their own experiencing. Rogers' and Gendlin's ways of working can be seen as ways of facilitating these two aspects of the therapeutic encounter, but that is not to say that other more specific procedures may not be very helpful for many clients. What is important, though, is that such procedures need to be employed in a focusing-oriented way, that is, in a way which continually checks back with the client what the impact of the procedure is on the client's experiencing. The important question is whether this procedure *here*, with *this* client, helps the client to move forward. From a focusing-oriented perspective, the procedures need to be employed within the overall felt sense of the therapy situation. They should not dominate a session, but be incorporated into it in a way which furthers the client's experiential process.

Yet while Gendlin's approach enables us to see that there can be many effective 'schools' of therapy, it also makes it clear that the philosophical principles behind person-centred practice are *fundamentally* different from the ways of thinking which characterise most schools of therapy. Most schools of therapy ground their practice in particular theories of personality or of human development (and such theories are there to a limited extent in the writings of Rogers and Gendlin themselves). However, Gendlin's way of thinking takes seriously the person-centred view that it is the *client's* way of conceptualising (interacting with) their experiencing which matters. Instead of another scientific theory of how people are, Gendlin provides a philosophical analysis of the relationship of experiencing to concepts in general.

Gendlin has little by way of a theoretical framework of personality or of human development into which the client's issues are to be fitted. He has a philosophical view of human beings as creatures in which there is a continuing interaction between experiencing and symbolic forms, but that is different from having a scientific theory of personality. Yet his approach is not anti-theoretical; theoretical ideas can be helpful to the client, but *which* theories will be helpful is a matter of how the client interacts with the theory. It is not decided in advance by the therapist which theoretical ideas will help the client. The more theoretical frameworks with which the therapist is familiar the better, since then there is a greater chance of the therapist responding in a way which will be helpful to *this* client. Similarly, the more therapeutic procedures with which the therapist is familiar the better, since then the therapist may be able to draw on something which will be helpful to *this* client. Gendlin's approach is radically *person*-centred; it is centred not on any scientific theory but on the 'person in there' who is to be helped in construing their lived experiencing in ways which carry *them* forward.

Gendlin's approach shows how the person-centred approach relates to other approaches. It is not on the same level as them. What is central to the person-centred approach – its *person*-centredness – needs to be there in *any* form of therapy if that therapy is to be effective. Classical person-centred therapy, that is, the form of therapy which pursues primarily the avenue of 'reflection of feeling', can reasonably be seen as one school of therapy amongst others, but this 'school' does not *constitute* person-centred therapy. Nor does the 'school' which emphasises 'the use of the self', in the sense of working with the specifics of client–therapist interaction. Person-centred therapy cannot be identified with *any* of the avenues of therapy; it is, rather, a matter of *how* one proceeds along an avenue.

Finally, Gendlin's position can help us to appreciate that any formulation of what is valuable in therapy, including the focusing-oriented formulation, can be used in ways which are unhelpful to the client. In a conference presentation Gendlin (1990, pp. 205, 206) said:

> What matters is to be a human being with another human being, to recognise the other person as another being in there. Even if it is a cat or bird, if you are trying to help a wounded bird, the first thing you have to know is that there is somebody in there, and that you have to wait for that "person", that being in there, to be in contact with you. . . .
>
> Do not let focusing, or reflecting, or anything else get in between. Do not use it as an in-between. Do not say: "I can stay here because I have my reflecting-method, I have my ping-pong-paddle, so you cannot get me. You say something? You get it back." There is a sense that we are armed, you see. We have methods, we know focusing; we have credentials; we have doctors. We have all this stuff and it is so easy for us to sit there with stuff in between. Do not let it be in between; put it out of the way.

This is, I believe, very close to the spirit of Carl Rogers' thinking. In an appreciative obituary of Rogers, Gendlin (1988, p. 128) records that on a video-recorded panel a few months before Rogers' death, 'there was an argument between those who uphold the pure client-centered method and those who integrate it with other methods. I said we need both groups. But Carl said, "I didn't want to find a *client-centered* way. I wanted to find a way to help people".'

Appendix A

The Wider Context

Psychotherapy does not exist in a vacuum. It is an activity which is inextricably connected with the rest of human life. Some relevant connections are:

- Principles and procedures in psychotherapy clearly have ethical and social implications.
- There is a creative element in psychotherapy which must in some way connect with creativity in the arts.
- Similarly, there must be connections with creative thinking in general.
- Views of psychotherapy are inevitably embedded in general philosophical conceptions of the nature of the world and our place in it.
- Human beings are embodied beings, so that ultimately there have to be connections between what goes on in psychotherapy, and the biological and physical underpinnings of our lives.
- Many of us feel that human beings have a spiritual dimension, and that too must stand in significant relationship with what goes on in psychotherapy.

In assessing any theory of psychotherapy it is important to take into consideration this wider context. Assessment of any form of psychotherapy should not be limited to empirical studies of process and outcome, as if therapy could be separated from everything else in our lives. The general principles which lie behind a psychotherapy will have implications elsewhere, and these implications need to be assessed as part of the assessment of the general principles. In this part of the book I will discuss briefly several areas in which Gendlin's principles can be seen to be illuminating or fruitful. In so far as this is so in these *other* areas, we have reason to take the general principles seriously. Then we can, with extra confidence, employ them in the field of psychotherapy.

To write at all adequately about these areas would require a whole chapter for each of them – or in some cases a whole book – but I hope at least to give some glimpses of the context and implications of Gendlin's thinking. What follows will be a set of swift, kaleidoscopic impressions, rather than a systematic survey.

Ethics and values

In wrestling with a moral problem we often seem to be pulled in two ways. There is often the immediate feeling of wanting to do something, but opposed to that is the pull of a moral principle, such as that of not hurting people or not taking what does not belong to us. Some philosophers, such as Kant, hold that morality is entirely a matter of acting from principle, from a sense of duty; if one also *wants* to do what duty prescribes, that creates the risk of doing the right thing for the wrong reasons. Others, such as Aristotle, hold that we *only* act morally when our character has developed to the point that we naturally want to do what is in accordance with moral principles. Both these views contrast with the view that people should simply do whatever they want to do, and ignore 'moral principles' which are seen as constrictions laid upon the individual by the society.

Gendlin (1986b, 1996, Chapter 21) gives us a novel way of looking at these issues. For Gendlin a human being is not an organism on which society *imposes* its values; a human being is an *interaction* between organic feeling, and the general concepts and principles of society. Much of what we feel about what is right and wrong, we have picked up from parents and others. Later we may come to sense that some of these absorbed principles do not fit our developing experience, and we modify or reject them. But the others we keep; the fact that we learned them from others is no reason for saying that they are not *our* principles, any more than it is for saying that what we have learned from others about history or science is not *our* knowledge.

Whether a way of thinking or feeling is ours is not a matter of where it came from, but of whether it connects *now* with our own experiencing. From our society we absorb some principles which naturally fit with our experiencing, others which are initially uncomfortable but with which we later come to appreciate and identify with, and still others which we cannot feel comfortable with and which we need to reject. We will only take the third kind of case as the norm if we mistakenly think of human beings as initially isolated organisms which later have to be 'socialised'. Rogers always held that as people become more themselves they become *more* sensitive to the needs of others, more 'moral', but his theoretical framework (which sets 'organismic experience' against 'conditions of worth' imposed by society) makes it difficult to understand *why* this is so. For Gendlin there is still a real distinction between moral principles which are our own, and principles which we live by in an inauthentic way, out of fear, or habit, or anything other than our immediate experiencing. But the distinction does not rest on where the principles come from; it rests on whether the principles in question are really alive for us in our immediate experiencing, or whether we are telling ourselves that we 'ought' to feel that way when really we do not.

Gendlin's thinking allows for the case where we *genuinely feel* that we ought to feel different from the way we do feel (e.g. we genuinely want to feel

accepting of certain kinds of people that we cannot yet feel accepting of).
It is not a matter of whatever we feel being right for us. In this connection
I think that Harry Frankfurt's (1971) distinction between first- and second-
order desires is helpful. It is characteristic of human beings that we not only
have our desires and feelings but also have desires and feelings *about* our
desires and feelings. It can seem that in Focusing, and in the person-centred
approach generally, we are encouraging people just to follow their feelings,
irrespective of the impact of this on others. But that is a misunderstanding.
Rather, we are encouraging people to notice their feelings, to stay with
them, to sense what needs to be acted on and what does not, taking into
account the whole of their experiencing *including their moral principles*.

It may seem that there is still a question of why we need moral principles
at all. Why can we not simply rely on our immediate felt experiencing in
making a moral choice? In terms of Gendlin's theory the answer is that
experiencing is always an interaction between the immediate feeling-process
and something general. An animal simply *reacts* to events in its *environment*
out of its feeling-process, but a human being *responds* to a *situation* which
is constituted as much by what is general and social as by the individual's
feeling-process. For example, an animal simply reacts to threat with
counter-threat or flight. A human being may be inclined to do the same, but
can also respond in terms of a general awareness that 'tit-for-tat' responses
can be harmful, or that giving in to bullying is not a good thing. In the
human response there are general principles involved. These are not imposed
on human beings, but partly constitute what *human* responses are.

There is then the vexed question of *which* moral principles we should
subscribe to, given the variety of such principles found in different societies
or within subgroups of a single society. This is a question which has become
especially acute as we have become more aware of the variety of moral positions which can be adopted. Here Gendlin's answer is that the moral principles
which are right for us are those which arise from our engaging fully with
the whole of our experiencing. Consider the example of a student who is
trying to decide whether he ought to abandon his university career. Suppose
he says after a short discussion that his parents really want him to stay and
that he does not want to let them down, that settles the matter. His friends
then criticise him for doing the wrong thing, on the grounds that young
people should not do what their parents tell them to do. Or suppose he says
that it's just silly doing something you do not want to do, so he's going to
leave. His parents then criticise him for doing the wrong thing, on the
grounds that people should make the most of the educational opportunities
which they have. Here there are conflicting moral reactions. It can seem
that the important issue is whether the friends or the parents are right, but
who is to say *who* is right?

Now a counsellor working with the student is unlikely to adopt the position
of either the friends or the parents. The counsellor helps the student to

reflect on what is right for the student to do, but *this* process of moral reflection does not begin with general principles. It begins with the student going into his experiencing, exploring new aspects of it, such as the general difficulty he has in making decisions, the associated self-doubt, his contempt for himself for being so indecisive and so on. Out of this process of exploration something will emerge. It may be that he decides to leave the university or it may be that he decides to stay, but *either way* it now seems appropriate to say that he has made the right decision. That the decision is a good one is not a matter of its content but of the process by which it is reached.

The process is one of going into one's experiencing and making new distinctions in terms of one's feelings. But this is not to say that moral principles are not involved. On the contrary, it may be that the moral principles with which the student is confronted by his friends and parents are exactly what stir up his feelings. In his counselling sessions he may well be reflecting on the principle that one should not waste one's opportunities. How does that feel? Does it make him feel trapped, or does it bring a sense of challenge? Then again the student may be confronted with the principle that young people should not be doing what their parents tell them to do. Does this bring a sense of excitement and novelty, or does it touch on a deep sadness that his parents have never understood him? When we bring moral principles up to our experiencing there is an interaction. Our experiencing changes, and so do our principles. Having had *that* experience I can no longer hold on to this moral principle, at least not in its original form. But also having looked at my life through the lens of this moral framework I no longer experience the situation in the same way.

Looking at moral principles in this process-oriented way frees us from the dilemma of having to choose between moral principles as statements either of absolute truths or of mere personal preferences. Moral principles do not tell us what to do, nor do they express what we want; rather, they provide an avenue along which we can explore what to do. They can be a means of carrying us forward in our quest for what is good.

It is axiomatic that in a person-centred therapeutic context the therapist should not try to impose their values on the client, but at the same time the therapist needs to be authentic with the client, and not pretend to be value-neutral. This has sometimes seemed a dilemma in the person-centred approach. But from Gendlin's perspective there is no difficulty in principle. The therapist can try out making value statements such as 'every child should be cared for' – such statements can have an experiential impact. A client may implicitly hold to this value without connecting it with certain aspects of their *own* childhood. When the therapist puts forward this value statement explicitly, the client may resonate with it, and begin to connect it to the fact that they were not themselves cared for.

Gendlin will sometimes try out value statements on the client which are experientially alive for him, and which he thinks *might* be experientially alive for the client: for example (1996, p. 265) 'People have a right to at least some times for themselves', (p. 266) 'Every child should be cared about', (p. 267) 'You shouldn't have had to try to give her what she needed.' Sometimes this helps the client carry forward, sometimes (p. 267) not. Where it does not help the client to carry forward Gendlin drops the value statement and goes back to what the client is feeling.

I think that Gendlin is saying that moral principles are pointless unless they move us in some way. In contexts where they do not move us it is best to drop them and go back to the feelings. But that is not to say moral principles are of no use – on the contrary they often do move us, but no one can know whether a particular person in a particular context will be so moved. If stating a moral principle evokes an experiential response in someone, then they are helped to that extent. Moral principles get a bad name through people trying to persuade other people to follow them without the experiential response being there. So we need to be value-neutral in the sense of having no fixed views about which moral principles will help which people and when.

Social and political implications

Gendlin has always been concerned with the social and political aspects of his work. He has from the beginning encouraged the development of groups, known as 'Changes' groups, in which listening and focusing can be learned and practised. Like Rogers, he has been sceptical about the professionalisation of the therapy world and has written about 'The politics of giving therapy away' (Gendlin, 1984c).

In addition to these practical measures Gendlin has written on the theoretical implications of his views for how we can understand the relationship between the individual and the society. He criticises the influential tradition, coming partly from thinkers such as Adorno and Foucault, according to which everything human is a 'social construction', so that there is then nothing in the individual human being which can resist the imposition of social controls. According to this view it is an illusion to suppose that by turning to one's own experiencing one can find anything which will provide an authentic basis for challenging the norms of one's society; for one's experiencing has been formed by just those norms.

Gendlin traces the origins of this view to the beginnings of modern science, when for the first time a mathematical grid was imposed on our experiencing. Kant's philosophy then developed the view that all our experiencing must conform with the principles of pure reason which exist *a priori*. Finally, the principles which determine the nature of our experiencing were identified with the structures of society which are imposed by the exercise of power. Then there is no longer anything significant in the human being which is independent of society. Even what we might think of as the basic needs of our body are so imbued by societal structures that it no longer makes any sense to speak of a human nature in itself. Gendlin (1987, p. 256) quotes Foucault's aim 'to expose a body totally imprisoned by history and the process of history's destruction of the body'.

Gendlin relates this development to Freud's insistence that the ego is formed by society; there *is* another part of the person, the id, but the id is unstructured impulse which has no form of its own. It could also be related to the theme of behaviourist psychology that all significant human behaviour is *learned*.

Gendlin accepts that there is no human experiencing which is independent of the structures of society. But for him the relationship between the structures and experiencing is not a one-way imposition of the former on the latter. Rather, it is an 'interaffecting' relationship, in which, it is true, experiencing is always already affected by society, but it is also true that society is always an expression of human experiencing. The answer to the question of what is in the human being apart from the structures of society is the intricate organisation and functioning of the human body. This is admittedly deeply affected by the societal structures, but the structures are also deeply affected by *it*.

Through the work of the ethologists in the last sixty years it has become abundantly clear that not all animal behaviour is learned. Amongst the lower forms of animal life most behaviour is innately determined, but even in mammals and primates there is a blend of social learning with a very significant innate element. In animal societies, social learning elaborates on inherited behavioural structures, and there is no reason to think that it is different for human beings. Not only is there, undoubtedly, such a thing as the imposition of social forms on the individual human being, but there is also something that the forms are *imposed on*.

Gendlin applauds Foucault's demonstration that medicine and psychiatry, for example, can be forms of social control, but he insists that they *need not* function in this way. Instead of imposing on and controlling our experiencing, these social forms can carry it forward. In the same way instruction does not have to be indoctrination; it can be genuine education. The difference between the two is that indoctrination imposes its content, whereas education is sensitive to the experiencing of the learner, and presents the content in a way which carries the learner's experiencing forward.

Gendlin believes that modern society has reached an important point at which a growing number of people have become aware of the structures within which they live, and wish to find their own ways of living within, or creatively modifying, those structures. Although in many quarters the movement towards standardisation, quality control, explicit mission statements, performance criteria and so forth continues unabated, there is an increasing number of people who resist this tendency. Some of them would like to destroy the structures entirely, but many see that the way forward is rather to work at ways of making the structures fit better with human experiencing, to adapt the machine-world to human needs, rather than human needs to the machine-world.

Artistic creativity

Writing

Focusing can be used very effectively in the teaching of writing. Sondra Perl, a professor of English at the City University of New York, and former director of the New York City Writing Project, has been teaching creative writing to students at all educational levels for the last twenty years, using a suitably adapted form of Gendlin's Focusing instructions. Perl (1994, p. 79) has created a set of Guidelines for Composing:

> They are tools that invite writers to work directly with the felt sense, to use it to discover what they want to write and to rely on it as a guide, both in choosing words and knowing whether those words capture their intended meanings. More often than not, they lead to writing that is powerfully connected to the writer and powerful in its own right. ... The Guidelines for Composing are, essentially, a series of questions intended to call up and draw out writers' felt sense. They invite writers to stop, relax, pause, and listen quietly so they hear not only their usual thoughts but the silences between them

Perl emphasises the importance of the instructor's stance, which needs to be one which embodies respect, trust, caring and patience. In the writing group, facing a blank page can be a frightening experience, and part of the instructor's role is 'to ease the panic that often accompanies composition, the anxiety or fear of not-knowing that hits us just before we begin to create something. This is perhaps the most valuable aspect of the process: that another person is there to accompany us along a path that initially appears daunting' (p. 80).

Having established an atmosphere of safety in the group, Perl then gets the students to relax, and to jot down an inventory of what is on their minds, what they are thinking about these days. She then asks them to look over the list and see if any item is asking for attention, if any item 'jumps off the page at you'. The students are then asked to take that item and write it at the top of a new page. They then note down whatever comes to them in connection with that item. They are asked not to go into any particular association too deeply. Perl (pp. 84–5) then asks them

> to set aside all the bits and pieces and picture yourself holding the topic or issue in your palm. Stay there and just picture the whole topic right there, stretched out in front of you. I want you to look at the whole of it, not the

bits and pieces that are so familiar to you, and ask yourself the following questions: What makes this topic or issue so compelling or important? What is at the heart of this issue for me? . . . Now wait until you get a word, or phrase, or an image that captures your sense of the whole topic. Once you get it, write it down and begin exploring it. . . . As you write, let your felt sense deepen. See if it says you are on the right track. Notice what else it may be telling you. Can you experience the shift in your body that says "Yes, this feels right. This begins to say it"?

The students are then encouraged to write for fifteen minutes or so, and then Perl asks some closing questions:

Ask yourself: Where's this all leading? What's the point I'm trying to make? And write again whatever comes to you . . . . Once you feel you are near or at the end, ask yourself: Does this feel complete? If so, write down your answer. If not, ask, again: What's missing? And, again, look to your felt sense of the topic for some guidance. . . . Once you have a felt sense of where this is leading, ask yourself: What form might this be written in? Is this a poem? A play? A narrative? Is it a dialogue or a story or an essay? . . . Can someone else tell this story? Make some notes to yourself about what forms you might use or from whose point of view you might work as you compose your piece.

Perl comments (p. 87):

When the Guidelines are effective, what works is not so much a technique as a philosophy . . . . One key idea is that our individual ways of being are also, intrinsically, ways of being with others. Genuine voices can be forged, against all the odds, in the most adverse circumstances. But individual authenticity flourishes where such authenticity is also valued by the group. When using the Guidelines, we do not *tell* students they have something valuable to say. We *show* them. We say, in effect, that there is more to each person present than he or she is usually aware of . . . And what we work with when articulating meaning creatively is a sensate knowing that we can refer to and draw upon, even though it may never be fully said. To uncover this sense and to let what we thereby contact speak through us is no mere deciphering or decoding. It deserves to be called a higher literacy, for we 'read' the hitherto unwritten, and 'hear' what is not yet spoken.

Painting

Gendlin (1992, p. 199) writes:

The artist adds a line and then stands back . . . and feels very exactly whether the line is what it needs or whether that new line was wrong and must be taken out again. The artist might stand before such a design for a long time – even years, sensing but not finding the needed line. The design needs something, but what? It's not just unbalanced, as if adding most anything to the left side would do. No, it needs – uhm, ah, hmm, ... That blank seems to know what the design needs. Certainly it knows to reject the line the artist just tried. And also to reject many more lines that come and are never even drawn. That ... knows what and where a right new line goes, and yet that line has never existed before – in the history of the world.

The artist and psychotherapist Mical Goldfarb, having heard Gendlin speak about creativity, began to explore her own experience of creating works of art, and that of some fellow artists. She writes (Goldfarb, 1992, p. 180):

Much has been written about the process of art, about its creation and its creators. However, even the notes and journals of artists give few glimpses into the creative process as it is lived and felt: into the actual, particular, sensed experience of bringing a work of art into being.

Goldfarb interviewed several painters in the Seattle area, with a view to seeing whether they worked with a felt sense in their painting.

None of the artists interviewed specifically identified, located or dialogued with [an] inner feeling in a direct manner. In fact ... none of them had really thought about the relationship between their inner felt sense of wanting to create a painting and the creative process itself until my questions pointed to it. What emerged were descriptions of an attunement to an inner sense of something wanting to be created, and of an attention to this sense as an essential feature of the process of creating a work of art.

One of the painters, Kevin Harvey, told the story of his painting of 'the universe over the telephone wires and the trees'. He had been looking out from a friend's front porch one evening,

looking up and just seeing these weird angles of trees and these weird telephone wires ... I liked that image for some reason, and ... going back to his house, looking at it again in the daylight, not so much to get an exact replica of it, but just to capture the feeling which I first had when I saw it ... and also knowing that whatever it was that I saw there was important and it was important to get that feeling across to somebody else ... to know that [the painting] had the same feeling that I originally saw when I looked out ... I moved those telephone wires around a lot, just to make them have some sense of purpose. They had to have direction and purpose, otherwise they just seemed like a bunch of lines crossing a page ... otherwise they wouldn't have been convincing. They would have been read as telephone wires, but they wouldn't have read the same way ... not fitting the internal image.

Here we see the artist having the initial experience which feels important and which he wants to get across to others. He goes back to the friend's house to recapture the experience. Then he paints, and has to try out various things and move the wires around, so that they convey the experience he is trying to convey, so that they 'fit the internal image'. He comments:

> You start with knowing what it's supposed to be and then you go through all these stages where it isn't what it's supposed to be, and then it ends up being what it's supposed to be, even if it's not what it was when you started.

Another of the painters interviewed by Goldfarb, Pat DeCaro, remarked:

> sometimes it's not even an image, but it's a feeling of it, ... Sometimes there is an image of it, but a lot of times you may not even know what it would look like. But [you have] a sense of just what it is going to be ... [and] you do find it, and it is part by part ... you're working over here, and suddenly it tells you what to do over here, and then that tells you what to do in another part ... I wouldn't say the work's speaking to you, I think your self is speaking to you as you're working ... but its not articulated in words.

Not infrequently artists experience a block to their creativity. Goldfarb quotes Paul Klee: 'I have very definite feelings, but have not yet transformed them into art. So now I have to struggle again, and chiefly against the inhibitions that prevent me from exploiting my original talent. ... As if I were pregnant with things needing form, and dead sure of a miscarriage.'

Goldfarb describes her own experience of working on a large painting of a group of rocks off the coast of Washington which had great significance for her. She felt deeply the exact experience she wanted to express, as well as the image of the rocks which would be its vehicle. But she could not move forward with the painting; there was an inner sense of being blocked. Then she began to approach the *block* as a feeling, made room for it, and asked it to help her find a solution. Weeks later, she

> felt a rush of excitement in my middle. The image of the rocks of Stonehenge loomed suddenly in my mind's eye. The awe and reverence I had felt when I visited the great circle of stones years ago was with me in that moment. I knew that *this* was the felt sense of my painting, struggling to find its way onto the canvas and I saw that my adherence to a literal realism was exactly what was standing in the way of my ability to express my felt experience. Returning to the studio, I worked for hours on the painting, grouping the great stones off the coast as the monoliths stand on Salisbury Plain. Clearly, this was what was needed! By making room for the blocked feeling and accepting it as a natural part of the process of creating the painting, I allowed the unknown to be made known.

Creative thinking

Gendlin has developed a systematic way of applying his philosophy to creative thinking and theory construction in general. This procedure, known as 'Thinking at the Edge' (TAE), in effect applies the Focusing procedure to intellectual rather than personal problems. As with Focusing, Gendlin has laid out a series of steps which are intended as guidelines rather than as a rigid prescription which must be followed exactly. A full account of TAE can be found in a special issue of *The Folio*, the Journal of the Focusing Institute (2000–2003). It contains Gendlin's own account of the procedure, three detailed examples of its use (in the philosophy of science, text translation and psychotherapy theory), and applications in industry and ecology. A version of the paper on unconditional positive regard in psychotherapy change has already appeared in Hendricks (2001). I can only give a first taste of the procedure here.

TAE begins with the situation in which we have a sense that we know something important (in a field which we are familiar with), but cannot yet articulate or communicate what we know. We may say, 'There is something odd here – it feels I'm on to something.' As in Focusing we first sit with the felt sense of this as yet unclear place.

Then we notice that because there is something *new* here, it has something of a paradoxical or contradictory aspect to it. From the felt sense emerges something like 'It is this, yet it is not', for example 'Separating from a situation lets one have the situation.'

We then notice which words seem to be crucial to what we want to say, and write these words down, together with their standard meanings.

When these words are used with their standard meanings they do not really say what we want them to say. But words can always be used in *new* ways. When we made the contradictory sentence we did not mean the words in quite their normal senses. What then did we mean by them? We move between the words and the felt sense.

We can then notice that other words can work just as well. Using these other words we can write down several sentences which catch the crux of what we mean. The different sentences pull out different aspects of the felt sense, different strands in what we mean.

Next we collect examples or facets *of this which we mean*: anything which resonates with the felt sense of it, anything which carries it forward.

We write down a sentence for each facet which *would not be intelligible to anyone who was unfamiliar with what we mean*. It is a sentence which only makes sense when understood the way *we* mean it (it may contain metaphors or poetic forms of expression or juxtapositions of elements that would not normally go together).

Then we can cross the structure of two facets – we ask how each looks when seen in the light of the other.

Finally, from all this, what can emerge is a way of expressing what we mean which *can* be put in the public language. Further steps are then provided, which enable what has emerged to be built into a formal, logical theory.

'Thinking at the Edge' has developed out of a course on Theory Construction which Gendlin taught at the University of Chicago for many years. There is a close, dual, relationship between TAE and his theoretical work: not only were his theoretical concepts developed through the kind of process which TAE formalises, but also the theory, as formulated especially in *A Process Model*, constitutes an explanation of how it is that TAE (and Focusing) works.

Biology

In the late nineteenth century there was a battle between those biologists (the 'mechanists') who held that living things can be thought of as essentially physical systems, and those (the 'vitalists') who thought that in addition to the mechanisms of organic life there is also a 'vital force' in virtue of which an organism is a living thing. This battle was for all practical purposes won by the mechanists, and the notion of a 'vital force' which would distinguish living things from non-living things has no place in modern biology. And yet, we may feel, there *is* a difference: there is something different about living things, which is not just a matter of the complexity of their physical structures.

The basic issue here goes back to Descartes' dichotomy between human beings which have minds and other things which are just physical systems. This dichotomy leaves no room for conceiving of plants or animals as beings which are neither human nor merely physical. Aristotle, on the other hand, thought in terms of a four-way division of: material things, living things, animals and people, in which each category includes but goes beyond the preceding one. Gendlin's system is like Aristotle's in this respect (Gendlin is, amongst other things, an Aristotelean scholar). In *A Process Model*, he develops an intricate account of how we can think about the difference between organisms, animals and human beings, an account which neither reduces organisms and animals to mere physical systems, nor introduces speculative entities such as the vital force.

For Gendlin, the modern account of living things as mechanistic systems confuses a mechanistic *way of looking* at things (which has its place and value) with a view of what living things *are*. For Gendlin the actual living organism is an interaffecting whole which can for certain purposes and in certain respects be regarded as a set of mechanisms. But there is always more to a living thing than can be specified in terms of specific mechanisms. These 'mechanisms' are specific aspects of the organism which are 'pulled out' (discovered, created), as we bring our mechanistic conceptual scheme up to the living thing itself.

Although Gendlin does not discuss the concept, I think that his account helps us to make sense of the notion of 'function' in biology. The notion of function is not easy to elucidate. In the case of a machine we can say that the function of each of its parts is to contribute to the overall 'purpose' of the machine, which of course is determined by the purposes of human beings. But living things are not created by human beings for human purposes; they in some sense have their own purposes. But in modern biology there is no place for purposes; there are just mechanisms. It might seem that biology will have to get along without the notion of function (Manser, 1973), but that is clearly impossible. Biological thinking is permeated by the notion of function (Purton, 1978a,b, 2004). For example, function largely determines what *counts* as an organ of a particular kind. The eye of a fly is a very different sort of physical structure from the eye of a cat. They both count as eyes because of their function, because of the role they play in the life of the animal.

Now various attempts have been made to re-interpret 'function' in terms of what contributes to the survival of the organism, or to the survival of the species, or to the maximisation of reproduction of the genes involved, but none of these ways of thinking about function has proved really satisfactory. (For instance, if we think of function in terms of what contributes to the survival of the individual we will have difficulties with such things as the kangaroo's pouch; if we think in terms of what contributes to the survival of the species, or propagation of the genes, what are we to say of the characteristics of animals such as mules, which do not reproduce?) What we want to say, I think, is that the function of an organ or of a behaviour pattern is what it contributes to the *life* of the organism, but there is no way of saying that in mechanistic biology.

I think that Gendlin's concepts may be of help here. For Gendlin an organism cannot be adequately conceptualised as a mechanistic system. It needs, rather, to be thought of as an interaffecting whole. The life of the organism is the 'totaling' and 'focaling' (Gendlin, 1997a, pp. 46–7) of all its interaffecting processes, and the function of any process is a matter of what that process contributes to the organism's life as a whole. It is the 'interaffecting whole' that cannot properly be formulated in mechanistic biology, but function is a matter of what contributes to that whole.

Animal behaviour studies

An area in which I worked a bit, many years ago (Purton, 1978b), is ethology, the biological study of animal behaviour. In Gendlin's writings (e.g. 1991b, pp. 110, 132–5; 1993, pp. 4–5; 1997a, pp. 116, 139) there are a number of references to ethology, and in a way ethology could be said to be quite central to his project of developing a way of thinking about the body which allows for the possibility of focusing. It is the ethologists who have shown that there is much in animal behaviour which cannot be accounted for in terms of learning. The findings of ethology make it very implausible to assume that human behaviour and experience are determined entirely by social and cultural factors. They make it much more plausible that the social context interacts with, and gives a cultural specificity to, that which is *not* culturally determined.

It seems clear that in human beings what is 'cultural' and what is 'natural' cannot in fact be separated, but we can appreciate that there are *two* factors involved, not just one, through considering what happens in focusing and in creative activity generally. In these activities what is physically felt is changed through interaction with cultural forms, but also new forms are created out of what is felt. The experiencing of a creative artist arises in part from historical and cultural factors, but what is created may transform those very factors. Ethology can help us to appreciate this fact that there is more to experience and behaviour than that comes from learning or society.

Reflection on ethology can help us to understand Gendlin's position better, but it may also be that Gendlin's ideas will be of use to ethologists. Ethology is a branch of biology, not of psychology; animals, for the ethologist, are organic physical systems to be understood in terms of physiological mechanisms, biological function and evolutionary origin. Yet in reality, of course, we see and relate to animals in ways other than in this detached 'scientific' way. My cat clearly shows affection for me; we are fond of each other. How does *that* connect with movement patterns or physiology? Ethologists look at animals, but animals can *look back at us*. The fact that there is no place for this fact in our 'scientific' way of thinking about animals was something that struck me very much when I was working in the philosophy of ethology, and I was delighted to find this passage in Gendlin's work (1995, p. 146):

> Since Descartes, the scientists have had to avoid noticing the absurdity of the assumption that animals are just pattern*ed* machines, that there is no one looking back at them, just bits of color. We seem unable to think about what obviously looks at us.

Gendlin has written more on this in an unpublished paper titled 'On animals':

> I know that there is somebody in every dog, cat and cow. They see you seeing them, and touching them can keep them from being lost in the night and fog ... our society treats animals − as mere raw material. To become accustomed to it, one must be able to ignore the one in there who looks out at us. As long as that one has to be ignored in them, people hardly relate to that one in each other.

Until fairly recently, such matters would simply have been ignored by ethologists. However, there is now a relatively small, but still significant, school of 'cognitive ethology', originating from the work of Donald Griffin, which is prepared to think of animals in terms of concepts such as 'wanting', 'hoping' and 'intention' which mainstream ethologists still tend to regard as 'anthropomorphic'. Yet this cognitive ethology has its difficulties. While from a common-sense point of view the cognitivists are surely right in speaking of 'intention' and 'hope' in the context of chimpanzee behaviour, it may seem not quite so right to apply these concepts to ants or amoebae. People's intuitions differ here, but for most of us there comes a point in the scale of life where we do not seriously think of an organism as hoping, intending or even wanting. At some point – perhaps we have to come down to the level of jellyfish or even cabbages – the kinds of concepts we employ in thinking about people no longer have an application.

Now I suspect that one of the difficulties in current cognitive ethology is that the concepts currently available cannot capture much of the intricacy of animal behaviour. Griffin (1981, p. 115) writes of a chimpanzee:

> I submit that it may actually clarify our thinking to entertain such thoughts as 'Washoe *hopes* to go out for a romp, and *intends* to influence her human companions to that end,' or 'This bee *likes* one cavity better than the other, and *wants* her swarm to occupy the preferred one.'

Traditional ethologists would object to this. They would see terms such as 'hope', 'intention', 'liking' and 'wanting' as referring to unobservable inner states of the animal which have no use in ethological theory. Such a view has long been abandoned by most philosophers, and Griffin is surely right that to *entertain* such thoughts can lead to better ethological descriptions and explanations. However, the unease which the traditional ethologists feel is not entirely misplaced. Terms like 'hope' and 'fear' have intricate patterns of connections rooted in our human form of life. They may not be applicable without modification to the context of animals. (This is the familiar concern over the 'anthropomorphization' of animals.) Wittgenstein (1963) remarked:

> One can imagine an animal angry, frightened, unhappy, startled. But hopeful? And why not?

> We say a dog is afraid his master will beat him, but not, he is afraid his master will beat him tomorrow. (I, 650)

I think many people would feel that there *are* contexts where we could speak of a dog as hoping, but what about bees or ants? It can seem that we have to make a decision about whether the animal in question 'has a mind or not'. If it has, we can apply all our 'mentalistic' concepts such as hope, intention and so on; if it does not have then we must describe it in purely mechanistic or functional terms. But creatures such as ants or bees do not fit this dichotomy. 'Hope' and 'intention' seem out of place in describing their behaviour (the details of why this is so – if it is – need close examination), but that does not mean that the only alternative is to explain their behaviour in terms of physical mechanisms.

Griffin's reference to the bee *liking* one cavity better than another does not strike me as out of place (though I would hesitate over bees hoping). But 'liking' here probably does not have quite the same web of connections which it would have if we were speaking of a human being liking one site for a house better than another. It is a different, though related concept. I suspect that we get to it by the procedure Gendlin (1991b, pp. 96–9; 1997a, pp. 51–4) calls 'crossing'; that is, we bring our notion of human liking up to what we observe of bee behaviour and let the human-liking concept draw out certain aspects of bee behaviour that would not otherwise be prominent. Certainly there are implications in saying that a bee likes something. We are not attributing to the bee some unobservable inner state (which traditional ethologists would rightly dismiss as irrelevant to their work). When we say that the bee likes this cavity we are saying that the bee is registering the cavity, and there is some 'press' or tendency for the bee to do what is needed to get the swarm to settle there. The bee's state is one which, in Gendlin's sense, *implies* behaving in ways which will lead to that cavity being selected.

Gendlin's concepts (which I have barely touched on here) provide ways of thinking about living things and animals which are neither anthropomorphic nor mechanistic. They are the kind of concepts which ethology needs if it is to do justice to the study of animal behaviour. (Some of the material in this section is taken from an article on 'Ethology and Gendlin's Process Model' (Purton, 2004) in which I discuss the issues more fully.)

Medicine

Focusing has been used in a number of medical and health-care settings. For example Katonah (1991) studied the impact of Focusing on depression, hardiness, body cathexis, body attitudes and physical activity level in twelve cancer patients, the results showing a significant decrease in depression and a significant improvement in body attitudes. A number of other studies on the effects of Focusing on cancer patients appeared in the 1999 issue of *The Folio: A Journal for Focusing and Experiential Therapy*.

There is some evidence that Focusing may have a positive impact on immune functioning. There is background evidence for this possibility in a study (Kiecolt-Glaser *et al.*, 1985) suggesting that some enhancement of cellular immunity is accomplished through a regular practice of relaxation, and a study by Pennebaker *et al.* (1988) suggesting that self-disclosure of traumatic events can enhance the immune capacity. A further study by Lutgendorf *et al.* (1994), using the Experiencing Scale, suggested that disclosure in itself did not increase immunity, but that after Focusing questions were used to increase the patient's experiential involvement there was an increase in immune function. Katonah (1999, p. *vii*) concludes that it may be 'the manner in which one engages in the expression of the trauma that makes the difference in immune functioning rather than just talking or writing.... Utilizing focusing to increase experiential involvement may be a key variable in this area of psychoneuroimmunology.'

The 1999 issue of *The Folio*, referred to above, was devoted to the theme of Focusing and medicine. In addition to the material on cancer and immune reaction just mentioned, it contains a number of other papers on these themes. There are also interesting articles on using Focusing in working with conditions such as AIDS, chronic pain, memory impairment, stress and mild concussion.

Education

In 1997 another special edition of *The Folio* was devoted to the theme of Focusing with children. It contains papers on topics such the use of Focusing in Schools, Focusing using art with adolescents, and Focusing and play therapy with a 6-year-old child. There have been three international conferences on Focusing with children, held in Hungary in 1998 and 2000, and in Canada in 2002. This is a flourishing area of the Focusing world, more details of which can be found on the Focusing Institute website.

Time and space

To see the changes which occur in psychotherapy, for example, as 'explications' or 'carryings-forward' of earlier states brings with it a novel view of time. We look back on something that happened when we were in Paris, and acknowledge that we were jealous, although we were 'not aware of it at the time'. We can remember how we felt at the time, and we really did not feel jealous. In the time series which we *remember* there was no jealousy, at that time in Paris. But now, through reflection, and talking things over, we have come to reconstrue the Paris events. Our experiencing of the Paris events has been carried forward by our reflecting and our talking and now there is a reconstrued past in which we *were* jealous. The usual way of thinking makes out that this jealousy *was there* at the time, and forces us into speaking of 'unconscious feelings'. Yet there is no way of confirming the presence of an 'unconscious feeling'; it is by definition unknowable to the person who has it. Of course other people might say at the time 'He is obviously jealous', but in saying that they are only saying that various consequences are likely to ensue; they are not claiming some x-ray insight into how we feel at the time. (And if they did, they would be wrong, for there were no jealous feelings at the time.)

'Unconscious feelings' are a conceptual impossibility, but there are real phenomena to which this phrase points, the phenomena of explication and carrying-forward, and the 'doubled' nature of time in which what happened in the remembered past is distinct from what happened in the explicated past. The explicated past (what we might *now* say 'really' happened) emerges from explication, from interaction with other people or our own process of self-examination. There is a sense in which the interaction creates (as much as reveals) what really happened. The remembered past, on the other hand, is the images we have of a sequence of events laid out as if along a line which stretches into the past. It is the past as we imagine it in the present. It is what we can be trapped in if we do not allow our feelings and images to interact with something or someone who can carry us forward.

For Gendlin (1991b, 1997a), the kind of time which stretches out in a line is a late and characteristically human development. Animals do not live in this sort of time, because they do not have the resources to symbolise their experience in this way. Linear time requires the ability to reflect and hence to experience the repetition of patterns, so that there can be the experience of 'this is like that which I experienced before'.

Something similar applies in the case of space. The ability to reflect and experience things as *kinds* of things, to experience *patterns*, is an essentially human ability. Animals have a sense of space, but it is the immediate lived space of their behaviour in context. Human beings can see things *as* of a certain kind, they can see *aspects* of things. They can imagine things as if seen from the point of view of someone else. The three-dimensional framework of space allows for the seeing of aspects, and Gendlin (1997a, Chapter 7) argues that conversely the development of symbolic behaviour, initially in the form of gestures, is what lies at the heart of our ability to envision the world as stretched out in space and time. Human space and time are thus not independent realities, but are generated from the human mode of interaction.

Physics

There has for a long time been a tension in physics between the conceptual frameworks of relativity theory on the one hand and quantum mechanics on the other. One aspect of this is that although relativity abandons Newton's notion of absolute space and time and makes the space–time co-ordinate frames relative to the observer, it nevertheless employs overall space–time co-ordinate frames within which events are specifiable. Quantum mechanics, on the other hand, thinks in terms of an interactional framework in which events cannot be specified at all except through the *interaction* by which they are detected and measured. The attempt to combine relativity with quantum mechanics leads to well-known anomalies which have to be dealt with in *ad hoc* and theoretically unsatisfactory ways.

Gendlin collaborated with the theoretical physicist Jay Lemke in looking at these difficulties (Gendlin and Lemke, 1983). In Gendlin's scheme of things interaction always comes first, which suggests that the general scheme of quantum mechanics should be seen as the fundamental one in physics, and that where relativity and quantum mechanics together generate anomalies, the reason is likely to be that relativity theory has not freed itself from the traces of 'absolute space and time' which still inhere in it. From Gendlin's perspective, space and time, as overarching frameworks within which events take place, are constructions which are derivatives from actual interactions. Particles, too, as specified in terms of energy intensities at particular space–time locations are a secondary construction out of interactions. A particle can only exist as an aspect of an interaction; there cannot be an isolated particle. For Gendlin, the physical world, as much as the human world, is an interactive order in which space, time, and individual particles and organisms exist only as manifestations of interaction.

So far as I know, Gendlin's work has not had any direct impact in theoretical physics, but Professor Mark Bickhard (2003) of Lehigh University writes in this connection:

> The 1983 paper seems roughly prescient about some developments in string theory, such as there being a proper space–time for each world tube, instead of a background space-time in which interactions take place, but this seems to have emerged from the mathematics rather than from that paper.

Philosophy

As we saw in Chapter 3, Gendlin originally trained as a philosopher, and about half of his published work is in that field. The main influence in his philosophical work comes from the tradition of phenomenology and existentialism, and reading works such as Merleau-Ponty's *Phenomenology of Perception* can be very helpful in understanding Gendlin's thinking. (In Spain Carlos Allemeny insists that his focusing-oriented psychotherapy trainees should study some of this philosophical background.)

Gendlin (1989, p. 404) sketches the beginnings of his philosophy in the following way. He writes:

> As an undergraduate I developed a method to communicate with religious people *and* atheists, Marxists *and* McCarthyites, Behaviorists *and* Freudians. My method was to accept anyone's entire system – for the moment – so as to use *their* terms to couch whatever point I wanted to make. I would explain that I didn't agree with all that, I was only postponing all other arguments, so that I could make one point. I found I could formulate any *one* point in *any* system. I knew that "the" point was not the same in different terms, since "it" had the different implications I postponed. The difference was clear. But what was the sameness? In what respects was "it" still "that" point, moving across the formulations?

On coming to the University of Chicago, Gendlin recognised one part of his puzzle in the work of Richard McKeon, who argued that there are a number of alternative philosophical frameworks through which the world can be viewed, each self-consistent, but incompatible with the others. Another part of his puzzle he found in the work of the phenomenologists who knew that there was more to a 'point' than its formulation. Thirdly in the writings of Dilthey he found the element of *creativity* that is present in all understanding: in reformulating a point we create something new; 'it re-makes itself out of us' (*ibid.*, p. 406).

Other influences on Gendlin's thinking were the American pragmatists, and indirectly, Heidegger, with whose ideas he became familiar through other people who had read him. Gendlin did not read Heidegger himself until 1963 because he had heard about Heidegger's one-time Nazi connections. However, having seen an 'unusable' translation of Heidegger's *Die Frage nach dem Ding* he set about making his own translation and wrote an analysis of it.

> I sent the book to Heidegger. I wrote him "In the Analysis I explained every point I did not understand at first". He answered: "You have written an illuminating afterword with great penetration. It will make my work more accessible in your country". He was always kind in these things. And/or he saw that I grasped and showed his more-than-conceptual thinking (*ibid.*, p. 408)

Gendlin's *Analysis* was published along with the English translation, which is titled *What is a Thing?* (Heidegger, 1967).

Although Gendlin formulated his position before the contemporary debates on postmodernism developed, he sees his philosophy as offering a way through the current difficulties. Like McKeon, postmodernism sees that there are many ways of conceptualising the world, but is unable to formulate the point that there is something that is conceptualised, or the point that some conceptualisations are better than others. To use one of Gendlin's examples, it is absurd to fly to a philosophy conference by aeroplane while arguing that the laws of aerodynamics are a mere 'social construction'. Gendlin's solution to this problem is not easy to explain briefly, but in essence he holds that the world is an implicit and interactional order which responds differently but precisely to the conceptual schemes we bring to it. Some schemes carry us forward, while others do not. The world *is not* what any of the schemes say, but it responds differentially to those schemes. The schemes draw forth different responses, just as in the special case of psychotherapy where a particular formulation of an issue can resonate with us and carry us on, whereas another formulation leaves us unmoved.

Gendlin's work has attracted some interest amongst philosophers of language who are concerned with these problems. A book edited by David Levin (1997) contains the comments of fourteen philosophers on different aspects of Gendlin's thought together with his responses and his own summary of his position.

One final aspect of Gendlin's philosophy should be mentioned. Like his teacher McKeon he is a significant Aristotelean scholar, and has for thirty years or so been working on a commentary to Aristotle's *De Anima*, a work which could rather anachronistically be described as 'Aristotle's psychology'. As I mentioned above, Aristotle, unlike Descartes, allows for categories of beings other than people and material objects, and in particular for living things as a distinctive kind of entity. Behind the more recent work of the phenomenologists and pragmatists I think that Gendlin's work can be seen as quite deeply rooted in Aristotle.

The philosophical aspects of Gendlin's work may seem rather daunting to the non-philosophical reader. However, I have along with Rob Foxcroft, Kye Nelson and Barbara McGavin, taught aspects of his philosophy to people interested in Focusing at a summer school in Scotland. Gendlin initially believed that this project could not succeed, but to my surprise almost as much as his, it has proved a success. For the last three years people have come to the Isle of Cumbrae and we have looked at the philosophical ideas which are most relevant to Gendlin's work, and examined in detail his first book *Experiencing and the Creation of Meaning*, and then the even more forbidding *Process Model*. Gendlin (2002) has commented 'I am becoming interested in this fascinating fact that there are people without philosophical training who can hear, feel, think this work . . .'

Spirituality

In Focusing we open ourselves to what may come. We are active in bringing our attention to a murky felt sense, and in asking questions such as 'What is this?' or 'What does this need?', but then we wait . . . and often there is a response. A word or an image 'comes', and there is a sense of release.

This opening of oneself to something else, to something unknown, clearly has something in common with spiritual practices such as prayer and meditation. There is also a parallel, Gendlin (1984d) suggests, with the notion of *obedience* to that which lies beyond ourselves. He suggests that there are many forms of obedience which are not to be commended: obedience to other people, to the dictates of one's superego (which Freud identified with God), to one's own wishes and plans, or to one's own fears. Nor should we immediately follow whatever comes from our opening to the (. . .), the felt sense. It is rather an obedience to what comes from the dialogue with the (. . .) over a series of steps. The (. . .) or 'edge of awareness' is to be valued (p. 196) because it is a porous borderzone through which new steps come that we could not have made.... That edge or border which we do sense has to be distinguished from the other side which is vastly more, and which we do not sense as such. What comes in one moment in such a sense is not the other side! It is only a little bit from the other side, and already mixed with how we are and have been. So we cannot simply obey one such step, sense or edge, either. After a while more steps come, and may change what seems right.

Gendlin's reference to 'the other side which is vastly more' is reminiscent of William James' remark at the close of *The Varieties of Religious Experience* (1902/1985, pp. 457–8):

Let me then propose, as a hypothesis, that whatever it may be on its *further* side, the 'more' with which in religious experience we feel ourselves connected is on its *hither* side the subconscious continuation of our conscious life.

In his book *Religious Experiencing: William James and Eugene Gendlin* (Shea, 1987), the Augustinian priest John Shea has drawn attention to other elements in James's account of religious experiencing which are echoed in Gendlin's views, especially the emphasis on feeling and the transformation of feeling.

Two other Catholic priests, Peter Campbell and Edwin McMahon, have founded an Institute for Bio-Spiritual Research, which is devoted to the exploration of spirituality through Focusing. Details of their approach can be found in their book *Bio-spirituality: Focusing as a Way to Grow* (1985/1997). In a rather similar way, although not from a specifically Christian perspective, Elfie Hinterkopf (1998) writes about her way of using Focusing in a spiritual context with counselling clients. Her book is titled *Integrating Spirituality in Counselling: A Manual for Using the Experiential Focusing Method*.

A number of Buddhist thinkers have been drawn to Gendlin's work. Roger Levin (2003) in 'Focusing and Spirituality' (Focusing Institute Website 2003) writes:

The American meditation master Robert Aitkins Roshi once suggested in an introduction to Zen Buddhism that students beginning serious study of Dharma could find no better preparation than to learn Focusing. Buddhist Dharma holds that our perception of self and the world, in fact our entire sense of reality, is constructed of less-than-conscious habits of fixated attention which become rigidified into conditioned patterns of defensive judgments designed to control experiencing in order to maximize pleasure or avoid pain. However, it is these very attachments or conditioned habits of experiencing which are, paradoxically, the root cause of human suffering in the Buddhist view.

In a book on Buddhist psychology John Welwood (2000, p. *xiii*) writes that 'Gendlin opened up the whole world of inner experiencing for me. He was the first person I ever met who spoke directly about the actual process of felt experience – how it works, how it unfolds and leads to sudden, unexpected breakthroughs.'

There are clearly connections between what goes on in Focusing and what goes on in meditation (King, 1979; Amodeo, 1981a,b; Moore, 2001), but Gendlin (1996, pp. 65–6) notes that some forms of meditation involve a more thorough letting-go of everyday awareness. In Focusing we need to retain awareness of the bodily felt sense, whereas in at least some forms of meditation there is the movement into a state of consciousness in which body-awareness plays no role.

Taoism is another form of spirituality which clearly resonates with Focusing. In their book *Grace Unfolding: Psychotherapy in the Spirit of the Tao-te Ching* (1991, pp. 2, 60) Greg Johanson and Ron Kurtz write:

> From the outset the *Tao-te Ching* points to both the inevitability and the inadequacy of words. . . . Words can name and create meaning, bringing experience to expression and understanding. However they can never capture precisely what *is*. We can get lost in words. They can separate us from experience . . . In his classes on the Focusing Method, Gendlin teaches ways in which people can concentrate on the alive, *felt sense* of an issue as opposed to wandering off into disembodied theories *about the issue*. Although experiential, bodily knowledge can be frightening because it is so radically raw and uncontained by our theories. Lao Tsu cautions against exchanging it for the conventional wisdom of abstractions which place a veneer over truth.

Kurtz (1990) has developed a form of therapy – Hakomi Therapy – which draws on Taoism and body-oriented forms of psychotherapy, and which is very consonant with focusing-oriented principles.

As well as connecting with various forms of spirituality, focusing may have implications for religious practice. Gendlin suggests that religious ceremonies can often lose their effectiveness because they become detached from the participants' immediate experiencing. He suggests a project (Gendlin, 2000) in which, after a religious service, participants might take time simply to say something about how the words of the liturgy connected with their own experiencing. This way of responding could be initially modelled by the person leading the service, for example by saying something such as

> 'He heals the sick and frees the bond' – where am I currently 'bound'? – Here is a promise that I could be free – ah – . . . there is my longing to be

free – what would it be like to be free? Can I 'taste' it? It would be right to be free – it says here that the Universe (or whatever All That should be called...) could free me – without any particular shape or answer I am relating to this promise of no longer being so bound – in that way I know myself to be bound, that I felt at the start.

Participants could also form Focusing partnerships which could meet after the service, or at some time before the next service, so that there could be further opportunities to express the experiences elicited by the service.

This procedure would bring religious experiencing into the community:

> Many people are lonely, not because they don't know community groups to which they could go, but because what happens there will feel superficial, and will not inwardly reach and touch them. Then attending is only an effort, an added expenditure of energy rather than the strengthening and support that community used to provide.... The present project proposes first connecting the communal meanings to the inner experiencing process, so that they can cross, enrich and be enriched by the unique and intricately detailed meanings that arise from experiencing. Secondly, the project builds into the structure of community a time and pattern of inviting, reaching for, and hearing from the unique individuals.

There is one further aspect of spirituality which Gendlin does not discuss explicitly, but to which his work seems clearly relevant. In his classic work *The Idea of the Holy*, the German theologian Rudolf Otto (1923/1958) suggests that the field of the holy has two dimensions. There is an ethical dimension (a holy person is a good person) and there is what he calls the 'numinous' dimension (a holy person is seen as being in touch with, or informed by, numinous power). Something of these two dimensions can also be seen in the use of the English word 'spiritual'. If we emphasise one dimension we come to the saintly person who lives by high ideals; if we emphasise the other we come to the shaman, the person who is in touch with the spirits. For Otto, both dimensions are essential to the holy. The holy without the numinous is the sphere of morality; the holy without the ethical is the realm of the uncanny.

Given the scientific world view which is dominant today the numinous has for many people shrunk to vanishing point. Of course the *phenomena* of the numinous, such as telepathy, clairvoyance, precognition and 'far memory' are still reported, but they are dismissed as fraudulent, or due to mere imagination or psychopathology. These phenomena form a category, investigated by the rather dubious discipline of 'parapsychology', only because they do not fit into the framework of scientific thought. That is, they break the space–time–causality model which is (in spite of the development of quantum mechanics) seen not just as a model, but as the *reality* of things.

However, in a philosophical framework such as that of Gendlin, all this looks different. For Gendlin the space and time with which physics deals is a lately developed human construction. *This* space and time is generated by human interaction, in perhaps the same sort of way that quantum interactions *generate* a space and time rather than occurring within an already established space–time framework. In Gendlin's philosophy space and time are not the substantial forms which we have inherited from Newtonian physics. It is not that space–time framework which is primary, but the framework of personal life and interaction. This kind of position is not new; it is there in phenomenology and, in different ways, in the work of philosophers such as Heidegger and Wittgenstein. What is given, where we start from, is the human form of life. Science develops *within* that form of life.

The scientific world is a *human* creation, though not an arbitrary one. In a way this is obvious, but because science is taught today as the discovery of a reality independent of human beings, we can lose sight of it. Gendlin (1991b, pp. 42–3) shows how the change from taking the scientific picture as a model which is useful for certain purposes, to taking it as a representation of reality took place gradually between the time of Galileo and that of Kant. Early in this period Descartes was clear that science needs to develop through imposing its conceptual grid on nature, and

[f]or a century or more, people kept their eyes on both the elegant logical-mathematical order, and the messy natural order. They thought of science not as people think of it today, as telling us the facts of nature. Rather, they thought of science as a hypothetical scheme of mathematical constructions that we invent and impose. For example, look at how Rousseau begins the *Second Essay on Inequality*: For a few pages he summarises naturalistic observations and history. Then he says: "Let us set the facts aside...as our physicists do every day...and let us proceed hypothetically."....Today, people must read Rousseau's paragraph several times before they can believe that they have read it correctly. "How can he say that scientists set the facts aside?" they ask....People have forgotten that science "sets the facts aside". Now they think there are no facts other than scientific ones.

But, the paragraph also puzzles sophisticated philosophers. Like Descartes and Rousseau, they think of science as a construction we impose, but now they also think that nothing else is possible. Isn't anything else just a construction too? What is that, which Rousseau asks us to set aside? That natural order has been lost! Before, it was always there. In Rousseau's time it was still obvious that "the facts" are far richer and more confusing than science's clean hypothetical grids.

With Rousseau the natural order has its last moment.

It is to the restoration of our sense of the natural order – the order of interactional experiencing – that Gendlin's work points. Then, I think, *many* phenomena, especially in the realm of the human and spiritual, and including the phenomena of focusing, will find their natural place.

Appendix B

Resources

The Focusing Institute

34 East Lane, Spring Valley, NY 10977, New York
www.focusing.org   Tel./fax 914 362 5222.   email: info@focusing.org

Focusing Resources

2625 Alcatraz Ave, PMB #202, Berkeley, CA 94705 USA
www.focusingresources.com   Tel. 510 666 9948.   email: awcornell
@aol.com

Some English-language websites

www.focusing.org (Focusing Institute, USA)
www.focusingresources.com (Ann Weiser Cornell, USA)
www.focusing.co.uk (Peter Afford, UK)
www.focusing.org.uk (Rob Foxcroft, UK)
www.innerrelationship.com (Barbara McGavin, UK)

Journals

The Focusing Folio, published by the Focusing Institute.
The Focusing Connection, published by Focusing Resources. Back copies are available.

Research

Network for Research on Experiential Psychotherapies
www.experiential-researchers.org

References

Amodeo, J. (1981a) The complementary effects of meditation and focusing. *The Folio: A Journal for Focusing and Experiential Therapy*, **2**(3), 9–16.

Amodeo, J. (1981b) Focusing applied to a case of disorientation in meditation. *Journal of Transpersonal Psychology*, **13**(2), 149–54.

Armstrong, M. (1998) Treating trauma with focusing and EMDR. *The Folio: A Journal for Focusing and Experiential Therapy*, **17**(1), 23–30.

Baker, N. (2004) Experiential person-centred therapy. In P. Sanders (ed.) *The Tribes of the Person-Centered Nation*. Ross-on-Wye, PCCS Books, pp. 67–94.

Baldwin, M. (1987) Interview with Carl Rogers on the use of the self in therapy. In M. Baldwin and V. Satir (eds) *The Use of the Self in Therapy*. New York: Haworth Press, pp. 45–52.

Baljon, M.C.L. (2002) Focusing in client-centred psychotherapy supervision: teaching congruence. In *Client-Centered and Experiential Psychotherapy in the 21st Century: Advances in Theory, Research and Practice*. Ross-on-Wye: PCCS Books, pp. 315–24.

Barrett-Lennard, G.T. (1998) *Carl Rogers' Helping System: Journey and Substance*. London: Sage Publications.

Battye, R. (2003) Beads on a string. In S. Keys (ed.) *Idiosyncratic Person-Centred Counselling*. Ross-on-Wye: PCCS Books, pp. 151–71.

Bergin, A.E. and Garfield, S.L. (1996) *Handbook of Psychotherapy and Behavior Change*. Fourth edition. Chichester: John Wiley.

Bickhard, M. (2003) Personal communication.

Bozarth, J. (1984) Beyond reflection: emergent modes of empathy. In R. Levant and J.M. Shlien (eds) *Client-Centered Therapy and the Person-Centered Approach*. New York: Praeger, pp. 59–75.

Bozarth, J.D. (1996) Reflections and reactions to Carl R. Rogers with Mr. Vac: implications for future therapeutic interactions with severely disturbed clients. In R. Hutterer, G. Pawlowsky and P. Schmid (eds) *Client-Centered and Experiential Therapy: A Paradigm in Motion*. Frankfurt am Main: Peter Lang, pp. 495–8.

Bozarth, J. (1998) *Person-Centred Therapy: A Revolutionary Paradigm*. Ross-on-Wye: PCCS Books.

Brodley, B.T. (1988) Does early-in-therapy experiencing level predict outcome? A review of research. Discussion paper prepared for the Second Annual Meeting of the Association for the Development of the Person-Centered Approach, New York, May 1988.

Brodley, B.T. (1990) Client-centered and experiential: two different therapies. In G. Lietaer, J. Rombauts and R. Van Balen (eds) *Client-Centered and Experiential Psychotherapy in the Nineties*. Leuven: Leuven University Press, pp. 87–107.

Brodley, B.T. (1991) The role of focusing in client-centred therapy. Paper presented at the 1991 Annual Meeting of the ADPCA in Coffeyville, Kansas, May 23–27.

Brodley, B.T. (1999) About the non-directive attitude. *Person-Centred Practice*, **7**(2), 79–82.

Bucher, C. (2000) Why it was crucial for me to quit Focusing, and what came next. *The Focusing Connection*, **17**(3), 3.

Campbell, P.A. and McMahon, E.M. (1985/1997) *Bio-Spirituality: Focusing as a Way to Grow*. Chicago: Loyola Press.

Clark, C.A. (1990) A comprehensive process analysis of focusing events in experiential therapy. Doctoral dissertation, University of Toledo.

Coffeng, T. (1996) The delicate approach to early trauma. In R. Hutterer, G. Pawlowsky and P. Schmid (eds) *Client-Centered and Experiential Therapy: A Paradigm in Motion*. Frankfurt am Main: Peter Lang, pp. 499–511.

Cornell, A.W. (1990) *The Focusing Guide's Manual*. Berkeley: Focusing Resources.

Cornell, A.W. (1993) Teaching focusing with five steps and four skills. In D. Brazier (ed.) *Beyond Carl Rogers*. London: Constable, pp. 167–80.

Cornell, A.W. (1995) Relationship = Distance + Connection: A comparison of inner relationship techniques to finding distance techniques in Focusing. Paper presented at the First Conference on Focusing Therapy, Lindau-Bodensee, August 1995. Available at www.focusingresources.com.

Cornell, A.W. (1996) *The Power of Focusing*. Oakland: New Harbinger.

Cornell, A.W. (2001) The power of listening. Paper presented at 13th International Focusing Conference, Shannon, Ireland, May 2001. Available at www.focusingresources.com.

Cornell, A.W. (2003) Personal communication.

Cornell, A.W. and McGavin, B. (2002) *The Focusing Student's and Companion's Manual*. Berkeley: Calluna Press.

Corsini, R. (1973) *Current Psychotherapies*. Itasca, Illinois: Peacock Publishers.

De Silva, P. (1984) Buddhism and behaviour modification. *Behaviour Research and Therapy*, **22**(6), 661–78.

Draper, I. (2002) Swimming with the dolphins. *Person-Centred Practice*, **10**(1), 45–48.

Durak, G.M., Bernstein, R. and Gendlin, E.T. (1997) Effects of focusing training on therapy process and outcome. *The Folio: A Journal for Focusing and Experiential Therapy*, **15**(2), 7–14.

Ellingham, I. (2001) Carl Rogers' 'congruence' as an organismic, not a Freudian, concept. In G. Wyatt (ed.) *Congruence*. Volume One of *Rogers' Therapeutic Conditions: Evolution, Theory and Practice*. Ross-on-Wye: PCCS Books, pp. 96–115.

Elliott, R. (1989) Comprehensive process analysis: understanding the change process in significant therapy events. In M. Packer and R.B. Addison (eds) *Entering the Circle: Hermeneutic Investigation in Psychology*. Albany, New York: SUNY Press, pp. 165–84.

Elliott, R. *et al.* (1996) A process-experiential approach to post-traumatic stress disorder. In R. Hutterer, G. Pawlowsky and P. Schmid (eds) *Client-Centered and Experiential Psychotherapy: A Paradigm in Motion*. Frankfurt am Main: Peter Lang, pp. 235–54.

Elliott, R., Davis, K. and Slatick, E. (1998) Process-experiential therapy for posttraumatic stress difficulties. In L. Greenberg, J. Watson and G. Lietaer (eds) *Handbook of Experiential Psychotherapy*. New York: Guilford Press, pp. 249–71.

Flanagan, K. (1998) *Everyday Genius: Focusing on Your Emotional Intelligence*. Dublin: Marino Books.

Frankfurt, H. (1971) Freedom of the will and the concept of a person. *Journal of Philosophy*, **68**(1), 5–20.

Freud, S. (1936) *The Problem of Anxiety*. New York: Norton.

Geggus, P. (2002) Zero Balancing: Person-centred bodywork – or body-centred personwork. *Person-Centred Practice*, **10**(2), 88–95.

Gendlin, E.T. (1959) The concept of congruence reformulated in terms of experiencing. University of Chicago Counselling Center Discussion Paper, **5**(12).

Gendlin, E.T. (1962/1997) *Experiencing and the Creation of Meaning*. Second edition. Evanston, Illinois: Northwestern University Press (1997).

Gendlin, E.T. (1963/1968) Subverbal communication and therapist expressivity: trends in client-centered therapy with schizophrenics. *Journal of Existential Psychiatry*, **4**(14) (1963). Revised version in C.R. Rogers and B. Stevens (eds) *Person to Person: The Problem of Being Human*. Lafayette, CA: Real People Press, pp. 119–28 (1968).

Gendlin, E.T. (1964a) Schizophrenia: problems and methods of psychotherapy. *Review of Existential Psychology and Psychiatry*, **4**, 168–79.

Gendlin, E.T. (1964b/1973) A theory of personality change. In A.R. Mahrer and L. Pearson (eds) *Creative Developments in Psychotherapy*. New York: Jason Aronson (1973). Originally published in P. Worchel and D. Byrne (eds) *Personality Change*. New York: Wiley (1964), pp. 439–89.

Gendlin, E.T. (1968) The experiential response. In E.F. Hammer (ed.) *Use of Interpretation in Treatment: Technique and Art*. New York: Grune & Stratton, pp. 208–27.

Gendlin, E.T. (1969) Focusing. *Psychotherapy: Theory, Research and Practice*, **6**(1), 4–15.

Gendlin, E.T. (1970) A small, still voice. *Psychology Today*, June, pp. 57–9.

Gendlin, E.T. (1973a) A phenomenology of emotions: anger. In *Explorations in Phenomenology and Existential Philosophy*. The Hague: Martinus Nijoff, pp. 367–98.

240 References

Gendlin, E.T. (1973b) Experiential psychotherapy. In R. Corsini (ed.) *Current Psychotherapies*. Itasca, Illinois: F.E. Peacock, pp. 317–52.

Gendlin, E.T. (1978/2003) *Focusing*. Revised and updated 25th anniversary edition (2003). London: Rider.

Gendlin, E.T. (1980) Client-centered therapy as a frame of reference for training: the use of focusing during therapy. In W. De Moor and H.R. Wijngaarden (eds) *Psychotherapy: Research and Training*. Amsterdam: Elsevier, pp. 279–97.

Gendlin, E.T. (1983) On client-centered and experiential psychotherapy: An interview with Gene Gendlin. In W.-R. Minsel and W. Herff (eds) *Research on Psychotherapeutic Approaches*. Frankfurt: Verlag Peter Lang, pp. 77–104.

Gendlin, E.T. (1984a) Imagery, body and space in focusing. In A.A. Sheikh (ed.) *Imagination and Healing*. New York: Baywood Publishing, pp. 259–86.

Gendlin, E.T. (1984b) The client's client. In R. Levant and J.M. Shlien (eds) *Client-Centered Therapy and the Person-Centered Approach*. New York: Praeger, pp. 76–107.

Gendlin, E.T. (1984c) The politics of giving therapy away: listening and focusing. In D. Larson (ed.) *Teaching Psychological Skills: Models for Giving Therapy Away*. Monterey: Brooks/Cole, pp. 287–305.

Gendlin, E.T. (1984d) The obedience pattern. *Studies in Formative Spirituality*, **5**(2), 189–202.

Gendlin, E.T. (1986a) *Let Your Body Interpret Your Dreams*. Wilmette: Chiron.

Gendlin, E.T. (1986b) Process ethics and the political question. In A.-T. Tymieniecka (ed.) *Analecta Husserliana*, Vol. 20, Boston: Reidel, pp. 265–75.

Gendlin, E.T. (1986c) What comes after traditional psychotherapy research? *American Psychologist*, **41**(2), 131–6.

Gendlin, E.T. (1987) A philosophical critique of the concept of narcissism. In D. Levin (ed.) *Pathologies of the Modern Self*. New York: New York University Press, pp. 251–304.

Gendlin, E.T. (1988) Carl Rogers (1902–1987). *American Psychologist*, **43**(2), 127–8.

Gendlin, E.T. (1989) Phenomenology as non-logical steps. In E.F. Kaelin and C.O. Schrag (eds) *American Phenomenology: Origins and Developments*. Dordrecht: Kluwer, pp. 404–10.

Gendlin, E.T. (1990) The small steps of the therapy process: how they come and how to help them come. In G. Lietaer, J. Rombauts and R. Van Balen (eds) *Client-Centered and Experiential Psychotherapy in the Nineties*. Leuven: Leuven University Press, pp. 205–24.

Gendlin, E.T. (1991a) On emotion in therapy. In J.D. Safran and L.S. Greenberg (eds) *Emotion, Psychotherapy and Change*. New York: Guilford, pp. 255–79.

Gendlin, E.T. (1991b) Thinking beyond patterns. In B. den Ouden and M. Moen (eds) *The Presence of Feeling in Thought*. New York: Peter Lang, pp. 21–151.

Gendlin, E.T. (1992) The wider role of bodily sense in thought and language. In M. Sheets-Johnstone (ed.) *Giving the Body Its Due*. New York: SUNY Press, pp. 192–207.

Gendlin, E.T. (1993) Human nature and concepts. In J. Braun (ed.) *Psychological Aspects of Modernity*. Westport: Praeger, pp. 3–16.

Gendlin, E.T. (1995) Ultimacy in Aristotle: in essence activity. In N. Georgopoulos and M. Heim (eds) *Being Human in the Ultimate: Studies in the Thought of John M. Anderson*. Amsterdam, GA: Rodopi, pp. 135–66.

Gendlin, E.T. (1996) *Focusing-Oriented Psychotherapy*. New York: Guilford Press.

Gendlin, E.T. (1997a) *A Process Model*. New York: Focusing Institute.

Gendlin, E.T. (1997b) Reply to Hatab. In M.J. Levin (ed.) *Language Beyond Postmodernism: Saying and Thinking in Gendlin's Philosophy*. Evanston: Northwestern University Press, pp. 246–51.

Gendlin, E.T. (1999) Authenticity after postmodernism. *Changes: An International Journal of Psychology and Psychotherapy*, **17**(3), 203–12.

Gendlin, E.T. (2000) Focusing as part of spiritual renewal. Focusing Institute website: www.focusing.org.

Gendlin, E.T. (2002) Personal communication.

Gendlin, E.T. and Berlin, J.I. (1961) Galvanic skin response correlates of different modes of experiencing. *Journal of Clinical Psychology*, **17**(1), 73–7.

Gendlin, E.T. and Lemke, J. (1983) A critique of relativity and localization. *Mathematical Modelling*, **4**, 61–72.

Gendlin, E.T. and Shlien, J.M. (1961) Immediacy in time attitudes before and after time-limited psychotherapy. *Journal of Clinical Psychology*, **17**(1), 69–72.

Gendlin, E.T. and Tomlinson, T.M. (1967) The process conception and its measurement. In C.R. Rogers (ed.) *The Therapeutic Relationship and its Impact: A Study of Psychotherapy with Schizophrenics*. Madison: University of Wisconsin Press, pp. 109–31.

Gendlin, E.T. and Zimring, F. (1955) The qualities or dimensions of experiencing and their change. University of Chicago Counselling Center Discussion Papers, **1**(3). Reprinted in *Person-Centered Journal*, **1**(2), 55–67 (1994).

Gendlin, E.T., Jenney, R.H. and Shlien, J.M. (1960) Counsellor ratings of process and outcome in client-centred therapy. *Journal of Clinical Psychology*, **16**, 210–13.

Gendlin, E.T., Moursund, J.P. and Rogers, C.R. (1967) Putting the design into effect. In *The Therapeutic Relationship and its Impact: A Study of Psychotherapy with Schizophrenics*. Madison: University of Wisconsin Press, pp. 39–62.

Gendlin, E.T. *et al.* (1968) Focusing ability in psychotherapy, personality and creativity. In M.M. Shlien (ed.) *Research in Psychotherapy* (Vol. 3, pp. 217–41). Washington, DC: American Psychological Association.

Ghosh, A. (2001) *The Glass Palace.* New York: HarperCollins.

Goldfarb, M. (1992) Making the unknown known: art as the speech of the body. In M. Sheets-Johnstone (ed.) *Giving the Body Its Due.* New York: SUNY Press, pp. 180–90.

Goldman, R. (1997) Change in thematic depth of experiencing and outcome in experiential psychotherapy. Doctoral dissertation, York University, Ontario.

Goldman, R. (2002) The empty-chair dialogue for unfinished business. In J.C. Watson, R.N. Goldman and M. Warner (eds) *Client-Centered and Experiential Psychotherapy in the 21st Century.* Ross-on-Wye: PCCS Books, pp. 427–47.

Greenberg, L.S. (1979) Resolving splits: The two-chair technique. *Psychotherapy: Theory, Research and Practice,* **16**, 310–18.

Greenberg, L.S. (2002) *Emotion-Focused Therapy: Coaching Clients to Work Through Their Feelings.* Washington, DC: American Psychological Association.

Greenberg, L.S. and Safran, J.D. (1987) *Emotion in Psychotherapy.* New York: Guilford Press.

Greenberg, L.S. and Van Balen, R. (1998) The theory of experience-centered therapies. In L. Greenberg, J. Watson and G. Lietaer (eds) *Handbook of Experiential Psychotherapy.* New York: Guilford Press, pp. 28–57.

Greenberg, L.S., Rice, L.N. and Elliott, R. (1993) *Facilitating Emotional Change: The Moment-by-Moment Process.* New York: Guilford Press.

Griffin, D. (1981) *The Question of Animal Awareness.* Revised edition. Los Altos: William Kaufmann.

Hatab, L.J. (1997) Language and human nature. In M.J. Levin (ed.) *Language Beyond Postmodernism: Saying and Thinking in Gendlin's Philosophy.* Evanston: Northwestern University Press, pp. 234–46.

Haugh, S. (2001) The difficulties in the conceptualisation of congruence: a way forward with complexity theory? In G. Wyatt (ed.) *Congruence.* Volume One of *Rogers' Therapeutic Conditions: Evolution, Theory and Practice.* Ross-on-Wye: PCCS Books, pp. 116–30.

Hayashi, S. *et al.* (1998) Client-centred therapy in Japan: Fujio Tomoda and Taoism. *Journal of Humanistic Psychology,* **38**(2), 103–24.

Heidegger, M. (1967) *What is a Thing?* Chicago: Henry Regnery.

Hendricks, M. (2001) An experiential version of unconditional positive regard. In J.D. Bozarth and P. Wilkins (eds) *Unconditional Positive Regard.* Ross-on-Wye: PCCS Books, pp. 126–44.

Hendricks, M. (2002) Focusing-oriented/experiential psychotherapy. In D.J. Cain and J. Seeman (eds) *Humanistic Psychotherapies: Handbook of Research and Practice.* Washington, DC: American Psychological Association, pp. 221–51.

Hendricks, M. (2003) Dialogue between Mary Hendricks Gendlin and Marge Witty. *Person-Centred Practice*, **11**(2), 61–9.

Hendricks, M. and Cartwright, R. (1978) Experiencing level in dreams. *Psychotherapy: Theory, Research and Practice*, **15**(3), 292–8.

Hinterkopf, E. (1998) *Integrating Spirituality in Counselling: A Manual for Using the Experiential Focusing Method*. Alexandria, VA: American Counselling Association.

Holdstock, T.L. (1996) Discrepancy between the person-centered theories of self and of therapy. In R. Hutterer *et al.* (eds) *Client-Centered and Experiential Psychotherapy: A Paradigm in Motion*. Frankfurt am Main: Peter Lang, pp. 395–403.

Iberg, J.R. (2001) Focusing. In R. Corsini (ed.) *Handbook of Innovative Therapy*. Second edition. Chichester: John Wiley, pp. 263–78.

Iberg, J.R. (2002) Psychometric development of measures of in-session focusing activity: The *Focusing-Oriented Session Report* and the *Therapist Ratings of Client Focusing Activity*. In J.C. Watson, R.N. Goldman and M. Warner (eds) *Client-Centered and Experiential Psychotherapy in the 21st Century*. Ross-on-Wye: PCCS Books, pp. 221–46.

James, W. (1902/1985) *The Varieties of Religious Experience*. London: Penguin.

Johanson, G. and Kurtz, R. (1991) *Grace Unfolding: Psychotherapy in the Spirit of the Tao-te Ching*. New York: Bell Tower.

Jung, C.G. (1983) *Memories, Dreams, Reflections*. London: Fontana.

Katonah, D.G. (1991) Focusing and cancer: a psychological tool as an adjunct treatment for adaptive recovery. Doctoral dissertation, Illinois School of Professional Psychology, Chicago.

Katonah, D.G. (1999) Introduction to focusing and medicine. *The Folio: A Journal for Focusing and Experiential Therapy*, **18**(1), pp. *vi–viii*.

Kiecolt-Glaser, J.D. *et al.* (1985) Psychosocial enhancement of immuno-competence in a geriatric population. *Health Psychology*, **4**, 25–41.

King, J.W. (1979) Meditation and the enhancement of focusing ability. Doctoral dissertation, Northwestern University.

King, M. *et al.* (2000) Randomised controlled trial of non-directive counselling, cognitive-behaviour therapy and usual general practitioner care in the management of depression as well as mixed anxiety and depression in primary care. *Health Technology Assessment*, **4**(19).

Kirschenbaum, H. (1979) *On Becoming Carl Rogers*. New York: Delacorte.

Kirtner, W.L. and Cartwright, D.S. (1958a) Success and failure in client-centered therapy as a function of client personality variables. *Journal of Consulting Psychology*, **22**, 259–64.

Kirtner, W.L. and Cartwright, D.S. (1958b) Success and failure in client-centered therapy as a function of initial in-therapy behavior. *Journal of Consulting Psychology*, **22**, 329–33.

Klein, M.H., Mathieu, P.L., Gendlin, E.T. and Kiesler, D.J. (1969) *The Experiencing Scale: A Research and Training Manual*. Madison: Wisconsin Psychiatric Institute.

Klein, M.H., Mathieu-Coughlan, P. and Kiesler, D.J. (1986) The experiencing scales. In L.S. Greenberg and W.M. Pinsof (eds) *The Psychotherapeutic Process: A Research Handbook*. New York: Guilford, pp. 21–71.

Kurtz, R. (1990) *Body-Centered Psychotherapy: The Hakomi Method*. Mendocino, CA: LifeRhythm.

Lambers, E. (2000) Supervision in person-centred therapy: facilitating congruence. In D. Mearns and B. Thorne (eds) *Person-Centred Therapy Today*. London: Sage, pp. 196–211.

Lambert, M.J. and Bergin, A.E. (1994) The effectiveness of psychotherapy. In A.E. Bergin and S.L. Garfield (eds) *Handbook of Psychotherapy and Behavior Change*. Fourth edition. Chichester: John Wiley, pp. 143–89.

Leijssen, M. (1993) Creating a workable distance to overwhelming images: comments on a session transcript. In D. Brazier (ed.) *Beyond Carl Rogers*. London: Constable, pp. 129–47.

Leijssen, M. (1996) Characteristics of a healing inner relationship. In R. Hutterer *et al.* (eds) *Client-Centered and Experiential Psychotherapy: A Paradigm in Motion*. Frankfurt am Main: Peter Lang, pp. 427–38.

Leijssen, M. (1997) Focusing processes in client-centered experiential psychotherapy: an overview of my research findings. *The Folio: A Journal for Focusing and Experiential Therapy*, **15**(2), 1–6.

Levin, D.M. (ed.) (1997) *Language Beyond Postmodernism: Saying and Thinking in Gendlin's Philosophy*. Evanston: Northwestern University Press.

Levin, R. (2003) Focusing and spirituality. Focusing Institute Website: www.focusing.org.

Levine, P. (1991) Revisioning anxiety and trauma: the body as healer. In M. Sheets-Johnstone (ed.) *Giving the Body Its Due*. New York: SUNY Press.

Levine, P. (1997) *Waking the Tiger: Healing Trauma*. Berkeley, CA: North Atlantic.

Lietaer, G. (1998) From non-directive to experiential: a paradigm unfolding. In B. Thorne and E. Lambers (eds) *Person-Centred Therapy: A European Perspective*. London: Sage, pp. 62–73.

Lutgendorf, S. *et al.* (1994) Changes in cognitive coping strategies predict EBV-antibody titre change following a stressor disclosure induction. *Journal of Psychosomatic Research*, **38**(1), 63–77.

Mahrer, A.R. (1996) *The Complete Guide to Experiential Psychotherapy*. Chichester: John Wiley.

Manser, A.R. (1973) Function and explanation. *Aristotelean Society Supplementary Volume*, **48**.

Mathieu-Coughlan, P. and Klein, M.H. (1984) Experiential Psychotherapy: key events in client–therapist interaction. In L.N. Rice and L.S. Greenberg (eds) *Patterns of Change*. New York: Guilford.

McEvenue, K. (2003) *Wholebody Focusing*. Video tape, available from The Focusing Institute, New York.

McGavin, B. (2000) The power of presence. *The Focusing Connection*, **17**(4), July.

McGuire, K.N. (1991) Affect in focusing and experiential psychotherapy. In J.D. Safran and L.S. Greenberg (eds) *Emotion, Psychotherapy and Change*. New York: Guilford, p. 251.

McMullin, R.E. (1972) Effects of counsellor focusing on client self-experiencing under low attitudinal conditions. *Journal of Counselling Psychology*, **19**, 282–5.

Mearns, D. (1997) *Person-Centred Counselling Training*. London: Sage.

Mearns, D. (2003) *Person-Centred Counselling Training*. 2nd edition. London: Sage.

Mearns, D. and Thorne, B. (1988) *Person-Centred Counselling in Action* (second edition 1999). London: Sage.

Mearns, D. and Thorne, B. (2000) *Person-Centred Therapy Today*. London: Sage.

Merry, T. (ed.) (1999) *Learning and Being in Person-Centred Counselling*. Ross-on-Wye: PCCS Books.

Merry, T. (ed.) (2000) *Person-Centred Practice: The BAPCA Reader*. Ross-on-Wye: PCCS Books.

Moore, J. (2001) Acceptance of the truth of the present moment as a trustworthy foundation for unconditional positive regard. In J.D. Bozarth and P. Wilkins (eds) *Unconditional Positive Regard*. Ross-on-Wye: PCCS Books, pp. 198–209.

Moore, J. (2002) Listening within: counselling women in awareness of the body. In F. Poland and G. Boswell (eds) *Women's Minds, Women's Bodies: An Interdisciplinary Approach to Women's Health*. Basingstoke: Palgrave.

Mountford, C.P. (2001) Jonah and the dark side. *Person-Centred Practice*, **9**(2), 85–91.

Orlinsky, Graw and Parks (1994) Process and outcome in psychotherapy – noch einmal. In A.E. Bergin and S.L. Garfield (eds) *Handbook of Psychotherapy and Behavior Change*. Fourth edition. Chichester: John Wiley, pp. 270–376.

Otto, R. (1923/1958) *The Idea of the Holy*. Oxford: Oxford University Press.

Pennebaker, J.W. *et al.* (1988) Disclosure of traumas and immune function: health implications for psychotherapy. *Journal of Consulting and Clinical Psychology*, **56**, 239–45.

Perl, S. (1994) A writer's way of knowing: guidelines for composing. In A.G. Brand and R.L. Graves (eds) *Presence of Mind: Writing and the Domain Beyond the Cognitive*. Portsmouth, NH: Boynton/Cook, pp. 77–87.

Perls, F. (1969) *Gestalt Therapy Verbatim*. Lafayett, CA: Real People Publishing.

Polanyi, M. (1958) *Personal Knowledge*. London: Routledge & Kegan Paul.

Polanyi, M. (1967) *The Tacit Dimension*. London: Routledge & Kegan Paul.

Prouty, G.F. (1976) Pre-therapy, a method of treating pre-expressive psychotic and retarded patients. *Psychotherapy: Theory, Research and Practice*, **13**, 290–4.

Prouty, G.F. (1990) Pre-therapy: a theoretical evolution in the person-centered/experiential psychotherapy of schizophrenia and retardation. In G. Lietaer, J. Rombauts and R. Van Balen (eds) *Client-Centered and Experiential Psychotherapy in the Nineties*. Leuven: Leuven University Press, pp. 645–58.

Prouty, G.F. (1998) Pre-therapy and pre-symbolic experiencing. In L. Greenberg, J. Watson and G. Lietaer (eds) *Handbook of Experiential Psychotherapy*. New York: Guilford Press, pp. 388–409.

Purton, C. (1978a) Biological function. *Philosophical Quarterly*, **29**, 10–24.

Purton, C. (1978b) Ethological categories of behaviour and some consequences of their conflation. *Animal Behaviour*, **26**, 653–70.

Purton, C. (1989) The person-centred Jungian. *Person-Centered Review*, **4**(4), 403–19.

Purton, C. (1998) Unconditional positive regard and its spiritual implications. In *Person-Centred Therapy: A European Perspective*. London: Sage, pp. 23–37.

Purton, C. (2000a) Empathising with shame and guilt. In J. Marquez-Teixeira and S. Antunes (eds) *Client-Centered and Experiential Psychotherapy*. Linda a Velha: Vale & Vale, pp. 33–54.

Purton, C. (2000b) Introjection and the aliens within. *Person-Centred Practice*, **8**(1), 15–20.

Purton, C. (2002) Focusing on focusing. In *Client-Centered and Experiential Psychotherapy in the 21st Century: Advances in Theory, Research and Practice*. Ross-on-Wye: PCCS Books, pp. 89–98.

Purton, C. (2004) Ethology and Gendlin's Process Model. *The Folio: A Journal for Focusing and Experiential Therapy*, **19**(1), 114–23.

Rennie, D.L. (1998) *Person-Centred Counselling: An Experiential Approach*. London: Sage.

Rice, L.N. (1974) The evocative function of the therapist. In D.A. Wexler and L.N. Rice (eds) *Innovations in Client-Centered Therapy*. New York: Wiley, pp. 289–311.

Rogers, C.R. (1942) *Counselling and Psychotherapy: Newer Concepts in Practice*. Boston: Houghton Mifflin.

Rogers, C.R. (1951) *Client-Centered Therapy*. London: Constable.

Rogers, C.R. (1954) The case of Mrs Oak: a research analysis. In C.R. Rogers and R.F. Dymond (eds) *Psychotherapy and Personality Change*. Chicago: University of Chicago Press, pp. 259–348.

Rogers, C.R. (1956) The essence of psychotherapy: moments of movement. Paper given at the first meeting of the American Academy of Psychotherapists, New York, October 20.

Rogers, C.R. (1957) The necessary and sufficient conditions of therapeutic personality change. *Journal of Consulting Psychology*, **21**, 95–103.

Rogers, C.R. (1958) A process conception of psychotherapy. *American Psychologist*, **18**, 142–59.

Rogers, C.R. (1959) A theory of therapy, personality and interpersonal relationships, as developed in the client-centered framework. In S. Koch (ed.) *Psychology: A Study of a Science, 3. Formulations of the Person and the Social Context.* New York: McGraw-Hill, pp. 184–256.

Rogers, C.R. (1961) *On Becoming a Person.* London, Constable.

Rogers, C.R. (1963) The actualizing tendency in relation to 'motives' and to consciousness. In M.R. Jones (ed.) *Nebraska Symposium on Motivation. Current Theory and Research in Motivation, Volume X1.* Lincoln: University of Nebraska Press, pp. 1–24.

Rogers, C.R. (1967) The findings in brief. In *The Therapeutic Relationship and its Impact: A study of Psychotherapy With Schizophrenics.* Madison: University of Wisconsin Press, pp. 73–93.

Rogers, C.R. (1980) *A Way of Being.* Boston: Houghton Mifflin.

Rogers, C.R. (1986a) Reflection of feelings. *Person-Centered Review*, **1**(4), 375–7.

Rogers, C.R. (1986b) Client-centered therapy. In I.L. Kutash and A. Wolf (eds) *Psychotherapist's Casebook.* San Francisco: Jossey-Bass, pp. 197–208.

Rogers, C.R. and Russell, D. (2002) *Carl Rogers: The Quiet Revolutionary. An Oral History.* Roseville, California: Penmarin Books.

Rogers, C.R. and Wallen, J. (eds) (1946) *Counselling with Returned Servicemen.* New York: McGraw-Hill.

Ross, C.A. (1999) Subpersonalities and multiple personalities: a dissociative continuum? In J. Rowan and M. Cooper (eds) *The Plural Self.* London: Sage Publications, pp. 183–97.

Rothschild, B. (2000) *The Body Remembers: The Psychophysiology of Trauma and Trauma Treatment.* New York: W.W. Norton.

Sachse, R. (1990a) Concrete interventions are crucial: The influence of the therapist's processing proposals on the client's intrapersonal exploration in client-centered therapy. In G. Lietaer, J. Rombauts and R. Van Balen (eds) *Client-Centred and Experiential Psychotherapy in the Nineties.* Leuven: Leuven University Press, pp. 295–308.

Sachse, R. (1990b) The influence of therapist processing proposals on the explication process of the client. *Person-Centered Review*, **5**(3), 321–44.

Sanders, P. (ed.) (2004) *The Tribes of the Person-Centred Nation.* Ross-on-Wye: PCCS Books.

Schmid, P. (2000) Prospects on further developments in the person-centred approach. In J. Marques-Teixeira and S. Antunes (eds) *Client-Centered and Experiential Psychotherapy.* Linda a Velha: Vale & Vale, pp. 11–31.

Schore, A.N. (1994) *Affect Regulation and the Origin of the Self.* Hillsdale, NJ: Lawrence Erlbaum Associates.

Schore, A.N. (2003) *Affect Regulation and the Repair of the Self.* New York: W.W. Norton.

Seeman, J. (1988) Self-actualisation: a reformulation. *Person-Centered Review*, **3**, 304–15.

Shapiro, F. (1995) *EMDR*. New York: Guilford Press.

Shea, J.J. (1987) *Religious Experiencing: William James and Eugene Gendlin*. New York: University Press of America.

Slack, S. (1985) Reflections on a workshop with Carl Rogers. *Journal of Humanistic Psychology*, **25**(1), 35–42.

Smith, M.L. and Glass, G.V. (1977) Meta-analysis of psychotherapy outcome studies. *American Psychologist*, **32**, 752–60.

Standal, S. (1954) The need for positive regard. A contribution to client-centered theory. Unpublished doctoral dissertation, University of Chicago.

Stiles, W.B., Shapiro, D.A. and Elliott, R.K. (1986) Are all psychotherapies equivalent? *American Psychologist*, **31**, 165–80.

Stinckens, N., Lietaer, G. and Leijssen, M. (2002) Working with the inner critic: fighting the enemy or keeping it company. *Client-Centered and Experiential Psychotherapy in the 21st Century: Advances in Theory, Research and Practice*. Ross-on-Wye: PCCS Books, pp. 415–26.

Tausch, R. (1990) The supplementation of client-centered communication therapy with other validated therapeutic methods: a client-centered necessity. In G. Lietaer, J. Rombauts and R. Van Balen (eds) *Client-Centered and Experiential Psychotherapy in the Nineties*. Leuven: Leuven University Press, pp. 448–55.

Thorne, B. (1992) *Carl Rogers*. London: Sage.

Thorne, B. (2002) *The Mystical Power of Person-Centred Therapy*. London: Whurr Publishers.

Warner, M.S. (1998) A client-centred approach to therapeutic work with dissociated and fragile process. In L. Greenberg, J. Watson and G. Lietaer (eds) *Handbook of Experiential Psychotherapy*. New York: Guilford Press, pp. 368–87.

Warner, M.S. (2000a) Person-centered psychotherapy: one nation, many tribes. *Person-Centered Journal*, **7**(1), 28–39.

Warner, M.S. (2000b) Person-centred therapy at the difficult edge: a developmentally based model of fragile and dissociated process. In D. Mearns and B. Thorne (eds) *Person-Centred Therapy Today*. London: Sage Publications, pp. 144–71.

Watson (1984) The empirical status of Rogers's hypothesis of the necessary and sufficient conditions for effective psychotherapy. In R.F. Levant and J.M. Shlien (eds) *Client-Centered Therapy and the Person-Centered Approach*. Westport: Praeger, pp. 17–40.

Weitzman, B. (1967) Behavior therapy and psychotherapy. *Psychological Review*, **74**(4), 300–17.

Welwood, J. (2000) *Toward a Psychology of Awakening*. Boston: Shambhala.

Wijngaarden, H.R. (1990) Carl Rogers, Carl Jung and client-centered therapy. In G. Lietaer, J. Rombauts and R. Van Balen (eds) *Client-Centered and*

Experiential Psychotherapy in the Nineties. Leuven: Leuven University Press, pp. 469–79.

Wilkins, P. (2003) *Person-Centred Therapy in Focus.* London: Sage.

Wittgenstein, L. (1963) *Philosophical Investigations.* Oxford: Basil Blackwell.

Wittgenstein, L. (1966) *Lectures and Conversations on Aesthetics, Psychology and Religious Belief.* Oxford: Blackwell.

Worsley, R. (2002) *Process Work in Person-Centred Therapy.* Basingstoke: Palgrave.

Worsley, R. (2004) Integrating with integrity. In P. Sanders (ed.) *The Tribes of the Person-Centred Nation.* Ross-on-Wye: PCCS Books, pp. 125–47.

Zimring, F. (1990) A characteristic of Rogers's response to clients. *Person-Centered Review*, **5**, 433–48.

Index

(. . .) device, 154–5, 175–81
  see also implicit, the

acceptance, *see* unconditional positive
    regard
action
  and felt sense, 95, 137–8
  focusing and, 95
  working with, 136–8
actualising tendency, 14–15
  and carrying-forward, 197
  and conditions of worth, 36–8
  revision of concept, 33, 35–6, 197–8
  and social restraint, 34–8
  and therapeutic conditions, 26–7, 69
Adorno, T., 214
agricultural metaphor, 7, 31–4
Aitkins, R., 231
Alexander Technique, 142
Allemeny, C., 228
Amodeo, J., 232
animal behaviour studies, *see* ethology
animal(s)
  consciousness of, 223–5
  emotion in, 75–6, 193–4
  life, 184–5
Aristotelean world view, 187–8
Aristotle, 187, 188, 211, 221, 230
Armstrong, M., 142
artistic creativity, 216–19
'asking' (focusing step), 87
  stages within, 92
attention, and felt sense, 56, 70, 74, 81,
    176, 180, 195
Augustine, St, 205
authenticity, 36, 84, 205
  and carrying-forward, 84
  and felt sense, 36–8
  see also congruence; genuineness
'avenues' of therapy, 96, 108, 128–42,
    156, 196
  and therapy training, 165

Baker, N., 24
Baljon, M.C.L., 173
Barrett-Lennard, G.T., 3, 12, 13, 65
Battye, R., 21
behaviourist psychology, 215
'being oneself', and social restraint, 34–8
Bergin, A.E., 2, 53, 156
Berkeley, Bishop, 50
Berlin, J.I., 56
Bickhard, M., 228
biological concepts, 34, 221–2
blocked process, 71–3, 185–6, 191,
    204–5
body
  'felt from inside', 83
  lived, 197
  registering changes in, 141
  sensations and felt sense, 74–5, 93–4
  sense, 86, 105–6, 194
  working with, 141–2
Bozarth, J., 26, 27, 39, 43, 57, 146
British Association for Counselling and
    Psychotherapy (BACP), 168
British Focusing Teachers'
    Association, 172
Brodley, B.T., 25, 42, 145, 146, 152, 157
Bucher, C., 95
Buddhism, 29, 231–2

Campbell, P., 89, 231
carrying-forward, 54, 71–3, 102–3,
    181–2
  and actualising tendency, 197
  and authenticity, 84
  'direction of fresh air', 103
  and listening, 193
  in psychotherapy, 190–1
  and structure-bound process,
    79–80
Cartwright, D.S., 55
Cartwright, R., 132
catatonia, 126–8

catharsis, 123, 132

chair work, *see* empty-chair procedure; two-chair procedure

change-step, 5–6
    see also felt shift; moments of movement

change, and insight, 77, 102, 134–5, 154, 196

'Changes' groups, 214

children, focusing with, 225–6

Clark, C., 150, 161, 162

clearing a space, 29, 30, 87–8
    in focusing-oriented therapy, 105, 134
    'inventory', 105, 147
    and stress reduction, 88
    see also 'putting down' (focusing step)

client-centred response, 48–52

client-centred therapy, 3–4, 11–12

client–therapist relationship, 138–40
    depth of, 149–52, 201, 203
    difficulties in, 115–16

client vulnerability, 110–12

'client's client', 29, 44, 98, 153–4

client's frame of reference, 97

Coffeng, T., 124

cognitive ethology, 224

cognitive therapy, 135

community group, 166

Comprehensive Process Analysis (CPA), 161

concepts, and experiencing, 5, 54, 69, 74, 83, 113, 177–8, 191

conditions of worth, 4, 199
    and actualising tendency, 36–8
    and empathy, 202
    and psychological disturbance, 39–41
    and self concept, 14
    in training, 165

Conditions of Worth Theory, 15, 16, 18
    difficulties with, 39–41
    and directivity, 146

configurations/parts of self, 91, 120, 121

congruence, 14
    geometrical metaphor of, 46, 206
    nature of, 45–8
    revision of concept, 47–8, 203–6
    and Wisconsin Project, 66–7

see also authenticity; genuineness; incongruence, and structure-bound process

conscience vs inner critic, 117

core conditions, 4, 7, 13, 115–16
    see also acceptance; congruence; empathy; therapist conditions

Cornell, A.W., 89–91, 94, 95, 114, 119, 121, 135

counsellor, *see* therapist

creativity, 176, 185, 191–2, 229
    artistic, 216–19
    thinking, 220–1

critic, inner, *see* inner critic

'crossing', 178–9

cultural differences, 110, 186

cultural relativism, 189

curtailed experiencing, 122–4

De Silva, P., 136

DeCaro, P., 219

denial, 15

Descartes, R., 221, 230, 234

desensitisation procedures, 162, 199

desires, first- and second-order, 212

diagnosis, 18, 24, 143–5
    vs sensitisation, 109–10, 144
    see also expert knowledge

Dilthey, W., 152, 229

direct referent, 59–60, 74, 176, 194
    referent movement, 77
    see also felt sense

'direction of fresh air', 103, 141

directivity, 3, 8–9, 42–5, 145–9
    and coercion, 43
    and Conditions of Worth Theory, 146
    and influence, 42
    in process-experiential therapy, 23
    purist view, 26–7
    towards experiencing, 43–5
    see also process direction

dissociated process, 90, 121
    see also 'too distant' process

dissociation, 124

distortion, 15

divided experiencing, 119–21

Draper, I., 166

dreams, 122, 132

Durak, G.M., 158

'edge of awareness', 20, 138, 203, 230–1
    see also felt sense
education
    focusing in, 225–6
    and indoctrination, 215
Ellingham, I., 47
Elliott, R., 22, 23, 161
EMDR (Eye Movement Desensitization
        and Reprocessing), 142
emotion-in-action, 75
emotion(s)
    in animals, 193–4
    and experiencing, 114
    and felt sense, 74–6, 93–4, 113, 133
    *mis*construal of, 124–5
    moderation of, 112
    overwhelm, 6, 8, 133–4
    in process-experiential therapy, 24
    schemes, 24
    and situations, 193, 194
    working with, 132–4
    see also feeling(s); 'too close' process
empathy
    and conditions of worth, 202
    and reflection, 100, 109, 202
    revision of concept, 201–3
empty-chair procedure, 23, 123
encounter, 83
    see also 'interaction first'
encounter groups, 17
ethics, 84, 200, 211–14
    process view of, 212–13
ethology, 215, 222–5
    cognitive, 224
evocative reflection, 22–3, 124
evolution, 33
'exiled' process, 90
    see also 'too distant' process
existence, preconceptual, 82–3
existential philosophy, 44
experience
    Rogers' concept of, 46–8
    unconscious, 15, 46–7, 70, 196,
        226–7
experiencing
    and concepts, 5, 54, 74, 83, 114,
        177–8, 191
    curtailed, 122–4
    depth of, 159–60

difficulties in relating to, 109–28
directed quality of, 84
directivity towards, 43–5
divided, 119–21
and emotion, 114
helping client relate to, 96–109
intricacy of, 37, 69, 72, 101–2, 133
misconstrued, 124–5
and moral principles, 213–14
paranormal, 151–2
'pointing' to, 100–2, 107–8
preconceptual, 82–3
reflexivity of, 30
religious, *see* spirituality
and society, 214–16
suppressed, 121–2
and theories, 4
    see also concepts, and experiencing
experiencing level
    in early sessions, 63–4, 157–8
    and therapeutic change, 63–9, 157–62
    and therapist conditions, 62–4, 68–9
Experiencing Scale, 56, 61
    schizophrenics, 62–3
experiential psychotherapy, 2, 22
    see also process-experiential therapy
expert knowledge, 51–2
    see also diagnosis
externalising, 6, 8, 67–8, 90, 113–14
    see also 'too distant' process

feeling-process, 175–8
    momentum of, 180
feeling(s)
    ambiguity of term, 37
    and experiencing, 114
    and felt sense, 37, 38, 74
    following, and social restraint, 35
    misconstrual of, 124–5
    reflection of, 27, 49–51, 100, 209
    and situations, 150, 193, 194
    unconscious, 15, 46–7, 70, 196, 226–7
    see also emotion(s)
felt sense, 69–70, 73, 87
    and action, 95, 137–8
    and attention, 56, 70, 74, 81, 176,
        180, 195
    and authenticity, 36–8
    'components' of, 94

development of concept of, 74, 194–5
and emotion, 74–6, 93–4, 113, 133
and feelings, 37, 38, 74
finding, 176
formation of, 115
'forward direction' in, 103
full, 93–4
in group work, 140–1
and imagery, 93–4, 132
intricacy in, 115
and life situation, 93–4
in poetry, 69
in reading, 176–7
and self, 153–4
and sensations, 74–5, 93–4
in teaching Focusing, 92
and thinking, 135–6
unfolding, 76–7
in writing, 177–8
see also direct referent; edge of
        awareness
felt shift, 5–6, 103, 195–6
see also change-step; moments of
        movement
Fiedler, F.E., 13
'finding the right distance', *see* 'putting
        down' (focusing step)
Flanagan, K., 89
'focaling', 195, 197, 222
focusing
and action, 95
as self-help procedure, 86
as taught procedure, 8, 20, 80–1,
        84–95, 172
attitude of friendliness, 105
global application, 77
interactive, 94
measurement scales, 161–2
origins of, 54–81
phases of, 73–80
in process-experiential therapy,
        23, 24, 25
referent movement, 77
solitary, 116
and subjectivity, 95
teacher training, 172
unfolding in, 76–7
Wholebody, 95
see also Experiencing Scale

focusing co-ordinators, 172
focusing instructions, 84–91
    classical, 86–8
    original, 84–5
    variants, 89–91
focusing-oriented psychotherapy, 96–142
    empirical evidence, 158–62
focusing partnerships, 168–9
Foucault, M., 214, 215
Foxcroft, R., 230
fragile process, 110–12
Frankfurt, H., 212
Freud, S., 46, 47, 55, 56, 215, 230
Freudian theory, 15, 16, 46–7, 70–3
    see also psychoanalytic concepts
fully-functioning person, 167
function, biological, 185, 222

Galileo, 234
galvanic skin-resistance studies, 56
Garfield, S.L., 2
Geggus, P., 142
Gendlin, E.T.
    appreciation of Rogers, 209
    basic concepts, 82–4
    directs Wisconsin project, 62
    early work with Rogers, 54–61
    and Freud, 70
    and Heidegger, 229
    impact of Wisconsin project results,
        65–6
    influences on his thought, 54,
        229, 230
    philosophical background, 5, 54,
        74, 228–30
    social/political work, 214
general principles, 186, 191
genuineness, 12, 19–20
    see also authenticity; congruence
Gestalt therapy, 23, 120, 122, 123
    experientially oriented, 162
gesturing, in Gendlin's theory, 185
Ghosh, A., 6
Glass, G.V., 53, 156
Goldfarb, M., 218, 219
Goldman, R., 124
Greenberg, L., 22, 23, 24, 33, 121,
        122, 124
Griffin, D., 224, 225

group supervision, 169–70
group work, 17, 20, 64–5, 140–1
 'Changes' groups, 214
 group size, 167
 listening/focusing groups, 168
 in therapy training, 166–8

Hakomi therapy, 142, 232
'handle' (focusing step), 87
Harvey, K., 218
Hatab, L.J., 154
Haugh, S., 48
Hayashi, S., 28, 29
Heidegger, M., 229, 234
Hendricks, M., 106, 132, 158, 159,
 160, 200, 220
'Herbert Bryan', case of, 28–9
Hinterkopf, E., 231
Holdstock, T.L., 35
holy, dimensions of, 233–4
human potential movement, 35

'I' and 'it', 91–2, 113, 199–201
Iberg, J., 106, 161, 162
identification, 90
 see also 'too close' process
image space, 92
imagery
 and felt sense, 93–4, 132
 working with, 131–2
immune functioning, 225–6
implicit, the
 and creativity, 192
 (. . .) device, 154–5, 175–81
 function in experiencing, 177–8
 and the unconscious, 48, 70–3,
  204–5
implying, 71–3, 180–2, 190, 200
 and psychotherapy, 204–5
incongruence, and structure-bound
 process, 205
indoctrination, and education, 215
inner critic, 116–19
 creation of, 119
 energy of, 117–18
 and introjection, 118–19
 superego as, 117
 vs conscience, 117
 working with, 117–19

insight, and change, 77, 102, 134–5,
 154, 196
Institute for Bio-Spiritual Research, 231
integrationists, 20–2
 variant theory, 20–1
intellectualising, 6, 8, 67–8, 90, 113–14
 see also 'too distant' process
interaction, 7–8
 client and therapist, *see* client–therapist
  relationship
 experiencing and society, 214–16
 feeling process and attention, 175–6
 feeling process and words, 175–7, 180
 organism and environment, 34
 tradition and felt needs, 189
'interaction first', 182–3
interactional order, restoration of, 235
Interactive Focusing, 94
interactive order, in physics, 227–8
interaffecting, 182–3
interpretation, 134–5, 148
intricacy
 experiential, 37, 69, 72, 101–2, 133
 in felt sense, 115
introjection, 4, 14, 15, 199
 and inner critic, 118–19
'inventory' (focusing step), 105

James, W., 231
Jenney, R., 55
Johanson, G., 232
Jung, C.G., 21, 152, 202

Kant, I., 211, 234
Katonah, D.G., 225, 226
Kiecolt-Glaser, J.D., 225
Kiesler, D.J., 157
King, J.W., 232
King, M., 53, 156
Kirschenbaum, H., 46, 62
Kirtner, W., 55, 58
Klee, P., 219
Klein, J., 94
Klein, M.H., 157
knowledge, 187–8
Kurtz, R., 142, 232

Lambers, E., 18, 173
Lambert, M.J., 53, 156

language
    in Gendlin's theory, 185
    learning, 32
    picture theory of, 205–6
Leijssen, M., 49–50, 93–4, 115, 150,
    154, 158
Lemke, J., 227
Levin, D., 229
Levin, R., 231
Levine, P., 124, 162
Lietaer, G., 43
life
    concept of, 32–4, 222
    levels of, 184–9
'life-forward' direction, 197–8
listening, and carrying-forward, 193
locus of evaluation
    external, 14
    internal, 18
Lutgendorf, S., 225

McEvenue, K., 95, 142
McGavin, B., 89–91, 95, 119, 121, 230
McGuire, K.N., 134
McGuire, M., 94
McKeon, R., 54, 229, 230
McMahon, E., 89, 231
McMullin, R.E., 161
Mahrer, A., 25
'making a list' (focusing step), 105, 147
Manser, A.R., 222
markers of process difficulties, 23, 29
Mathieu-Coughlan, P., 157
Mearns, D., 4, 17, 18, 19, 20, 35, 36,
    42, 121, 148, 149, 164, 166, 201
medicine, focusing in, 225–6
meditation, 29, 232
memory, 226–7
'merged' process, 90
    see also 'too close' process
Merleau-Ponty, M., 228
Merry, T., 18
metaphor, 178
    agricultural, 7, 31–4
    creation of, 179–80
mirroring
    in childhood, 50–1
    in focusing-oriented therapy, 98
    and psychological disturbance, 40

Rogers' view, 49
    see also reflection
misconstrued experiencing, 124–5
moments of movement, 5–6, 57–8,
    59, 141
    see also felt shift; change-step
momentum, 180, 191
Moore, H., 50, 50
Moore, J., 37, 232
moral principles, 211–13
    and experiencing, 213–14
morality, see ethics
Mountford, C., 167
multiple personality disorder, 121
mysticism, 150, 151–2
    see also spirituality

Nelson, K., 230
non-directive reflective psychotherapy,
    3, 12, 16, 42, 48–52
non-directive 'rules', 67
'nothing between', 97, 209
numinous, 233–4

obedience, 230–1
organic life, 221–2
    as metaphor, 31–4
    see also agricultural metaphor
organism
    development of, 15
    and environment, 183–4
Orlinsky, D., 8, 159
Otto, R., 233
overwhelm, emotional, see emotion(s),
    overwhelm, emotional

painting, focusing in, 217–19
paranormal experiencing, 151–2
parts/configurations of self, 91, 120, 121
Pennebaker, J.W., 225
Perl, S., 216, 217
Perls, F., 120
person-centred therapy
    and procedures, 129–30
    relation to other approaches, 21–2,
        96, 130, 156, 196, 209
    standard view, see 'standard'
        person-centred therapy
'person in there', 98, 111, 112, 209

personal development groups, 166–7
personal interaction, working with, 138–40
phenomenology, 229
philosophy, 228–30
    existential, 44
physics, interactive order in, 227–8
plant life, 184
    as analogy for human life, 31–4
poetry, 69, 181–2
'pointing' to experiencing, 100–2, 107–8
Polanyi, M., 191
politics, 214
post-traumatic stress difficulties, 124, 162
postmodernism, 189, 205, 229
'pre-therapy', 128
preconceptual experiencing, 82–3
    see also concepts, and experiencing
presence, 90, 91
    of therapist, 19
problematic reaction points, 22–3, 124
process
    blocked, *see* blocked process
    dissociated, 121
    fragile, 110–12
    'too close', 90, 112–15
    'too distant', 90, 112–15
process difficulties, 24
    markers, 29
process direction, 29, 30
process-experiential therapy, 22–5
    and directivity, 147
    focusing in, 23, 161
    and focusing-oriented therapy, 109
    therapist conditions in, 23–4
process identification, 29, 30
Process Scale, 56, 61
process skipping, 144–5
process stages, 59–61
process/content distinction, 24, 147–8
Prouty, G., 126, 128
psychoanalytic concepts
    and client-centred concepts, 130
    see also Freudian theory
psychodynamic therapy, 138–9
psychological contact
    and 'pre-therapy', 128

psychological disturbance
    conceptualisation of, 125–6
    and conditions of worth, 39–41
    Gendlin's view of, 7–8
    and structure-bound process, 56, 192–3
psychopathology, 18
psychotherapy
    Gendlin's view of, 70–81, 175–206
    and politics, 213
psychotherapy theories, 130
    assessment of, 155, 162, 210
'purists', 19, 20, 25–7, 38–9
purpose, in organic world, 33
Purton, C., 88, 92, 118, 124, 129, 194, 201, 222, 225
'putting down' (focusing step), 87
    alternatives to, 92
    in focusing-oriented therapy, 105, 134
    imagery of, 88
'putting nothing between', 97–8, 209

quantum mechanics, 227–8
Quinn, R.D., 13

reading, felt sense in, 176–7
'receiving' (focusing step), 87
receptive attitude, 59, 96–7
referent movement, 77
reflection, 3
    body, 126
    discrimination in, 99
    and empathy, 100, 109, 202
    evocative, 22–3, 124
    of feeling, 27, 49–51, 100, 209
    in focusing-oriented therapy, 98
    functions of, 48–52
    situational, 126
    word-for-word, 126
    see also mirroring
reflexivity, 30
relational depth, 149–51, 201, 203
relativity theory, 227–8
release, 103
    see also moments of movement; felt shift
religious practice, 232–3
Rennie, D., 25, 29–30
repression, 15, 46–7
'resonating' (focusing step), 87

Rice, L.N., 22, 23, 29, 124
Rogers, C.R.
 appreciation of Gendlin, 58, 59, 62
 early work, 2, 3, 11–16, 100
 empathic reflections, 109
 and Freud, 15–16, 46–7, 55
 and group work, 17, 20
 impact of Wisconsin project results,
  64–5, 66
 later work, 7, 19–20, 27
 move to California, 64–5
 and 'schools' of therapy, 52–3, 129
 terminology, 3, 4
 theory of self, 12
 view of theories, 1
role-play, 137
Ross, C.A., 121
Rothschild, B., 124, 162
Rousseau, J.-J., 234, 235

Sachse, R., 159, 160, 162
Safran, J.D., 24
Sanders, P., 17
Sartre, J.-P., 44
schizophrenia, 7, 16, 61–4, 65–7,
  126–8
 see also Wisconsin Project
'schools' of therapy, 2, 21, 129–30,
  207–8
 equal effectiveness of, 52–3
Schore, A.N., 51, 112
science, as human creation, 234
Seeman, J., 33
self
 configurations/parts of, 91, 120, 121
 and experience, 91–2, 113, 113,
  199–201
 and felt sense, 153–4
 Rogers' theory of, 12
 use of, 20, 139, 209
self-concept, 12
 and conditions of worth, 14
self-defeating modes of expression, 103–4
self-propelled feeling-process, 78
sensations, and felt sense, 74–5, 93–4
sensitisation, vs diagnosis, 109–10, 144
Shapiro, F., 142
Shea, J., 231
Shlien, J., 55, 56

simile, 178
situations
 and emotions, 193, 194
 and experiences, 83
 and feelings, 150, 193, 194
 and felt sense, 93–4
skills training, 168
skin-resistance studies, 56
Slack, S., 49
Smith, M.L., 53, 156
social construction of reality, 54, 186–7,
  213, 229
social restraint, and 'being oneself',
  34–8
society
 and experiencing, 214–16
 modern, 215–16
'something', 91, 107, 113
space
 between 'I' and 'it', 91–2
 Gendlin's view of, 226–7, 234
 image, 92
spirituality, 151–2, 200, 230–5
Standal, S., 12
'standard' person-centred therapy,
  17–20
 training, 164
standards, 187, 188
Stiles, W.B., 53, 156
Stinckens, N., 119
stress reduction, 88
structure-bound process, 56, 59, 61,
  72–3, 79
 extreme, 125–8
 and incongruence, 205
 and psychological disturbance,
  192–3
 in training, 165
subjectivity, 95
superego, and inner critic, 117
supervision
 group, 169–70
 individual, 172–4
suppressed experiencing, 121–2
symboling, in Gendlin's theory, 185

'tacit dimension' (Polanyi), 191
Taoism, 232
Tausch, R., 21

techniques, 21
Tennyson, A., 33
theory(ies)
    construction of, 221
    correspondence with reality, 129
    empirical testing, 155–62
    evidence for, 159
    and experiencing, 4
    in psychotherapy, 208
    in training courses, 169
therapeutic change
    client variables, 4, 55, 64
    empirical studies, 156–62
    focusing not necessary for, 152–5
    and therapeutic conditions, 63–4
    therapist variables in, *see* therapist
        conditions
therapeutic conditions, 13–15, 18
    and actualising tendency, 26–7, 69
    necessary/sufficient debate, 38–9
    necessity of, 27, 38–9
    in process-experiential therapy, 22
    Rogers' view of, 13–15
    sufficiency of, 19, 27, 29, 38–9
    and therapeutic progress, 39, 63–4
    see also individual conditions
Therapeutic Conditions Hypothesis,
        15, 48, 52–3
    tests of, 155
therapeutic progress, *see* therapeutic
        change
therapeutic relationship, depth of,
        149–52, 201, 203
therapist
    as well-functioning, 51–2
    power of, 44–5
    presence of, 78–80
therapist conditions, 13
    balance between, 16
    and experiencing level, 62–4,
        68–9
    and 'pre-therapy', 128
    in process-experiential
        psychotherapy, 23–4
    purist view, 27
    Rogers' view, 27
    Tomoda's view, 29
    see also core conditions
therapy, *see* psychotherapy

thinking
    creative, 220–1
    and felt sense, 135–6
    working with, 134–6
Thinking at the Edge (TAE), 172, 220–1
Thorne, B., 4, 18, 19, 20, 31, 35, 36,
        42, 121, 149, 150, 164
time, Gendlin's view of, 134, 200–1,
        226–7, 234
Tomlinson, T.M., 157
Tomoda, F., 27–9, 27–9
'too close' process, 90, 112–15
    see also emotions, overwhelm,
        emotional; identification
'too distant' process, 90, 112–15
    see also externalising; intellectualising
'totaling', 197, 222
tradition(s), 187–9, 190
    alternative, 187, 189
    and creativity, 192
    and felt needs, 189
training, 163–72
transference, 138–9
trauma, 123, 124, 162
    and Conditions of Worth Theory, 40
Treasure Maps to the Soul, 95
truth(s), 186, 188
    general, 187
two-chair procedure, 23, 120

unconditional positive regard, 12, 13
    paradoxical nature of, 199
    revision of concept, 198–201
    superficial, 201
unconscious feelings, 15, 46–7, 70,
        196, 226–7
unconscious, the, 15–16, 46–7,
        70–3, 196
    and the implicit, 48, 70–3, 204–5
unfinished business, 23, 123

value(s), 84
    see also morality
Van Balen, R., 33
vulnerability, client, 110–12

Wallen, J., 11
Warner, M., 17, 21, 111, 112, 121
Watson, N., 39, 155

Weitzman, B., 162
Welwood, J., 232
Wholebody Focusing, 95, 142
Wijngaarden, H.R., 20
Wilkins, P., 42
Wisconsin Project, 7, 56, 61–8,
    156–7
    clinical implications, 65–8
    theoretical implications,
        68–70

Wittgenstein, L., 32, 188, 205, 205,
    224, 234
Worsley, R., 20, 21, 24
writing
    felt sense in, 177–8
    focusing in, 216–17

Zen Buddhism, 29
Zero Balancing, 142
Zimring, F., 56, 58, 59

34533317R00153

Made in the USA
Lexington, KY
09 August 2014